D1593764

Lincoln Reshapes the Presidency

LINCOLN RESHAPES

THE PRESIDENCY

Edited by
Charles M. Hubbard

Mercer University Press
Macon

ISBN 0-86554-817-X
MUP/H619

First Edition.

Library of Congress Cataloging-in-Publication Data

Lincoln Symposium (2001 : Lincoln Memorial University)
 Lincoln reshapes the presidency / edited by Charles M. Hubbard.
    p. cm.
Developed from papers presented at the Lincoln Symposium, held at the
Abraham Lincoln Library and Museum on the campus of Lincoln Memorial
University on April 26-28, 2001.
Includes bibliographical references.
 ISBN 0-86554-817-X (alk. paper)
1. Lincoln, Abraham, 1809-1865—Congresses. 2. Lincoln, Abraham, 1809-
1865—Influence—Congresses. 3. Political leadership—United
States—History—19th century—Congresses. 4. Executive power—United
States—History—19th century—Congresses. 5. United States—Politics
and government—1861-1865—Congresses. 6. Presidents—United States--
Biography--Congresses. I. Hubbard, Charles M., 1939- II. Title.

E457.2.L834 2001
973.7'092—dc21

                                                        2003004186

Dedicated to
Dr. Jerry C. Bishop,
President Emeritus, Lincoln Memorial University,
with the appreciation of all the contributors
for his interest and support of Lincoln scholarship

TABLE OF CONTENTS

viii

ACKNOWLEDGMENTS

The essays in this book were developed from papers presented at the Abraham Lincoln Library and Museum on the campus of Lincoln Memorial University on 26–28 April 2001. The occasion was the Lincoln Symposium that is conducted every four years and sponsored by Lincoln Memorial University. The Symposium provides an opportunity for scholars and Lincoln enthusiasts to gather to share ideas and hear the most recent scholarly research in the Lincoln field.

The staff of the Abraham Lincoln Library and Museum, led by Carol Campbell and Steven Wilson, deserves the gratitude of all who attended the conference. Organizing a large symposium requires unusual attention to detail and all of the museum staff worked hard to assure that the event went well. Lisa Barrick, Ann Justice, and Angela Marx deserve our thanks for assisting the guests and speakers in numerous ways. I am especially grateful to Lisa Barrick and Martha Wiley who tirelessly labored typing and proofing this manuscript. Their patience was especially tested by my extended absence from the office. Without the support of Lincoln Memorial University and the Friends of the Abraham Lincoln Library and Museum, the symposium and this collection of essays could not have happened.

The late Henry Spencer deserves our enduring thanks for first suggesting the idea of the symposium and working to secure the support of the University and the Lincoln community to enable the symposium to become the prestigious event to which we all look forward.

Finally, I wish to thank the contributors for their cooperation and patience. I'm sure that throughout the editing process most of them tired of hearing from me with requests for changes, rewording, footnote clarification, and other nagging details. Everyone was gracious and I am certainly grateful for their cooperation.

Charles M. Hubbard
Harrogate, Tennessee

INTRODUCTION

Charles M. Hubbard

The essays in this book are about an extraordinary American president, Abraham Lincoln, and how his actions reshaped the executive branch of government for future generations. Lincoln was committed to the restoration of the Union and the abolition of slavery. To accomplish these objectives he took control of the government as no other president had before him. Historians, political scientists, and a variety of scholars in other academic disciplines generally agree that the American Civil War redefined the fundamental structure of the United States. Those monumental changes are reflected in the relationships of government to the governed. The document that defines the relationship of the American people to their government is the American Constitution, and the writers sought to protect the people from the abuses of government power by separating the government into three independent branches. This concept was remarkable and unique in the late eighteenth century and represents a significant contribution to the art of government by America's earliest citizens. While the Constitution is a "work in progress" and continues to evolve and change, the changes forged in the fires of the Civil War are unparalleled during any other period of American history.

Not only did the Civil War change the Constitution dramatically, but it also changed the power of the executive office. Many of the changes Lincoln made and the actions he took during the Civil War contributed ultimately to making the president of the United States the most powerful person in the world.

The men who drafted the Constitution sought to achieve their objectives, of guaranteeing personal liberty and freedom, by dispersing power and authority between the independent branches of government. They wanted to create a strong nation with a weak central government. The adversarial struggles that ensued between the branches were expected to guarantee the people freedom from oppression by the government. This concept was described in the fifty-first Federalist paper, when it was proposed that each branch be equipped with the "necessary constitutional means and personal motives to resist encroachments on the others."[1]

The United States that emerged from the Civil War found increased power in all branches of central government, but the executive branch garnered substantially more authority and power than the other two. Obviously, this resulted from the need to prosecute the war by consolidating power in the office of the commander in chief. It took the unique combination of a visionary and determined president combined with the exegesis of war to provide opportunities to reshape and strengthen the office of the American presidency. Lincoln was confronted with the ultimate threat to the nation's existence—a political rebellion backed by a powerful military force. A nation governed by the parameters of the Constitution was vulnerable in such circumstances because of the limited powers reserved for the commander in chief. Lincoln quickly recognized the need to take control of situations that threatened the federal government's ability to end the rebellion. The rebellion and the Civil War forced Abraham Lincoln to assume certain powers that had heretofore not been within the powers granted to the executive branch by the Constitution.

One of the first things Lincoln did when he was confronted with the secession crisis was to postpone the next session of Congress until summer. He was concerned that the Constitutionalists, through their interpretation of the war powers in the Constitution, would encumber his ability to deal with the grim reality of secession and rebellion. Lincoln delayed the convocation of Congress from 12 April 1861 until 4 July.

---

[1] The Fifty-first Federalist Paper, Federalist Papers, Library of Congress, Washington, DC.

This decision allowed him an opportunity to act as he deemed necessary to save the nation. During this political grace period Lincoln chose to ignore several laws and constitutional provisions. For example, he assembled the militia, enlarged the army and navy beyond their authorized strength, spent public funds without congressional appropriation, suspended habeas corpus, and arrested people who were involved in "disloyal practices." During this period of crisis Lincoln called for volunteers for three years of service. Some historians have argued that this latter act provoked the border states with their moderate views on secession to renounce the Union and join the Confederacy. Another decision the president made was to institute a naval blockade of the Confederate States. A blockade, as pointed out by Secretary of the Navy Gideon Wells, was a violation of international law and certainly would raise legal questions in Europe. Lincoln, by way of explaining his actions to Congress, said, "Whether strictly legal or not, were ventured upon what appeared to be a popular demand and a public necessity; trusting then as now that congress would readily ratify them."[2] And Congress did approve most of Lincoln's extra-constitutional acts, albeit after the fact.

Throughout the war, with and without congressional approval, Lincoln continued to exercise wide powers independently of those authorized by the Constitution or Congress. As the war went on he seized private property, suppressed dissent newspapers, proclaimed martial law behind the lines, and prevented the post office from delivering "treasonable correspondence." All of these actions took place without a formal declaration of war. Lincoln believed a declaration of war was inappropriate because a section of the country was in rebellion.[3]

Throughout the early nineteenth century the executive branch strengthened its control of information, secured its monopoly of diplomacy, and enlarged its theory of defensive war. However, Congress still maintained its control over any hostilities against foreign states. The

---

[2] In a message to Congress in special session, 1861. Roy Basler, *The Collected Works of Abraham Lincoln* (New Brunswick NJ: Rutgers University Press, 1955) 4:429.

[3] Arthur M. Schlesinger, Jr., *The Imperial Presidency* (Boston: Houghton-Mifflin Co., 1973) 58–59.

Constitution was very clear that the country could not engage in war without the consent of Congress, but when presidents were confronted by situations calling for the armed protection of American citizens abroad or the protection of property and the respect for law that involved stateless or lawless peoples, the Constitution was less specific. Early nineteenth-century presidents were confronted by a number of threats: the so-called Indian menace, pirates, slave traders, smugglers, cattle-rustlers, frontier ruffians, and all manner of foreign brigands. These limited, but frequent, responses relied on the orders of the president because they were not acts of war against foreign nations. Interventions to provide protection for American citizens abroad had clear precedent in international law and did not require special congressional approval or appropriations. In general, Congress was content to leave these special situations to the president. It did however, authorize the United States Navy (in an 1819 act) to take action against pirates and among other things to protect the rights and property of American citizens in danger overseas. The navy was under the direct command of the president as commander in chief.[4]

There was little resistance on the part of Congress to the concept of the president as the commander in chief. By the time the southern states rebelled against national government and seceded from the Union, there was ample precedent for the president to use force to subdue the rebels without a formal declaration of war. President Lincoln used the war powers associated with the presidency to strengthen the office and conduct military action to subdue the rebellion and unite the country. Lincoln identified the war power with the "law of necessity." It was his means of constitutionalizing this situation. He argued that a free government, in order to deal with such a monumental crisis, had "no choice but to call out the war power." When confronted by questions on the suspension of *habeas corpus* Lincoln went on to say, "Certain proceedings are constitutional when in cases of rebellion or invasion, the public safety requires them, which would not be constitutional when, an absence of rebellion or invasion, the public safety does not require them." Lincoln seems to suggest in this comment that in times of war the Constitution should be suspended or at least temporarily modified. He

---

[4] David H. Donald, *Lincoln Reconsidered* (New York: Vintage Books, 1956) 187.

pointed out on another occasion that these "measures otherwise unconstitutional might become lawful by becoming indispensable to the preservation of the constitution through the preservation of the Union."[5]

Clearly Lincoln saw the war powers in the presidency as expanding the role of the executive as commander in chief. This seems to contradict his long held view that the power of the presidency should be limited. After all, Lincoln had been a faithful Whig and the Whig Party was founded by opponents of Andrew Jackson. Jackson, it was feared, sought too much power for the office of the president. Lincoln believed in government activism and supported the use of public funds and land to provide economic opportunities for the people. However, he was committed to the concept that it was the responsibility of Congress to enact legislation to carry out this domestic agenda and not the executive branch. In matters of national security, however, Lincoln exercised the power of his office to protect the country. He was convinced that without union and a nation, the Constitution had no value.

Lincoln's strong personality is further reflected in the issuance of the Emancipation Proclamation. The Emancipation Proclamation deprived citizens, although they were in "rebellion," of their property. This property was tainted by slavery, but Lincoln understood that an amendment (the thirteenth) would be required to abolish slavery permanently, and the Emancipation Proclamation was a temporary war measure. The Constitution guarantees that no citizen should be deprived of his property without due process of law. When Lincoln told his cabinet of his decision to issue the Emancipation Proclamation, he explained that he did not "wish your advice about the main matter, for that I have determined for myself."[6] It is clear that he understood the constitutional implications of the Emancipation Proclamation and saw it as a temporary power vested in the executive branch. He certainly knew that only an amendment to the Constitution could properly remedy the contradiction between slavery and a country committed to freedom with liberty for all.

---

[5] Lincoln to Erastus Corning, 12 June 1863, *Collected Works,* ed. Basler, 6:261–69; Letter to A. G. Hodges, 4 April 1864, Ibid., 7:281–82.

[6] Donald, *Lincoln Reconsidered,* 201.

Arthur Schlesinger, Jr., the insightful historian and political analyst, has written in the *Imperial Presidency* about the struggle for power among the branches of government. He points out that presidents become powerful in times of crisis, national emergency, and war, because the people demand a stronger leader.[7] In a democracy, the people have the power and are willing to surrender some of that power to the chief executive in exchange for a powerful and forceful leader in a time of crisis. The president is the axis around which the whole population revolves in a time of national emergency. The president represents all the people as no other governmental branch does. Although in recent years demands by the press and organizations committed to transparency in government and informing the body politic have had success in penetrating presidential confidentiality, the office can be and traditionally has been closed to public scrutiny. Certainly it was during the Lincoln administration. Congress and the Supreme Court have maintained meticulous records, but the executive branch did not leave such detailed records. It remains to historians to ferret out the documents, personal papers, and other primary sources that provide the true story of the ever-changing, evolutionary system as it developed in the executive branch.

The following essays demonstrate how Lincoln changed the office of the presidency. They examine areas that are subtle yet significant in the transformation of the sixteenth president and the office he held. The issues discussed shed light on both the personal relationships of Abraham Lincoln as well as the political and military changes that occurred during the time of his presidency.

Frank Williams, in a well-organized essay, addresses many of the questions surrounding Lincoln as the commander in chief operating within the war powers. Judge Williams points to Lincoln's frustration and disappointment in the performance of his generals and how he exercised his authority to change field commanders.

Gerald Prokopowicz elaborates on one of Lincoln's responsibilities in his essay on military pardons and reveals the compassionate side of Abraham Lincoln when dealing with the military. John Sellers and

---

[7] Schlesinger, *The Imperial Presidency,* 59.

Michael Burlingame explain how Lincoln's two young secretaries helped the president with political liaisons and assisted, particularly with the press, to build a political base that was unique and original for American politics. John Nicolay and John Hay also assisted the president in numerous ways to gain support for his military and domestic policies with the congressional leadership. Philip Paludan follows with a discussion of Horace Greeley and his influence on American opinion. Throughout his administration Lincoln maintained an active dialogue with the New York publisher and was well aware of Greeley's influence, through the press, on public sentiment toward the war.

William Lee Miller in his essay examines the values that motivated Lincoln to expand the powers and reshape the presidency. Miller is interested in why Lincoln reacted as he did to the actions of the secessionists and those people who surrounded him at such a time of crisis. The issues of slavery, emancipation and the African-American experience form the basis of two powerful essays by Lucas Morel and Michael Vorenberg. Morel seeks to find a deep, spiritual meaning in Lincoln's drive toward emancipation. Vorenberg is interested in slavery and its overwhelming meaning for Americans and Lincoln in particular. William Harris in the next essay explains the importance of the election of 1864 in reshaping the country. Without reelection Lincoln's power could not have influenced the drive for the thirteenth amendment.

Mary Todd is the subject of Jennifer Fleischner's contribution. The role of the First Lady and her personality influenced both the president and the public's expectations for wives of future presidents. James McPherson, in his essay titled, *Lincoln's Legacy for Our Time,* provides interesting insights into a wide range of issues that have had a lasting impact on future generations of Americans. He explains how Lincoln and his legacy of his leadership continue to inform presidents and political leaders.

Many students of government and the Lincoln presidency might agree with political scientist Wilfred E. Binkley when he states that Lincoln "unquestionably set the high water mark of the exercise of executive power in the United States."[8] It is difficult to imagine why

---

[8] Wilfred E. Binkley, *President and Congress* (New York: A. A. Knopf, 1947) 36.

anyone would disagree with the statement so often quoted that "George Washington founded this nation and Abraham Lincoln saved it." Lincoln's commitment and persistence allowed him to use the office he held both to save and to redefine the government of the United States.

ABRAHAM LINCOLN AND THE CHANGING ROLE OF COMMANDER IN CHIEF

Frank J. Williams

As historian Alan Brinkley made clear, "Great presidents are products not just of their own talents and ambitions but of the circumstances they inherit."[1] Theodore Roosevelt, inspired by Abraham Lincoln, said, "A man has to take advantage of his opportunities but the opportunities have to come. If there is not the war, you don't get the great general; if there is not the great occasion, you don't get the great statesman; if Lincoln had lived in times of peace, no one would know his name now."[2]

Despite a successful presidency, Roosevelt was in the end greatly disappointed that World War I erupted after he had left office. He remained bitter that Woodrow Wilson, and not he, had been given the opportunity for greatness.[3]

T. R.'s concerns, of course, relate to the president's power as commander in chief. The Constitution states: "The President shall be Commander-In-Chief of the Army and Navy of the United States."[4] These sixteen words confer a vast undefined power, the limits of which have never been fully explored.

---

[1] Alan Brinkley, "The 43 Percent President," *The New York Times Magazine* (4 July 1993) 23.

[2] Ibid.

[3] Ibid.

[4] US Constitution, Article II, Section 2.

For all his seeming power, the president is not the sole master of the military enterprise. He shares power with a vast array of associates: Congress, the courts, public opinion, the nation's allies, and the professional military, among others. There are times when he may well wonder whether he really is the "chief," given the powers of his associates. He may also wonder whether his function actually involves "command." His highest task may be to "persuade" Congress and the allies, whom he cannot command, and the professional military, whose resistance is often common, to unite in a natural cause.

Lincoln the Captain

When he became commander in chief in 1861, Abraham Lincoln lacked serious military experience, especially in contrast to Jefferson Davis, a West Point graduate and Mexican War hero. Indeed, Lincoln often joked about his brief army career: three months' service with several rag-tag militia companies in the Black Hawk War. After he was elected a captain by his New Salem friends, Lincoln inspired more humor than gallantry as a leader. Once, when marching his company toward a narrow gate, he forgot the proper command to form his troops into a single column so they could advance. "Halt!" Lincoln finally shouted. "This company is dismissed for two minutes, when it will form again on the other side of the gate."[5] Lincoln was a civilian by habit, experience, and vision. Yet, his background served him well when he led the citizen soldiers who fought in the Civil War.

In truth, Lincoln's service in the Black Hawk War should not be underestimated. His election as captain led him to reflect almost thirty years later that no subsequent success of his life gave him as much satisfaction.[6] It was a defining moment in his life, much like that of Captain Harry Truman during World War I. Both drew many lessons

---

[5] Francis Fisher Browne, *The Ever—Day Life of Abraham Lincoln* (Lincoln: University of Nebraska Press, 1995) 107.

[6] Roy P. Basler, ed., *The Collected Works of Abraham Lincoln*, 9 vols. (New Brunswick: Rutgers University Press, 1953) 4:64.

from their experiences; the most important for young Lincoln was that exuberant young men could not make the transition from civilians to soldiers overnight and would never fully transform themselves into full-time military men. He also learned that raw recruits came from a democratic culture with a high disregard for authority. Many of these civilian soldiers in the end simply could not, and would not, recognize the right of the military to keep them in service longer than they wished to stay. Such attitude owed little or nothing to cowardice, laziness, or lack of patriotism, but had a great deal to do with a cultural instinct for independence. Lincoln shared their privations, especially hunger. The military supply system worked imperfectly at best, and the soldiers often went without rations. When his men went hungry, so did he, on one occasion passing two days without food. Instinctively he understood that good humor, patience, a willingness to share equally in the hardships of the privates, and an absence of self-importance were the primary bases to provide leadership and to bind the men to him.[7] Fortunately, these characteristics were already a part of his mid-western nature.

In most wars, the American president confined the exercise of his commander-in-chief power to the selection of commanding officers without participating in the formulation of strategy. Forces of circumstance and the character of the presidents rather than a formal conception of the power of the presidential office worked against an expanded role. This was true in the War of 1812.[8] But a strong and active president like James K. Polk would participate in decisions of military strategy.[9]

Captain to Commander in Chief

In the War Between the States circumstances existed that required a full exercise of the president's power as commander in chief. For a

---

[7] William C. Davis, *Lincoln's Men: How President Lincoln Became Father to an Army and a Nation* (New York: The Free Press, 1999) 9, 10.

[8] Donald R. Hickey, *The War of 1812: The Forgotten Conflict* (Urbana: University of Illinois Press, 1989) 301–302.

[9] Robert W. Johannsen, *To the Halls of the Montezumas: The Mexican War in the American Imagination* (New York: Oxford University Press, 1985) 14–15.

considerable time, its outcome remained highly uncertain. Initially, many of the Union commanders were incompetent. Their military plans frequently miscarried, so changes in strategy had to be swiftly devised and implemented. Abraham Lincoln, a strong and active president, had little choice but to take part in the conduct of the war. He did so from the outset. His first major problem arose in regard to Union forts in the South. Should they be surrendered or held? If held, should men and supplies be sent to relieve and replenish the troops? Lincoln sent a relief expedition to Fort Sumter in Charleston Harbor. Jefferson Davis ordered General P. G. T. Beauregard to open fire and the war began.[10]

From the beginning Lincoln set a pattern. His war power would not be limited to strictly military measures. On 20 April 1861, he ordered United States marshals to seize the originals of all telegrams sent and copies of all received during the preceding year from the principal telegraph offices in the northern states.[11] On 27 April 1861, without action by Congress, he suspended the writ of habeas corpus[12] and simply ignored the individual ruling of the longtime chief justice of the United States, Roger B. Taney, that his action was unconstitutional.[13] Shortly thereafter, again without congressional authorization, he enlarged the army by calling for volunteers.[14] The ex-captain soon felt it was necessary to disregard his professional military advisors, too. Both General Winfield Scott, who headed the army, and General Irwin McDowell, the field commander, advised against fighting the first battle of Manassas on the ground that more time was required for disciplining and drilling the troops. The public, however, clamored for action, and Lincoln, always in tune with political necessity, overruled the generals. The battle was fought—with disastrous result. Not daunted, the

---

[10] Richard N. Current, *Lincoln and the First Shot* (Philadelphia: J. B. Lippincott, 1963) 149–53.

[11] James G. Randall, *Constitutional Problems Under Lincoln* (Urbana: University of Illinois Press, 1951) 481–83.

[12] Basler, *Collected Works*, 4:347.

[13] *Ex parte* Merryman, 17 Fed. Cas. 144 (1861).

[14] Basler, *Collected Works*, 4:359.

following night, Lincoln went ahead and prepared a detailed plan of strategy.[15]

He did not always attempt to force his tentative strategy on others. Often he submitted to the advice of his generals. Occasionally they disregarded his wishes if not his direct orders. Early in the war Lincoln was eager for General Don Carlos Buell to capture Cumberland Gap, through which his grandfather and grandmother had once made their way westward. Buell, more than once, promised to take this course, but in the end turned his back on the Gap and moved toward Nashville.[16]

As the war developed, Lincoln became even more concerned with questions of strategy. He was greatly troubled by his inability to stir into action General George B. McClellan, the commander of the Army of the Potomac. The ever-serious commander in chief went so far as to educate himself on military strategy. The autodidact read Henry W. Halleck's translation of Jomini[17] and held long conversations with officers on the art of war. In December 1861 he presented an elaborate memorandum to McClellan that asked technical questions and made suggestions about an advance.[18] The over-confident McClellan returned it with penciled replies and a note rejecting all the suggestions.

On 27 January 1862 Lincoln issued his General War Order No. 1, in which he fixed 22 February as "the day for a general movement of the land and naval forces of the United States against the insurgent forces."[19] The Army of the Potomac and others, as well as certain naval forces, were named as ordered to "be ready for a movement on that day."[20] Four days later he supplemented this with "President's Special War Order No. 1," commanding the Army of the Potomac, after providing for the defense of Washington, to move on 22 February to seize Manassas Junction.[21] This was followed on 3 February by a note to McClellan

---

[15] Ibid., 457.

[16] Ibid., 5:90, 91, 98.

[17] Henry Wager Halleck, *Elements of Military Art and Science*, 2d ed. (New York, 1861).

[18] Basler, *Collected Works*, 5:34–35.

[19] Ibid., 111–12.

[20] Ibid.

[21] Ibid., 115.

insisting upon Lincoln's own plan for an attack on the Confederate army near Washington rather than an expedition by water against Richmond.[22] However, plans, suggestions, and orders were alike ineffective to move McClellan or his army.

Shortly after this, Lincoln told his secretary, John Hay, of his impulse to take charge of the Army of the Potomac and see what he could do as a field commander.[23] He did not yield to this impulse at this time or later, though on 23 May 1863, the *Chicago Tribune* urged him to take the field as actual commander. During the week of 5 May 1862, however, he did assume personal command of the operations that resulted in the capture of Norfolk. The president not only ordered the advance on Norfolk, but personally selected the place where the attack was to begin and gave the order to fire. Moreover, he countermanded the orders of Major General John E. Wool as to the disposal of some of his troops.[24]

Perhaps encouraged by this success, when Stonewall Jackson made one of his forays into the Shenandoah Valley, Lincoln gave specific orders to Generals McDowell, Buell, and John Fremont to surround and capture Jackson and his army.[25] Fremont disobeyed two of Lincoln's orders, resting his men one day when they were ordered to march and again taking a different route from the one selected by Lincoln. Even if the orders had been obeyed, the capture of Stonewall Jackson's army would not have been a simple task. After this experience, Lincoln did not again attempt to direct the field movements of several armies a long distance from the White House.

Several presidents have faced major crises either in bringing their field generals to engage in battle or in keeping them within bounds, not simply on the battlefield but within the framework of constitutional government. General McClellan, the most lagging of field generals, was a great trial to Abraham Lincoln in both spheres. Bold in his strategic

---

[22] Ibid., 118–19.

[23] John Hay, Tyler Dermett, ed., *Lincoln and the Civil War in the Diaries and Letters of John Hay* (New York: Dodd, Mead & Company, Inc., 1939) 36.

[24] Bruce Catton, *Terrible Swift Sword* (New York: Doubleday & Company, Inc., 1963) 279.

[25] Basler, *Collected Works*, 5:230–33.

conceptions, McClellan nevertheless dreaded the actual execution of his plans. A repetitive pattern for him was to demand more reinforcements after overestimating the enemy's strength and depreciating his own. He was a wonderfully imaginative procrastinator. If he had Robert E. Lee at a disadvantage, he almost invariably failed to exploit it. He must wait, McClellan would report to his impatient superiors at Washington, until the Potomac rose to be sure that Lee would not recross it; he must finish drilling new recruits, reorganize his forces, and procure more shoes, uniforms, blankets, and camp equipment.

McClellan compensated for battlefield inaction by spending his battle-idle time pouring his irrepressible arrogance into his letters, including one to Lincoln on 7 July 1862, pointing out that it was high time the government established a civil and military policy to cover the full canvass of the nation's troubles and "generously" informed the president what precisely that policy should be.[26] McClellan's behavior became critical after his failure to follow up his victory at Antietam by pursuing Lee's fleeing army. Lincoln worked mightily, as his secretary John Nicolay put it, at "poking sharp sticks into little Mac's ribs." When the general included among his ingenious excuses that an epidemic had afflicted the horses with sore mouths and weary backs, Lincoln was goaded into a sharp reply. "I have just read your despatch about sore tongued and fatiegued horses," he telegraphed. "Will you pardon me for asking what the horses of your Army have done since the battle of Antietam that fatigue anything?"[27]

Lincoln and his administration were now at a critical juncture. Winter was approaching and would assure that, with the exception of Antietam, the long record of eastern defeat and stalemate would remain intact. Congress, restive with this state of affairs, was soon to convene. Governors were nervous, the cabinet was divided, and both the extreme war and peace men were thundering against the president. Nor was Lincoln unmindful of McClellan's personal softness toward the South,

[26] George B. McClellan, Stephen W. Sears, eds., *The Civil War Papers of George B. McClellen: Selected Correspondence 1860–1865* (New York: Ticknor & Fields, 1989) 344–45.

[27] Basler, *Collected Works*, 5:474.

and the presence on his staff of some who advocated a waiting game to prolong the war until both sides were exhausted and the Union might be preserved with slavery intact. Should he replace McClellan? Alternative generals were a sorrowfully undistinguished lot, many already scarred with failure, and others abysmally inexperienced.

After serious deliberation, Lincoln relieved McClellan on 5 November 1862 and appointed General Ambrose E. Burnside in his place.[28] Upon reading the president's order, McClellan exclaimed, "Alas for my poor country."[29] Some among his officers even urged him to disobey the presidential order. McClellan later wrote that he could easily have marched his troops into Washington and taken possession of the government. If so, it would have been the first successful forward movement of the war! Instead, McClellan turned over the command of his 120,000 men in an elaborate ceremony. But this was by no means the last encounter between McClellan and Lincoln. In 1864, two years after his removal, McClellan met Lincoln on new terrain—as the Democratic nominee for the presidency. He lost that battle too.

Nearly a century later another former captain and then president, Harry Truman, confronted another field general, but one who was prone to do too much rather than too little. General Douglas MacArthur, commander of the United Nations forces in Korea, possessed a military career of rare distinction. His short stature (five foot two inches), his photographic, handsome, erect presence and majestic eloquence were marks of an imperious figure. MacArthur made public statements that did not reflect President Truman's policy. The autodidact Truman borrowed books from the Library of Congress to study the method Abraham Lincoln used to relieve George B. McClellan.[30] On 11 April 1951 the president announced MacArthur's removal from his command. Though the top military unqualifiedly supported President Truman, the Congress, the media, and the public initially condemned him.[31]

---

[28] Ibid., 485.

[29] McClellan, *The Civil War Papers of George B. McClellen*, 520.

[30] David McCullough, *Truman* (New York: Simon & Schuster, 1992) 837–38.

[31] Ibid., 843–56.

Presidential power was eventually vindicated by Truman, as it had been earlier by Lincoln. In both episodes, civilian supremacy was upheld over the professional military, a cardinal arrangement of the democratic state. Both presidents faced grave political risks: the possibility that the successors of the deposed generals would compile a less favorable military record, that public opinion would feel affronted, and that legislators would exploit the situation for personal political gain. But both former captains performed their presidential duty and brushed aside political expediency and the temptation not to act. The military rallied around them, the public came to understand, and ultimately the chief executive prevailed.

An Active Commander in Chief

Functioning as he does in a democratic state, the president requires legal authority to pursue military purposes. In wartime, of course, the need and the quest become most compelling. Presidents in the nation's major wars have invoked two contrasting patterns of legal justification for their acts. One, the Lincolnian, asserts an expansive view of the president's independent authority based on the commander-in-chief clause of the Constitution[32] and on the duty "to take care that the laws be faithfully executed."[33] In the ten weeks between the outbreak at Fort Sumter and the convening of Congress in special session on 4 July 1861, Lincoln employed these clauses to sanction measures whose extraordinary magnitude suggests dictatorship.

In the 10-week interval Lincoln added 23,000 men to the regular army and 18,000 to the navy, called 40,000 volunteers for 3 years' service, summoned the state militias into a 90-day volunteer force, paid $2 million dollars from the Treasury's unappropriated funds for purposes unauthorized by Congress, closed the Post Office to "treasonable correspondence," imposed a blockade on southern ports, suspended the writ of habeas corpus in certain parts of the country, and caused the

---

[32] US Constitution, Article II, Section 2.
[33] Ibid., Section 3.

arrest and military detention of persons "who were represented to him" as engaging in or contemplating "treasonable practices."[34] He later instituted a militia draft when voluntary recruiting broke down[35] and extended the suspension of the habeas corpus privilege nationwide for persons "guilty of any disloyal practice."[36] Lincoln did not intend to fight a rebellion with a powder puff.

His first Emancipation Proclamation was also couched as a military order from the commander in chief. It freed the slaves in states in rebellion against the United States and pledged "the Executive Government of the United States, including the military and naval authority thereof," to protect the freedom conferred.[37] Lincoln invited Congress to "ratify" his enlargement of the armed forces, which it did,[38] and it bolstered his handling of the writ of habeas corpus.[39]

The World War presidencies of Woodrow Wilson and Franklin D. Roosevelt afford contrasting patterns. The spreading character of war, its encroachment upon the economy, the involvement of growing numbers of people, and the resort to propaganda, fostered an executive-legislative partnership in war leadership. In both of the World Wars, statutes were passed delegating broad powers to the chief executive. Selective service laws in both wars enabled the president to administer a vast man-powered draft.

All wartime presidents had to reckon, too, with a favorite pre-occupation of Congress in the military realm: investigation. Harry Truman's Senate Committee to Investigate the National Defense Program was a model of searching, but constructive, criticism that produced faithful change in the administration of World War II.[40] Success as a wartime investigator established Truman's chief claim upon his subsequent vice-presidential nomination in 1944. A contrasting view of the investigatory power was the great cross Lincoln had to bear in the

---

[34] Randall, *Constitutional Problems Under Lincoln*, 33–41.
[35] Ibid., 37.
[36] Basler, *Collected Works*, 5:438.
[37] Ibid., 434.
[38] Randall, *Constitutional Problems Under Lincoln*, 128.
[39] Ibid., 130; US Stat. at Large, XII, 755 (Habeas Corpus Act of 1863).
[40] McCullough, *Truman*, 256–80.

Civil War: the Joint Committee on the Conduct of the War. Spotty and arbitrary, the committee concentrated upon the Army of the Potomac and investigated selected specific generals—George B. McClellan, Charles P. Stone, Fitz-John Porter, and William B. Franklin—as their investigative targets. In contrast, John C. Fremont and Benjamin Franklin Butler were favorites who could do no wrong.[41] The committee investigated its selected victims with preconceived notions of guilt, employed rumor and irresponsible publicity, and became a factional instrument of the Radical Republicans. Its busiest members were the staunch anti-Lincoln men, Benjamin Franklin Wade, George Washington Julian, and Zachariah Chandler. Chandler, in a typically unflattering estimate, wrote that the administration was timid and ineffective.[42] Lincoln reciprocated in his judgment of the committee. He insisted: "I have never faulted in my faith of being ultimately able to suppress this rebellion and of reuniting this divided country; but this improvised vigilant committee to watch my movements and keep me straight, appointed by Congress and called the 'committee on the conduct of the war,' is a marplot, and its greatest purpose seems to be to hamper my action and obstruct the military operations."[43]

Civil Liberties and Rights in a Civil War

As commanders in chief, presidents face additional tensions with the remaining governmental branch's concern with military affairs: the federal courts, with their high duty in a democratic state to protect the Constitution and the laws against encroachment. The most perplexing and consequential issues between the executive and the courts may arise during actual war, when the president is driven to curtail, or even suppress, key liberties sanctioned in the Bill of Rights. To further the

---

[41] Bruce Tap, *Over Lincoln's Shoulder: The Committee on the Conduct of the War* (Lawrence: University Press of Kansas, 1998).

[42] Ibid., 19.

[43] Ward Hill Lamon, Dorothy Lamon Teillard, eds., *Recollections of Abraham Lincoln, 1847–1869* (Washington: A. C. McClurg Co., 1911) 183, 191.

progress of war, to safeguard the nation's imperiled safety, the president may have to set aside political and economic liberties that in peacetime are inviolable.

The Civil War, fought within the nation's borders and jeopardizing its capital, was actually resisted in many sectors of the North, to the point that president Lincoln promulgated several orders and proclamations restrictive of individual liberty. The most important of these was his suspension of the constitutional privilege of the writ of habeas corpus, protecting the civilian against arbitrary arrests. Lincoln's first habeas corpus proclamation, issued in the war's early weeks, was triggered by events in Maryland. In early 1861 underground resistance and open defiance were rampant in that state. Federal troops were attacked by mobs in Baltimore, communications to the capital were severed, and the mayor and police chief were unabashedly pro-Confederate and anti-Lincoln. Bridges were destroyed to hamper the passage of Union troops, and newspapers hostile to the administration fanned disunion sentiment. The state legislature was soon to convene, with some of its members seeking to have the state secede from the Union.

To their credit, Union generals moved to nip the growing conspiracy by arresting the mayor, the chief of police, and several police commissioners. Even more sensational was the arrest of members of the Maryland legislature. To forestall the passage of an act of secession, Union General Nathaniel P. Banks barred the legislature from meeting and arrested nine of its members and the chief clerk of the Senate. Still other Marylanders were arrested, including one John Merryman "charged with various acts of treason." Merryman was languishing in Fort McHenry when the chief justice, Roger B. Taney, on circuit duty, ordered the "body of John Merryman [produced] and…the day and cause of his [capture and detention]"[44] made known. A head-on clash between the president and the Supreme Court, between the war and the Constitution, was in the making. Taney, to the administration's great relief, confined himself to declaring that the power to suspend the writ, which should be exercised with "extreme caution," belonged to

---

[44] Randall, *Constitutional Problems Under Lincoln*, 120–21.

Congress, and not to the president.[45] Taney's opinion, nevertheless, put the administration under the cloud of the likelihood of a hostile Supreme Court decision, an event Attorney General Edward Bates said would "do more to paralyze the Executive…than the worse defeat our armies have yet sustained."[46]

The administration's position was strengthened when Congress, after much struggle, passed the Habeas Corpus Act of 1863, affirming the president's power to suspend the writ. Despite several procedural devices incorporated to placate the courts, the act left to the executive the setting of policy concerning arrests and imprisonments. As before, prisoners were tried by military tribunal and punished or released under authority of the War Department. Arrests continued apace. Clement L. Vallandingham, the well-known Copperhead, after his arrest, trial, and sentencing by a military commission, appealed to the United States Supreme Court to transfer his case to civil court, but the Supreme Court ruled that it had no jurisdiction, since a military commission was not a "court" over which the federal judiciary had jurisdiction.[47]

Although Vallandingham never lived to see it, his legal position was ultimately vindicated in the celebrated case of *Ex parte* Milligan.[48] Milligan too was a Copperhead, tried by a military commission for "treasonable" speeches. Condemned to hang, he invoked the habeas corpus writ. But by then the war was over, and the Court was prepared to act boldly. It ruled that Indiana, where Milligan resided and spoke, was not part of the "theater of war" and that the civil courts there were "open" and therefore available to conduct his trial. Under such circumstances, military tribunals were unlawful. The Court did not rule that suspension of habeas corpus was illegal. But even the Milligan case, needless to say, has become the source of permanent consternation to the friends of presidential power. It establishes the principle that the courts shall determine, even to the point of overriding the executive, what is the

---

[45] Ibid.
[46] Ibid., 132; Letter from Bates to Edwin M. Stanton.
[47] *Ex parte* Vallandigham, 68 US 243, 1864.
[48] *Ex parte* Milligan, 4 Wallace 2, 1866.

area of war and public danger, a principle that could well cause havoc with presidential effectiveness in an actual emergency.

Despite the hazards of the Milligan doctrine, the Supreme Court proved tolerant of presidential power in the two World Wars. In *Ex parte* Quirin[49], the Court, during World War II, broadly construed the commander in chief's capacity as executor of the Articles of War, enacted by Congress to further the United States' obligations under the laws of war, a branch of international law. The case concerned eight saboteurs who were trained in a Berlin espionage school and deposited on Long Island and the Florida coast by German submarines. Arrested by the FBI before they could begin operations, they were tried, by order of President Franklin D. Roosevelt, before a military commission for violating the laws of war by not wearing fixed emblems revealing their combatant status. Midway in the trial the defendants petitioned the United States Supreme Court for habeas corpus. The court rejected the writ.

The assertion of a president's wartime power can go too far. The most extreme application of the commander in chief's power to designate the theater of military operations was Franklin Roosevelt's executive order of 19 February 1942, directed at the presumed danger of Japanese sabotage on the West Coast. In the high excitement over the Japanese bombing of Pearl Harbor, Roosevelt blundered into one of the serious mistakes of his presidency against the advice of the FBI director and his attorney general. He willingly gave into the pressures of the military, Congress, West Coast groups, and the newspapers to remove persons of Japanese ancestry from that area. By Executive Order No. 9066 Roosevelt empowered the Secretary of War to establish "military areas" from which "any or all persons" [of Japanese ancestry] might be excluded to prevent espionage and sabotage, and he designated military commanders to police these areas. In all, some 112,000 persons were removed from their homes, of whom the vast majority—70,000—were United States citizens.[50] The "relocation" and the president's exercise of

---

[49] *Ex parte* Quirin, 317 US 1, 1942.

[50] James MacGregor Burns, *Roosevelt: The Solider of Freedom* (New York: Harcourt) 213–17.

this power was sustained by the Supreme Court in *Hirabayashi v. United States*[51] and in *Korematsu v. United States*.[52] Yet decades later the three branches of government would admit they were wrong in their treatment of Japanese-American citizens. Token compensation was provided.

Lincoln's Adaptive Methods

But a wartime president's principal role, as Lincoln came to see it, was to press his generals into action. McClellan was not the only commander who tested the president's patience. On 16 October 1863, he sent to George Gordon Meade, through his chief of staff General Henry Halleck, a curious letter that was in effect an order to attack Lee, and that concluded: "The honor will be his if he succeeds, and the blame may be mine if he fails."[53] The letter was widely publicized and administration newspapers hailed the president as a great strategist.

Lincoln himself laid no claim to military genius and frankly admitted that his interference with his commanders was partly the result of their dilatoriness and ineptitude, and partly the result of political pressure. As capable commanders emerged Lincoln interfered less and less. He became less inclined personally to direct the strategy of the various campaigns but he became more insistent upon generals who could work out a plan of campaign and fight.

In the beginning hundreds of commissions were issued, many to high ranking officers, for purely political reasons—because they had powerful friends, could raise troops, or because it was desired to obtain their full support of the war. The criticism was made—not without justification—that favoritism had officered the army with incompetence. Even when such men as Benjamin Butler and George McClellan had repeatedly demonstrated their incapacity, there was long hesitation in removing them for fear of unfavorable political reaction. Butler had Radical Republican friends. McClellan had Democratic admirers. Both

---

[51] *Hirabayashi v. United States*, 320 US 81, 1943.
[52] *Korematsu v. United States*, 323 US 214, 1944.
[53] Basler, *Collected Works*, 6:518.

elements were crucial to maintain the coalition support for the war at home. After Donelson, Shiloh, and Vicksburg, Ulysses S. Grant had Lincoln's complete confidence, and his reply to voluble criticism of him was: "I can't spare this man—he fights."[54] After Grant moved to Virginia, there was little interference and, indeed, on no other basis could the president and his chief commander have worked together. Grant was determined to go his own way and, though he attempted to conceal his feelings, was not particularly pleased when Lincoln visited his headquarters.

In the latter months of the war, finding in Grant, William T. Sherman, and Phillip Sheridan a triumvirate upon whom he could depend, Lincoln, while he keenly followed the movements of the armies, permitted his commanders free conduct of their own campaigns. On one occasion he said to Secretary of War Edwin M. Stanton, who was insisting that Grant was exceeding his authority: "You and I, Mr. Stanton, have been trying to boss this job and we haven't succeeded very well with it. We have sent across the mountains for Mr. Grant, as Mrs. Grant calls him, to relieve us and now I think we had better leave him alone to do as he pleases."[55]

Lincoln withheld from Grant only the decision or questions that were within the political zone as when he instructed him to have no conference with Robert E. Lee except for the surrender of Lee's army or upon some minor or purely military matter. All proposals for peace were to be passed on by Lincoln.

Lincoln had reason to believe that sentiment in the army favored his reelection in 1864, so he was not reluctant to take advantage of this factor. No restriction was placed upon electioneering for the soldier vote—the first in history.[56] Leaves of absence were fully granted to officers, so they might participate in the campaign. Many of them spoke at public meetings on behalf of the Lincoln-Johnson ticket. Furloughs

---

[54] Alexander K. McClure, *Abraham Lincoln and Men of War Times* (Philadelphia: Times Publishing Co., 1892) 196.

[55] William Conant Church, *Ulysses S. Grant and the Period of National Preservation* (New York: Garden City Publishing Co., 1897) 248–49.

[56] Frank J. Williams, *A View From the Field: The Soldiers' Vote for Abraham Lincoln's Re-election* (Redlands: The Lincoln Shrine, 2000).

were given to privates, so their influence might be felt in their home districts. Men on detached service and convalescents in hospitals were sent home to help. The situation in Indiana was a special problem since it was the only large state whose soldier-citizens could not vote in the field. It was felt that the loss of the state election in October would be a severe blow to the Republicans. Because General Sherman's army contained twenty-nine regiments and two batteries of Hoosiers, Indiana Governor Oliver Morton pressured Lincoln to write Sherman to permit the Indiana soldiers to return home to cast their ballots. Sherman, feeling that their absence would endanger his army, declined to order the soldiers home, and Lincoln refused to overrule him. Nonetheless, a few Indiana regiments from posts in Tennessee and Kentucky did return home for the state election. In addition, Lincoln ordered all Indiana soldiers either hospitalized or unfit for service sent to their home state. Moreover, he sent from Sherman's army six prominent Hoosier officers along with Major Generals John Logan and Frank Blair to stump Indiana and nearby states.

Lincoln justified this conduct, just as he justified his yielding to political pressure and granting pardons and cotton-trading permits, on the ground that in seeking his own reelection and strengthening the political influence of his administration, he was working not for personal ends but for the salvation of the Union.

The greatest exercise of Lincoln's power as commander in chief was in regard to subjects that he could not delegate to any general. There was no other basis for the governments that during the war were set up in the occupied southern states. In occupied territory in wartime the president believed he had the power to do what must be done. As commander in chief of the army the president was alone the judge. It was on this theory that Lincoln proceeded.

The Emancipation Proclamation was, of course, the culmination of Lincoln's exercise of his power as commander in chief. Only on this ground could it be valid and on this ground alone Lincoln defended it: "You dislike the emancipation proclamation. You say it is unconstitutional—I think differently. I think the Constitution invests its commander-in-chief, with the law of war, in time of war."[57]

Some of Lincoln's acts as commander in chief may have been questionable, some unwise, and others of doubtful constitutionality, but in retrospect it seems clear that he was in each instance motivated not by any thought of personal aggrandizement but by his desire to save the Union and that taken together they contributed greatly to that end.

Expediency shaped Lincoln's military thought. He recognized that he had to break with the old tenets of war. Among the president's more radical moves was his decision to free and arm the slaves. With this bold strike at the South's "peculiar institution" Lincoln accomplished three goals: he provided needed manpower for the Union armies (178,000 black soldiers), he weakened the South's labor force, and he inspired African-Americans, North and South, to suppress the rebellion.

Other innovations reveal Lincoln's understanding of the concept of total war. He authorized the devastating marches led by Sherman in Georgia and North Carolina and Philip H. Sheridan in Virginia. Late in the war he refused to exchange prisoners with the Confederacy. Each rebel soldier returned to his unit, reasoned Lincoln, would help prolong the war. Lincoln also was the first commander in chief to declare medicines contraband of war.

Innovative Command Legacy

Although Lincoln made mistakes as a war leader, he learned from them. Lincoln grew as a strategist; he asked questions; he read; he probed—anything within his power to win and shorten the war. Ironically it was Lincoln, a most unlikely military man, who became America's apostle of modern war.

When George B. McClellan took the field in the spring 1862, Lincoln relieved him as general in chief on the grounds that one man could not direct an army engaged in active operations and at the same time plan moves for other armies. The president did not appoint another

---

[57] Basler, *Collected Works*, 6:408.

officer to the position until July 1862. In the interim, Lincoln acted as his own general in chief. There can be little doubt that by this time he had come to have serious misgivings about the judgments of professional soldiers. Inclined at first to defer to their opinions, he now felt a growing confidence in his own powers to decide military questions, and he was perhaps a little too ready to impose his opinions on his generals.

Nevertheless, even in this period, Lincoln did not presume to dispense completely with expert advice. Secretary of War Stanton had convened an agency known as the Army Board, consisting of the heads of the bureaus in the War Department. This was only the general staff brought together under a chairman, but the transformation of the bureau chiefs into a collective body was a forward step in command. Lincoln frequently consulted the board before arriving at an important decision.

Lincoln seemed to sense that there was something wrong in the existing arrangement. He, a civilian, was doing things that should be done by a military man. Again he decided to fill the post of general in chief. In July 1862 he named to the position Henry W. Halleck, who had been a departmental commander in the Western Theater.[58]

General Halleck seemed to be the ideal man for the job. Before the war he had been known as one of the foremost American students of the art of war and a capable departmental administrator. Lincoln intended that Halleck should be a real general in chief, that he should, under the authority of the president, actually plan and direct operations.

At first Halleck acted up to his role—but not for long. His great defect was that he disliked responsibility. He delighted to provide technical knowledge and to advise, but he shrank from making decisions. Gradually he divested himself of his original function and deliberately assumed the part of an advisor and an informed critic.

Halleck's refusal to perform the requirements of his position forced Lincoln to act again as general in chief, but he kept Halleck as titular head of the office. The president had discovered that Halleck could do one valuable service for him—in the area of military communications. Often Lincoln and his generals had experienced serious misunderstandings because, almost literally, they spoke different

---

[58] Ibid., 5:312–13

languages: Lincoln the words of the lawyer-politician, and the generals the jargon of the military. Halleck had lived in both the civil and military worlds, and he could speak the language of both. Increasingly, Lincoln came to entrust the framing of his directives to Halleck.

In those years of lonely responsibility when Lincoln directed the war effort he grew steadily in stature as a strategist. Usually he displayed greater strategic insight than most of his commanders. But he was willing, as he had been earlier, to yield the power to frame and control strategy to any general who demonstrated that he could do the job—if he could find the general. By 1864 both he and the nation were certain they had found the man—Ulysses S. Grant. And in that year the United States finally achieved a modern command system to fight a modern war.

Lincoln's most important legacy as a strategist was his establishment of the modern command system: a commander in chief to establish overall strategy; a general in chief to implement plans; and a chief of staff to relay information. Thus Lincoln, without recognizing his long-range contribution to our modern command system, laid its foundation in 1864.

Under this new system, a joint product of Lincoln and Congress, Ulysses S. Grant was named general in chief, charged with the function of planning and directing the movements of all Union armies. Because he disliked the political atmosphere in Washington, Grant established his headquarters with the army in the eastern theater, but did not technically command that army. In the new arrangement Halleck received a new office, "chief of staff." He was not, however, a chief of staff in today's sense of the term. Primarily, he was a channel of communication between Lincoln and Grant and between Grant and the seventeen departmental commanders under Grant. The perfect office soldier, he had found at last his proper niche. Lincoln, as president, would be commander in chief.

As general in chief, Grant justified every belief Lincoln had in his capacities. He possessed in superb degree the ability to think of the war in overall terms, but his grand plan of operations that ended the war was at least partly Lincolnian in concept. Grant conformed his strategy to Lincoln's known ideas: hit the Confederacy from all sides with pulverizing blows and make enemy armies, not cities, his main objective.

The General submitted the broad outlines of his plan to Lincoln and the president, trusting in Grant, approved the design without seeking to know the details.

The 1864-command system embodied the brilliance of simplicity: a commander in chief to lay down policy and grand strategy, a general in chief to frame specific battle strategy, and a chief of staff to coordinate information. It contained elements that later would be studied by military leaders and students in many nations. Abraham Lincoln, without fully realizing his part, had made a large and permanent contribution to the story of command organization.

WORD OF HONOR:
ABRAHAM LINCOLN AND THE PAROLE SYSTEM IN THE CIVIL WAR

Gerald J. Prokopowicz

This message is sent to you with the hope you will forward it to everyone you know.

I had just finished a salad at Neiman-Marcus Cafe in Dallas and decided to have the "Neiman-Marcus Cookie." It was so excellent that I asked if they would give me the recipe, but they refused. Well, I said, "Would you let me buy the recipe?" With a cute smile, she said, "Yes." I asked how much, and she responded, "Two-fifty." I said with approval to just add it to my tab.

Thirty days later, I received my VISA statement from Neiman-Marcus, and it was $285.... As I glanced at the bottom of the statement, it said, "Cookie Recipe—$250." I called Neiman's Accounting Deptartment and told them the waitress said it was "two-fifty," and I did not realize she meant $250 for a cookie recipe.

I asked them to take back the recipe and reduce my bill, and they said they were sorry, but all the recipes were this expensive so not just everyone could duplicate their bakery recipes. So I told her that I was going to see to it that every cookie lover will have a $250 cookie recipe from Neiman-Marcus for nothing.

Anyone who has an email account or who has spent much time on the internet has probably read this story already. What is remarkable about it is not that it has gained such wide circulation, but that it has done so in spite of its inherent improbability. The most obvious indication that the story is not true is the amount of money in question; $250 is certainly a lot for the average person to spend for a cookie recipe, but to a commercial enterprise the size of Neiman-Marcus, it's nothing. If Neiman-Marcus really was concerned about protecting a trade secret from its competitors, it would hardly make the information available for such a paltry sum.

Why then have so many people accepted the story and kept it alive via email for so long? One reason is that on a personal scale, $250 is not insignificant. Most people would be pretty upset about losing that much money and would regard anyone who cheated them out of it as a villain deserving of the sort of comeuppance that N-M receives in this story. It takes at least a moment of reflection to realize that the standards that govern interpersonal conduct among individuals, where $250 matters, don't apply to large organizations.

Implausible and inaccurate historical stories or interpretations occasionally gain wide public circulation for the same reason: they feature actors who behave in ways that conform closely to the expectations and understandings that we apply to our day-to-day lives. That, however, is the tip-off that the stories are legend, folklore, or even intentional falsehood. Just as institutions like Neiman-Marcus don't really behave like individuals, people in other historical times and places did not necessarily behave like twenty-first-century Americans. Thus it is possible for a contemporary author to draw massive amounts of media attention by claiming that Abraham Lincoln was a proslavery racist, while at the other end of the political spectrum, defenders of the Confederacy argue insistently that as many as 30,000 African-Americans fought for the South in the Civil War. These claims continue to gain adherents, despite overwhelming evidence against both of them, in part because it is hard for people today to imagine any motive except racism for some of the anti-egalitarian statements that Lincoln made in the 1850s or to believe that any national independence movement could really be so ideological as to disdain to take advantage of 30 percent of its available manpower for self-defense. Arguing directly against the zealots who promote such ideas is rarely productive; a more fruitful approach for those interested in strengthening the public's historical judgment is to emphasize, by illustration, just how much the past differs from the present.

The treatment of prisoners of war from 1861 to 1863 provides one such illustration. Today the phrase "prisoner of war" conjures up all kinds of dreadful images: the psychological torture and political exploitation of US airmen in the Hanoi Hilton, the sufferings of the victims of the Bataan Death March, or the hollow-eyed stares of living skeletons at Andersonville. It is disheartening, but not surprising, to read of young American army officers near the end of the Cold War discussing how in wartime they planned to use Soviet prisoners as human guinea pigs to test for the presence of nerve gas on the battlefield or to shoot them outright rather than take the trouble of caring for them, in part because they expected no better treatment if they were captured.[1]

In contrast, in 1861 when Americans faced the sudden and unexpected problem of dealing with thousands of enemy soldiers captured in battle, no one on either side spoke seriously of torture or killing. There were at first no plans to confine military prisoners. Instead, it was generally expected that once they gave their word of honor, or parole, prisoners taken in battle could safely be released. The paroled prisoners would then return home to await formal exchange, unless their government for some reason refused to recognize their paroles, in which case they would be honor-bound to return themselves to captivity.[2]

The first government to face the issue of handling enemy prisoners was that of the state of Texas, where General David E. Twiggs surrendered the federal property under his command on 18 February 1861 on condition that his troops be allowed to march out of the state. On 11 April, a few days before war began at Fort Sumter, the

---

[1] Dave Grossman, *On Killing: The Psychological Cost of Learning to Kill in War and Society* (Boston: Little, Brown, 1995) 203–204.

[2] "If a prisoner's government refuses to recognize the instrument, the prisoner is bound in honor to return to captivity." Holland Thompson, *Prisons and Hospitals*, vol. 7 of *Photographic History of the Civil War*, 10 vols., ed. Francis Trevelyan Miller (New York: Review of Reviews, 1911) 32.

Confederate government directed General Earl Van Dorn to keep Twiggs's men in Texas as prisoners of war. They were not to be jailed, however; the officers were offered paroles that began, "I give my word of honor as an officer and a gentleman," promising not to bear arms against the Confederacy until exchanged for a rebel prisoner or released from the parole by the president of the Confederate States. The signer of such a parole was deemed free to go wherever he pleased, including back to his home, with the single restriction that he was not to enter or leave a Confederate military installation without permission from the local commander. The enlisted men, not having the social status of "gentleman" that would enable them to give a meaningful word of honor, were simply sworn under oath not to bear arms against the Confederacy and kept within the state until exchanged in 1863.[3]

For the federal government, the idea of releasing rebel prisoners based on nothing more than their pledges of honor was initially more problematic. In his proclamation immediately following the attack on Fort Sumter, President Lincoln characterized the Confederacy as a set of "combinations," meaning criminal conspiracies, "too powerful to be suppressed by the ordinary course of judicial proceedings."[4] If Confederates were criminals, they could hardly offer the honor of officers and gentlemen to secure their paroles. More realistically, Lincoln and his advisers were concerned that paroling rebels or honoring paroles given by their own soldiers to rebel authorities might imply recognition of the Confederacy. Secretary of War Simon Cameron initially ordered Twiggs's paroled officers back to duty on the ground that their paroles were of no validity. This placed the officers in the awkward position of having to violate their words of honor or disobey their superiors. Captain Isaac Reeve appealed to the president for relief, and Lincoln overruled Cameron.[5]

---

[3] See William B. Hesseltine, *Civil War Prisons: A Study in War Psychology* (Columbus: Ohio State University Press, 1930) 4–5.

[4] [Abraham Lincoln,] "Proclamation Calling Militia and Convening Congress," 15 April 1861, *The Collected Works of Abraham Lincoln,* 9 vols., ed. Roy P. Basler (New Brunswick NJ: Rutgers University Press, 1953–1955) 4:332.

[5] Thompson, *Prisons and Hospitals,* 30.

The Lincoln administration was equally reluctant to exchange prisoners with the rebels either by trading actual captives or by releasing parolees from their pledges not to fight for the same reasons. But the pressure of events proved overwhelming. As the war got underway in earnest, both sides found themselves with growing numbers of prisoners on their hands. On 13 July 1861 Major General George B. McClellan wrote to the War Department that he was accepting the surrender of some 1,000 Rebels in western Virginia. He did not know what to do with them and described the problem as "embarrassing." He reported that he had agreed "to treat them with the kindness due prisoners of war," but needed "immediate instructions by telegraph as to the disposition to be made of officers and men."[6] At the First Battle of Bull Run on 21 July 1861, Confederate troops captured approximately 1,000 Union soldiers and one United States congressman, Alfred Ely of New York, who had been among the picnickers come down from Washington to watch the battle. On 8 February 1862 Ambrose Burnside's amphibious expedition to North Carolina netted 2,500 prisoners, and at Fort Donelson just over a week later, Ulysses S. Grant captured the opposing force whole, giving the North some 14,000 new prisoners. Like McClellan, Grant wondered what to do with his new charges and was relieved to write to his superior's chief of staff on 17 February: "I am now forwarding prisoners of war to your care and I shall be truly glad to get clear of them. It is a much less job to take than to keep them."[7]

The laws of war were not explicit on what Grant was to do with his prisoners or on many other points concerning prisoners of war because there existed no formal written international agreements governing the conduct of war in 1861. This is not to say, however, that there was no international law. As the Nuremberg court was to observe in 1947: "The law of war is to be found not only in treaties, but in the customs and practices of states which gradually obtained universal recognition, and

---

[6] G. B. McClellan to E. D. Townsend, US War Department, 13 July 1861, *The War of the Rebellion: A Compilation of the Official Records of the Union and Confederate Armies*, 128 vols. (Washington, DC: Government Printing Office, 1880–1901) ser. 2, vol. 3, p.9. (Hereinafter cited as *OR.*)

[7] U. S. Grant to G. W. Cullum, 17 February 1862, *OR,* ser. 2, vol. 3 p. 271; H. W. Halleck to L. Thomas, 25 December 1861, *OR,* ser. 2, vol. 3 p. 169.

from the general principles of justice applied by jurists and practiced by military courts."[8] In 1861 a body of widely recognized customs, usages, and principles regulated the taking, exchanging, and paroling of prisoners. Union Major General Henry W. Halleck, who published a volume on international law in 1861, served as a sort of adjunct attorney general, offering his legal opinion on various issues regarding prisoners.[9]

In Halleck's opinion, expressed in the aftermath of the battle of Belmont in November 1861, the Union government could safely exchange prisoners with the Confederacy: "After full consideration of the subject I am of the opinion that prisoners ought to be exchanged. This exchange is a mere military convention. A prisoner exchanged under the laws of war is not thereby exempted from trial and punishment as a traitor. Treason is a state or civil offense punishable by the civil courts; the exchange of prisoners of war is only a part of the ordinary *commercia belli*."[10] Even without Halleck's permission, individual generals had from the first moments of the war already been arranging with their immediate opponents to conduct special exchanges of individuals or small batches of captives.[11]

Negotiations for a formal cartel governing exchanges and for the general exchange of all prisoners on both sides faltered over the issue of Confederate privateers in Union hands. Refusing to recognize letters of marque issued by Jefferson Davis, the federal government held captured Confederate sailors, including the crew of the CSS *Savannah*, as pirates, which led the Confederate government to hold an equal number of Union prisoners hostage for the treatment of the *Savannah*'s crew. Under mounting pressure from the Northern public to bring home the men who were languishing in Southern prisons, the administration yielded. Operating at first under the terms of the exchange cartel established between the United Sates and Great Britain during the War of 1812 and

---

[8] Quoted in W. Michael Reisman and Chris T. Antoniou, eds., *The Laws of War: A Comprehensive Collection of Primary Documents on International Laws Governing Armed Conflict* (New York: Vintage Books, 1994) xix.

[9] Henry W. Halleck, *International Law; or, Rules Regulating the Intercourse of States in Peace and War* (San Francisco: H. H. Basecroft and Co., 1861).

[10] Halleck to McClellan, 3 December 1861, *OR*, ser. 2, vol. 3 pp. 150–51.

[11] See Hesseltine, *Civil War Prisons*, chapter 2.

later under a cartel negotiated specifically for the current situation, the blue and the gray were exchanging prisoners regularly by mid-1862. The cartel of 22 July 1862 established values based on rank—one colonel was worth fifteen private soldiers, for example—allowing exchanges of equivalent values of prisoners.[12]

Under the July cartel, all captured soldiers were to be paroled and sent back within ten days and were to remain out of service pursuant to the terms of their paroles until exchanged. Many of the prisoner exchanges of 1862 took place entirely on paper, as the two sides exchanged lists of men freed from their paroles. After his unhappy experience trying to care for the prisoners taken at Fort Donelson, Grant was one general who approved of this system: "I would suggest the policy of paroling all prisoners hereafter and taking a receipt for them from the commanding officer, so that exchanges may all be made on paper."[13]

By August 1862 there were widespread expectations that this practice would be adopted and that the North and South would soon conduct a general exchange of prisoners that would empty all the military prisons across the country. Lincoln authorized Major General John A. Dix to negotiate such an exchange,[14] and the Union Commissary-General of Prisoners, Colonel William Hoffman (himself a parolee from Twiggs's force) ordered his camp commanders to prepare careful rolls of their prisoners, whom he expected to send home shortly. Neither side particularly wanted to feed and house the other's soldiers, and both were eager to send every prisoner back, with those in excess of the enemy's numbers being paroled to await future exchanges.

One reason such a general exchange seemed possible was that the parole system was so effectively self-enforced. Most soldiers were punctilious in carrying out the terms of their paroles. The men of the 9th Michigan infantry regiment, captured and paroled by Nathan Bedford Forrest's cavalry at Murfreesboro in July 1862 refused to obey an order

---

[12] E. M. Stanton to John A. Dix, enclosure, 23 July 1862, *OR,* ser. 2, vol. 4, pp.266–68.

[13] U. S. Grant to G. W. Cullum, 17 February 1862, *OR,* ser. 2, vol. 3 pp. 271–72.

[14] Stanton to Dix, 12 July 1862, *OR,* ser. 2, vol. 4, p. 174.

from Brigadier General William Nelson to help build fortifications at Nashville, where they had stopped on their way north, because to do so would have violated their paroles not to take part in the war. They were so outraged at Nelson's orders that they break their words of honor and at the abusive fashion in which he delivered those orders, that when word came to 9th Michigan's parolees at Camp Chase a month later that Nelson had been assassinated by a fellow Union general, "Instead of mourning, some of our boys cheered and swung their caps."[15]

Unlike Nelson, most officers were just as careful as their men in respecting paroles. Article 4 of the exchange cartel specified that prisoners on parole "shall not be permitted to take up arms again, nor to serve as military police or constabulary force in any fort, garrison, or field-work held by either of the respective parties, nor as guards of prisons, depots, stores, nor to discharge any duty usually performed by soldiers, until exchanged under the provisions of this cartel."[16] When McClellan became aware that some of his officers were ordering men back to duty before they had been exchanged, he issued Special Orders No. 226, forbidding the practice and quoting the above passage from the cartel.[17]

Fear caused that soldiers and their officers to be reluctant to break their paroles. A soldier on parole who fought again before being properly exchanged was liable to execution if captured again. This was the sad fate of some members of the 13th Missouri regiment, captured at Lexington in September 1861. After giving their paroles, returning home, and being discharged, they were ordered to report back to their regiment or suffer the punishment for desertion. When they fought at Shiloh in April 1862, several of the Lexington captives were taken prisoner again and shot by the Confederates for violating their paroles. After

---

[15] Charles W. Bennett, *Historical Sketches of the Ninth Michigan Infantry (General Thomas' Headquarters Guards) with an Account of the Battle of Murfreesboro, Tennessee, Sunday, July 13, 1862: Four Years Campaigning in the Army of the Cumberland* (Coldwater MI.: Daily Courier Print, 1913) 19.

[16] *OR,* ser. 2, vol. 4, p. 267.

[17] Special Orders 226, Army of the Potomac, 4 August 1862, *OR,* ser. 2, vol. 4 p. 336; see also L. Thomas to C. H. McNally, 13 April 1862, *OR,* ser. 2, vol. 3 p. 449, prohibiting paroled troops from guarding prisoners of war.

investigating the matter, the men of the 13th Missouri discovered that they had never been exchanged, as they thought they had. They signed a petition to Secretary of War Edwin Stanton explaining, "We have been innocently and unknowingly violating our oath given at Lexington to General Price," after which they were allowed to leave the service.[18]

While fear was a factor in guaranteeing adherence to paroles, a more important motive was honor. For a Southern officer, fighting to defend a society and culture that placed a high premium on the concept of personal honor, it would have been self-defeating to violate a solemnly given word of honor.[19] But Northern culture valued honor almost as highly. Douglas Wilson argued persuasively that Abraham Lincoln's personal honor was his primary motivation for agreeing to fight a duel with James Shields that would surely have ended Lincoln's political career, and Shield's life, had it been consummated, and that it was Lincoln's honor that led him to fulfill his promise to marry Mary Todd, regardless of consequences.[20] As president, Lincoln invoked the concept of honor regularly in his public and private pronouncements. When he angrily rejected the pleas of a committee from Baltimore that he essentially give up the Union rather than fight, he replied, "There is no Washington in that—no Jackson in that—no manhood nor honor in that." When he sought the support of Congress for emancipation policy in December 1862, he knew that he could make no stronger appeal than the half-promise-half-warning that "the fiery trial through which we pass, will light us down, in honor or dishonor, to the latest generation." Lincoln's papers show that he received numerous requests to grant or extend the terms of paroles granted to various federal prisoners: Confederate soldiers, Copperhead rebel sympathizers, or just plain

---

[18] See James M. Newhard to Stanton, 27 August 1862, *OR,* ser. 2, vol. 4 pp. 455–56; B. L. E. Bonneville to T. S. Griffing, with enclosures, 25 September 1862, *OR,* ser. 2, vol. 4 pp. 556–61.

[19] For an introduction to the voluminous literature on the role of honor in antebellum Southern culture, see Kenneth S. Greenberg, *Honor & Slavery*...(Princeton NJ: Princeton University Press, 1996) and Bertram Wyatt-Brown, *Southern Honor: Ethics and Behavior in the Old South* (New York: Oxford University Press, 1982).

[20] Douglas Wilson, *Honor's Voice: The Transformation of Abraham Lincoln* (New York: Random House, 1998).

Democrats. He was not a sentimentalist or a weakling, yet Lincoln repeatedly granted such requests, apparently confident that he could rely on a pledged word of honor that the writer would refrain from any actions that would hurt the Union.[21]

The behavior of Colonel Augustus Moor stands as a particularly vivid illustration of how Northern officers could place honor above all other values. On 12 September 1862, five days before the battle of Antietam, Brigadier General Jacob D. Cox's division of the Army of the Potomac marched into Frederick, Maryland, as part of McClellan's campaign to try to catch and destroy the Confederate Army of Northern Virginia. Colonel Moor, commanding one of the division's two brigades, entered the town some distance ahead of his troops accompanied by the brigade staff. As Moor and his escort rounded a corner into the streets of Frederick, they unexpectedly came upon a rear guard of rebel cavalry led by Wade Hampton. Moor was taken prisoner.

Two days later, as Cox watched his other brigade advancing across South Mountain through Turner's Gap, he had an unexpected encounter. Cox wrote:

> I was surprised to see Colonel Moor standing at the roadside. With astonishment, I rode to him and asked him how he came there. He said that he had been taken as prisoner beyond the mountain, but had been paroled the evening before, and was now finding his way back to us on foot. "But where are *you* going?" said he. I answered that Scammon's brigade was going to support Pleasonton in a reconnoissance [sic] into the gap. Moor made an involuntary start, saying, "My God! be careful"; then, checking himself, said, "But I am paroled!" and turned away.[22]

---

[21] Reply to Baltimore Committee, 22 April 1861, *Collected Works,* ed. Basler, 4:341; Annual Message to Congress, 1 December 1862, *Collected Works,* ed. Basler, 5:537; for Lincoln's paroles, see, e.g., *Collected Works,* ed. Basler, 5:300, 403; 6:135, 219; 7:199, 373, 430, 446–47, 480; 8:51, 226, 259, 302, 303, 310, 314, 317.

[22] Jacob D. Cox, "Forcing Fox's Gap and Turner's Gap," *Battles and Leaders of the Civil War,* 4 vols., ed. Robert Underwood Johnson and Clarence Clough Buel (New York: Century, 1884–1887): 2:583–86.

Moor preferred to let the comrades of his own division, including his commanding officer, ride into the teeth of a Confederate ambush rather than violate his parole. No Southern officer could have done more for personal honor. Moor's behavior is strong evidence of the importance of honor among Northern officers, but Cox's is even stronger; as the person who was about to be sacrificed on the altar of Moor's honor, he must have fully concurred in Moor's values to record the incident with such cool approval.

Just as wholesale violations of paroles would have cut at the heart of Southerners' self-image as a members of an honorable society, in contrast to what they saw as the venal and corrupt North, so would such violations have struck at Northern self-conceptions as pioneers in an experimental nation based on law and morality. It was not in Augustus Moor's self-interest to refrain from warning his fellow soldiers of the danger they faced; on a larger scale, it was not necessarily in the military self-interest of the North to adhere to the parole system after Fort Donelson, when the Union began to hold more prisoners than the Confederacy. Neither, however, was it acceptable for Northern men openly to place self-interest above concepts like justice and fairness, which was exactly what many of them accused Southerners of doing by owning slaves. Abraham Lincoln made this point in his speech in Peoria on 16 October 1854, when he argued that slavery was wrong not only because it was unjust to the slaves, but because it distorted the political principles of those who would defend it and "forces so many really good men amongst ourselves into an open war with the very fundamental principles of civil liberty—criticizing the Declaration of Independence, and insisting that there is no right principle of action but self-interest."[23]

Lincoln clearly rejected the idea that there is no right principle of action except self-interest. He demonstrated this when he refused to postpone the presidential election of 1864 and when he refused to modify his unpopular Emancipation Proclamation in order to enhance his reelectability, in both cases acting against his immediate self-interest. Although either action might have benefited Lincoln personally and

---

[23] 16 October 1854, *Collected Works,* ed. Basler, 3:255.

perhaps given a temporary boost to the Union war effort, either would have undercut what had become the fundamental war aims of the North by 1864. As Lincoln said on 10 November 1864: "We can not have free government without elections; and if the rebellion could force us to forego, or postpone a national election, it might fairly claim to have already conquered and ruined us."[24]

While the keeping of one's parole could demonstrate a commitment to honor above self-interest, by mid-1862 increasing numbers of Union soldiers were discovering that the two values tended to coincide, as surrender and parole offered a safe and honorable way out of the war. As soon as a Union soldier surrendered, his name was removed from the roll of his regiment and transferred to that of a "skeleton regiment" consisting entirely of captured men, thus opening a vacancy in his original unit, so it could replace him and keep itself up to strength.[25] Before the cartel of 22 July 1862 the prisoner might have to wait for some time until his former commander could agree to an exchange with the local Confederate general, but under the cartel's terms he could expect to be returned within ten days. Once back in friendly territory, he could almost put the war behind him. In April 1862 the War Department declared that paroled prisoners were to be considered on leave of absence. They were free to go home, responsible only for reporting their addresses to their state governments, so they could be called back when officially exchanged.[26] On 12 June the War Department authorized military commanders to discharge parolees upon request and granted furloughs to all those who did not request discharges.[27]

Union soldiers who returned home under parole in 1862 enjoyed the status of veterans who had done their duty. As long as they had put up enough of fight to surrender honorably, they suffered no disgrace in giving their paroles. When the federal garrison at Munfordville, Kentucky, fought bravely before surrendering to an overwhelming force in September 1862, its members held their heads high as they marched

---

[24] 10 November 1864, *Collected Works,* ed. Basler, 8:101.

[25] General Orders No. 102, 25 November 1861, *OR,* ser. 2, vol. 3 p. 141.

[26] General Orders No. 36, 7 April 1862, *OR,* ser. 2, vol. 3 pp. 429.

[27] General Orders No. 65, 12 June 1862, *OR,* ser. 2, vol. 3 p. 679.

north, under parole, exchanging jibes with Yankees they passed who were marching south into danger ("Where are you going?" "Going to get your guns back for you?"). The friendly banter between regiments heading in opposite directions suggests that neither group attached any dishonor to the status of the parolees, who had earned the right to wait out the war in relative safety, protected by their words of honor that they would not fight again.

Gerald Linderman showed how the virtue of courage was gradually devalued over the course of the Civil War as soldiers came to realize that a minie bullet fired from 300 yards away was just as likely to kill a brave man as a coward and that displays of individual gallantry on the battlefield tended only to cause unnecessary casualties while having no perceptible effect on the outcome of the war.[28] The virtue of honor followed a similar trajectory of decline, as reflected in the abuses of the parole system. In August 1862 the commander of the Union's third largest field army, Don Carlos Buell, issued an order to his troops stating that the "system of paroles as practiced in this army has run into intolerable abuse." He prohibited his men from giving their paroles in the future without his written permission, which he promised to withhold in cases where the capture had resulted from the "neglect or misbehavior" of the prisoner.[29]

To make surrender a less tempting option, the government gradually tightened its regulations regarding paroled soldiers. Recognizing that the regiment was the soldier's military home on 10 May 1862 the War Department revoked the order removing captured soldiers from the rolls of their regiments.[30] The order of 12 June, granting discharges or furloughs to paroled prisoners, was the next to go. General Buell, who was trying to enforce military discipline on a body of 1,500 paroled men at Nashville, complained of the order that "the effect of course is

---

[28] Gerald F. Linderman, *Embattled Courage: The Experience of Combat in the American Civil War* (New York: Free Press, 1989).

[29] General Orders No. 41, Army of the Ohio, 8 August 1862, *OR*, ser. 2, vol. 4 p. 360; see Sam. Jones to D. C. Buell, 21 August 1862, *OR*, ser. 2, vol. 4 pp. 414–15 for Confederate objections to Buell's rules.

[30] General Orders No. 51, 10 May 1862, *OR*, ser. 2, vol. 3 p. 529; General Orders No. 52, 14 May 1862, *OR*, ser. 2, vol. 3, p. 534.

virtually to disband them but still allow them pay."[31] Although Halleck refused Buell's request not to discharge the Nashville men, he recognized the accuracy of Buell's statement.[32] Two weeks later, the War Department instituted a harsh new policy. General Orders No. 72 prohibited the discharge of paroled men, recalled those already on furlough, and decreed that all paroled prisoners were henceforth to report to detention camps, called "camps of instruction," located at Annapolis, Maryland (Camp Parole); Columbus, Ohio (Camp Chase, where Confederate POWs were also held), and Benton Barracks near St. Louis, Missouri. There they would be organized into temporary regiments and held under military discipline just like their comrades still in the ranks.[33]

This order was understandably unpopular with the parolees. The parole camps were ill prepared to absorb their new tenants.[34] Nor was it clear exactly how they should be treated, as some were being held for exchange while others were about to be mustered out, and all of them had suddenly fallen in status from "heroes home from the war" to virtual prisoners.[35] The assistant secretary of war described conditions at Camp Parole in Maryland as "deplorable," and the general responsible for the camp admitted that the men "no doubt were badly treated or rather neglected."[36]

Even worse for the parolees than the physical and psychological discomfort of their new surroundings was the fear that they were violating their words of honor. Many of them interpreted their paroles to mean that they could not do any military duty at all, including the police and fatigue duty necessary to maintain order and cleanliness in their own

---

[31] Buell to Halleck, 12 June 1862, *OR,* ser. 2, vol. 3, p. 678; Buell to Halleck, 31 May 1862, *OR,* ser. 2, vol. 3, p. 617.

[32] Halleck to Buell, 12 June 1862, *OR,* ser. 2, vol. 3, p. 678; Halleck to Buell, 14 June 1862, *OR,* ser. 2, vol. 4, p. 18; Halleck to N. H. Brainard, 28 June 1862, *OR,* ser. 2, vol. 4, p. 95.

[33] General Orders No. 72, 28 June 1862, *OR,* ser. 2, vol. 4 p. 94.

[34] Hesseltine, *Civil War Prisons,* 75.

[35] See, e.g. B. L. E. Bonneville to W. S. Ketchum, 13 July 1862, *OR,* ser. 2, vol. 4, p. 191.

[36] P. H. Watson to John E. Wool, 25 August 1862, *OR,* ser. 2, vol. 4, p. 430; N. Brewer to [Surgeon-General, US Army], 28 August 1862, *OR,* ser. 2, vol. 4, pp. 459–60; Wool to Col. Townsend, September 4, 1862, *OR,* ser. 2, vol. 4, p. 489.

camps.[37] In response to complaints that paroled troops were being forced to perform illegal duty,[38] Halleck minced no words: "Paroled prisoners are obliged to do guard, police, and fatigue duty for the proper order of their own corps."[39] The Iowa troops and their friends back home continued to write to the War Department, Secretary Stanton, and Lincoln himself, until the camp commander reasserted order by showing Halleck's message to the prisoners, explaining that they were being held in camp "for the purpose of feeding, clothing, mustering and paying them, and [having] them properly accounted for and in readiness for an exchange, and not with the view of ordering them to take the field or take up arms against the Southern Confederacy." After he assured them "they would not be required to violate the parole by the Government or its agents," the trouble subsided.[40]

By putting paroled soldiers into what amounted to prison camps and keeping them under military discipline, the federal government sharply reduced the temptation for individual soldiers to take advantage of the parole system. At the same time, it created a great temptation for military and civil officials to find ways to put the parolees to work whether or not permitted by the rules of the exchange cartel. Governors bombarded Stanton with requests that paroled men be sent to their home states, to be kept in state-run camps.[41] The secretary of war peremptorily refused most of these requests, responding to Governor Oliver P. Morton of Indiana, "Sending prisoners to their own State operates as an inducement for shameful surrender."[42]

The one request to which Stanton responded favorably came from Governor Ramsey of Minnesota, who asked on 22 August that the 3d

[37] See, e.g., Robert F. Winslow to Stanton, 19 July 1862, *OR,* ser. 2, vol. 4, p. 246.

[38] N. B. Baker to [Stanton], 21 July 1862, *OR,* ser. 2, vol. 4, pp. 250–51; Samuel J. Kirkwood to Stanton, 22 July 1862, *OR,* ser. 2, vol. 4, pp. 257–60.

[39] Halleck to N. B. Baker, 19 July 1862, *OR,* ser. 2, vol. 4, p. 242.

[40] Ketchum to Lorenzo Thomas, 28 July 1862, *OR,* ser. 2, vol. 4, p. 299; Robert F. Winslow to Lincoln, 28 July 1862, *OR,* ser. 2, vol. 4, p. 300.

[41] Examples include Austin Blair to Stanton, 8 August 1862, *OR,* ser. 2, vol. 4, p. 359; O. P. Morton to Stanton, 26 September 1862, *OR,* ser. 2, vol. 4, p. 562; J. F. Robinson to Stanton, 2 October 1862, *OR,* ser. 2, vol. 4, pp. 588–89; Robinson to Stanton, 3 October 1862, *OR,* ser. 2, vol. 4, p. 594.

[42] Stanton to Morton, 26 September 1862, *OR,* ser. 2, vol. 4, p. 562.

Minnesota, on parole at Benton Barracks, be sent "with arms and ammunition" to help defend its home state against "the overwhelming force of Indians" who were attacking there. "This service would not be a violation of their parole," Ramsey concluded, without explanation.[43] There is no record of Stanton's reply, but on 9 September when Governor David Tod repeated the suggestion of sending paroled troops to Minnesota, Stanton answered that the idea was "excellent and will be immediately acted upon."[44]

Despite Ramsey's assurance to the contrary, military service on the frontier was clearly in violation of the parole provisions of the exchange cartel. To disregard the cartel's explicit prohibition of the use of paroled troops would have been an unthinkable violation of the honor of the United States government, but there are few military measures that cannot be rationalized once they come to seem necessary. The first step in the process of remilitarizing the paroled men was to require them to perform the "guard, police, and fatigue duty for the proper order of their own corps," which Halleck had declared acceptable for paroled men. Halleck, however, had offered his opinion before the cartel was signed on 22 July 1862, and he did not read it until October. The cartel was clear on this point: in addition to Article 4's prohibition against active duty, quoted above, Article 6 reiterated that one of the underlying principles of the agreement was "that the parole forbids the performance of field, garrison, police, or guard, or constabulary duty."[45]

In a hair-splitting effort to get around this provision while still maintaining order at Camp Chase, the assistant adjutant general instructed the camp's commander that he could order paroled officers "to take command of paroled men to drill and do camp-guard duty for mere purposes of discipline" as long as they did not actually guard prisoners of war "or relieve any other officer from duty so the latter would be disengaged to serve against the enemy."[46] Of course, by commanding their troops for camp guard duty, the paroled officers at Camp Chase

---

[43] Alex. Ramsey to Stanton, 22 August 1862, *OR,* ser. 2, vol. 4, p. 417.

[44] Stanton to Governor Tod, 9 September 1862, *OR,* ser. 2, vol. 4, p. 499.

[45] *OR,* ser. 2, vol. 4, pp. 266–68.

[46] E. D. Townsend to C. W. B. Allison, 4 August 1862, *OR,* ser. 2, vol. 4, p. 336.

were relieving other troops of the necessity to do the same. At Annapolis, where paroled officers were apparently not so employed, Major General John E. Wool had to ask Halleck for a "full regiment" to serve as guards; the absurdity of having to detail volunteer citizen-soldiers to guard other volunteers galled the administration, including the secretary of war and the president. Not long after, the commander of Camp Parole issued an order informing paroled officers that they were not exempt from commanding their men and were "bound to perform police duties and anything that may be necessary to the welfare and comfort of the paroled troops."[47]

After the idea of employing paroled troops to police themselves gained general acceptance, the next step was to accuse the prisoners of dishonorable behavior in surrendering to the enemy, thus weakening their claim to the moral high ground if they tried to assert their honor when ordered to violate their paroles. Governor Tod pointed out to Stanton that if the troops who surrendered en masse at the battle of Richmond, Kentucky, on 30 August had refused to give their paroles, it would have taken the victorious rebel general Edmund Kirby Smith's entire army to guard them.[48] Stanton agreed that the parole system was offering too many troops an easy way out of the war, writing, "There is reason to fear that many voluntarily surrender for the sake of getting home."[49] A correspondent wrote to Stanton that the parole system was ruining the army, and it had become "an inducement not only for cowards, but for men discontented with their officers, or even homesick to surrender."[50] In summer and fall 1862 Union troops surrendered in large numbers at Murfreesboro, Tennessee; Richmond and Munfordville, Kentucky; and most spectacularly, at Harper's Ferry, Virginia, where Stonewall Jackson's men gobbled up more than 10,000 Yankee prisoners. The vast influx of paroled prisoners that followed gave some credence to Stanton's fears, and on 24 September he ordered parolees from Annapolis as well as those still at Harper's Ferry to go west and

---

[47] Special Orders No. 40, Headquarters Paroled Prisoners near Annapolis, MD, 18 September 1862, *OR,* ser. 2, vol. 4, p. 540.

[48] Tod to Stanton, 9 September 1862, *OR,* ser. 2, vol. 4, p. 499.

[49] Stanton to Tod, 9 September 1862, *OR,* ser. 2, vol. 4, p. 499.

[50] J. H. Geiger to Stanton, 29 September 1862, *OR,* ser. 2, vol. 4, p. 576.

report to General John Pope in Minnesota. "It is important to have them replaced by troops from the West and also to relieve the troops that are guarding them now," he wrote.[51]

Lincoln himself expressly endorsed Stanton's plan. On 20 September he wrote, "I know it is your purpose to send the paroled prisoners to the seat of the Indian difficulties, and I write this only to urge that this be done with all possible dispatch." That good regiments should be occupied guarding parolees, Lincoln stressed, "should not be endured beyond the earliest possible moment.... Each regiment arriving on the frontier will relieve a new regiment to come forward."[52]

Two weeks later Lincoln had second thoughts. When he learned that the Confederate cavalry general J. E. B. Stuart was issuing paroles that specifically forbade fighting against Indians, he initially thought that his officers should refuse to recognize such paroles. Before acting, however, he asked for Halleck's legal opinion, "based both upon the general law and cartel" because he wished "to avoid violations of law and bad faith."[53] Halleck replied immediately that Lincoln was right and that the rebels had no right to require anything but what he called "the usual parole—not to bear arms against the Confederate States during the war or until exchanged." A few hours later, Halleck actually read the cartel for the first time and changed his mind, explaining to Lincoln that the agreement prohibited all military duty for paroled prisoners.[54]

The next day, after a meeting between Stanton and Halleck, Halleck reported to Lincoln that Stanton's idea was legal after all. "After full consultation with the Secretary of War and Colonel Holt it is concluded that the parole under the cartel does not prohibit doing service against the Indians, " Halleck wrote, using the passive voice in a final effort to salvage his integrity as a legal scholar by deflecting responsibility for such an egregious misinterpretation.[55] Lincoln had once observed that the

---

[51] Stanton to [Lorenzo] Thomas, 24 September 1862, *OR,* ser. 2, vol. 4, p. 550.

[52] Lincoln to Stanton, 20 September 1862, *Collected Works,* ed. Basler, 5:432.

[53] Lincoln to Halleck, 3 October 1862, *Collected Works,* ed. Basler, 5:449.

[54] Halleck to Lincoln, 3 October 1862, *OR,* ser. 2, vol. 4, 593, pp. 593–94.

[55] Halleck to Lincoln, 4 October 1862, *OR,* ser. 2, vol. 4, p. 598. Stanton did not like Halleck, and vice versa; see Benjamin P. Thomas and Harold M. Hyman, *Stanton:*

financial self-interest of the slaveholder prevented him from understanding the clear meaning of the Declaration of Independence because the "plainest print cannot be read through a gold eagle"; now military self-interest had blinded Stanton and Halleck to the plain meaning of the exchange and parole cartel.[56]

Not every Union official was as pliant as Halleck. After Robert Ould, the Confederate commissioner for prisoner exchanges, protested that using paroled men to fight Indians was "in direct conflict with the terms of the cartel," Union Adjutant General Lorenzo Thomas agreed and pointed out to Stanton that the practice "would seem to be contrary to the fourth article of the cartel."[57]

More important, the paroled men themselves recognized that they were being ordered to do something inappropriate. They had already shown considerable resistance to the assignment of fatigue and camp duty, which were of questionable legality. When ordered to the West to take up arms against the Indians, in plain violation of their paroles, they simply refused. "This movement is very distasteful to them and many complaints are made that it is a violation of their parole," Adjutant General Thomas told Stanton, regarding the men at Annapolis.[58] Many of them deserted en route to Chicago, where their commander warned Thomas that answering Pope's request for a regiment was "impossible as the men are unarmed and in a state of sure mutiny"; their mood did not improve after the Chicago *Tribune* strengthened their legal position by publishing the terms of the cartel.[59]

From Camp Chase in Ohio, General Lew Wallace reported that the paroled men "generally refuse to be organized or to do any duty

The Life and Times of Lincoln's Secretary of War (New York: Alfred A. Knopf, 1962) 139–40.

[56] 26 June 1857, *Collected Works,* ed. Basler, 2:409.

[57] L. Thomas to Stanton, 14 October 1862, *OR,* ser. 2, vol. 4, p. 621–22; Robt. Ould to W. H. Ludlow, 5 October 1862, *OR,* ser. 2, vol. 4, pp. 600–603. Ould wrote: "This is in direct conflict with the terms of the cartel. Its language is very plain." Ould to Ludlow, 602.

[58] L. Thomas to Stanton, 22 September 1862, *OR,* ser. 2, vol. 4, pp. 546–47.

[59] Daniel Tyler to L. Thomas, 3 October 1862, *OR,* ser. 2, vol. 4, pp. 595–96; Daniel Tyler to L. Thomas, 5 October 1862, *OR,* ser. 2, vol. 4, p. 600.

whatever" and begged Stanton not to send any more men to him.[60] He was unable to control the men he had, who were "lousy, ragged, despairing and totally demoralized." They jeered and groaned at Wallace when he tried to organize them, and when he finally put together a unit that he called "First Regiment Paroled Prisoners," most of them deserted at the first opportunity. Wallace thought it pointless to organize any more units of paroled men, asking, "But what will such regiments be worth? Of what profit will they be?"[61]

These questions were never answered because on 8 October Pope telegraphed abruptly that the Indian war in Minnesota was over.[62] The conflict between the government's military needs and the personal honor of its soldiers was not, however. Wallace wrote of the Camp Chase men that "every objector intrenched [sic?] himself behind his parole," and Commissary-General Hoffman observed that as long as paroles were seen as personal obligations, the men were honor-bound to do as they had done. Further, the equally honor-conscious officers of the court might well support any officer court-martialed over the issue.[63]

In the same message in which he pointed out the problem, Hoffman suggested a solution. If paroles were understood as the obligation of the government not to use prisoners as soldiers, rather than as the personal pledges of the prisoners not to allow themselves to be so employed, then questionable interpretations or even outright violations of parole no longer compromised the personal honor of any individual, nor could any soldier protest at anything he was ordered to do. The Union officer was henceforth to be treated in matters of parole as an unthinking tool of the state rather than a free moral agent, with the bleak consolation that if ordered to violate his parole, then like Henry V's men at Agincourt, "If / his cause be wrong, our obedience to the king wipes / the crime of it out of us."[64]

---

[60] Lew. Wallace to Stanton, 26 September 1862, *OR,* ser. 2, vol. 4, p. 563.

[61] Lew. Wallace to L. Thomas, 28 September 1862, *OR,* ser. 2, vol. 4, pp. 569–71.

[62] John Pope to Halleck, 9 October 1862, *OR,* ser. 2, vol. 4, p. 607.

[63] W. Hoffman to L. Thomas, 25 October 1862, *OR,* ser. 2, vol. 4, pp. 652–53.

[64] Hoffman to Stanton, 3 November 1862, *OR,* ser. 2, vol. 4, pp. 674–75; Shakespeare, *Henry V,* act 4, scene 2.

The theory that "the parole is virtually given by the Government and not by individuals," as Halleck wrote in November 1862, may have worked for English peasants in 1415, but was less satisfactory for the volunteer citizen-soldiers of the Republic.[65] By early 1863 the entire parole system was in a shambles. The parole camps were neglected by the government and filled with men who still refused any sort of duty or discipline. Conditions were so bad at Annapolis that a group of prisoners from Pennsylvania petitioning their governor said that they would prefer to be returned to Confederate captivity rather than remain at Camp Parole.[66]

With the enforcement of paroles now in the hands of the government, rather than those of honor-bound individuals, the spirit that initially animated the system soon disappeared. General Orders No. 49, issued in February 1863, sharply restricted the circumstances under which Union troops could give or accept paroles.[67] After the battle of Gettysburg in July of that year, the War Department unilaterally declared free all the prisoners that Lee had captured and paroled because they had not been properly "reduced to possession" and released at one of the previously agreed-upon points of exchange. The Confederates reached the limit beyond which they were willing to enforce the strictures of parole upon themselves after the fall of Vicksburg, when Ulysses S. Grant similarly issued battlefield paroles to some 20,000 prisoners. When Union officers complained about some of Pemberton's paroled men fighting at Chickamauga, Lincoln dismissed the matter by telling the story of the annoying dog that was fed gunpowder by the neighbors—after it exploded, the owner looked at the pieces and mournfully concluded, "Well, I guess he'll never be much account again—*as a dog*." Lincoln, as usual, was more strategically astute than were his generals in recognizing that, paroled or not, "Pemberton's forces will never be much account again—*as an army*."[68]

---

[65] Halleck to H. G. Wright, 10 November 1862, *OR,* ser. 2, vol. 4, p. 697.

[66] A. G. Curtin to Stanton, 14 October 1862, *OR,* ser. 2, vol. 4, p. 620.

[67] General Orders No. 49, 28 February 1863, *OR,* ser. 2, vol. 5 pp. 306–307.

[68] Francis F. Browne, *The Every-day Life of Abraham Lincoln* (New York: N. D. Thompson, 1887) 616–17.

The parole system likewise ceased to be of much account by the end of 1863. The exchange of prisoners had broken down over the issue of Africans in arms, whom the Confederacy refused to regard as prisoners of war. On 7 May 1864, claiming that the rebels had unilaterally "exchanged" their paroled men, the War Department ordered all parolees back into active service.[69] Soldiers who surrendered any time in the last year of the war could look forward to nothing but indefinite confinement under inhuman conditions.

The photographs of those men tend to come to mind when we think of Civil War prisoners. Blinded by the shocking similarities between the starvation victims at Andersonville and Buchenwald or the mass graves at Camp Douglas and Katyn, it is easy to assume that the atrocities of the twentieth century were the rule in the nineteenth century as well. The premodern values that persisted through the first year and half of the Civil War are too often forgotten, even by professional historians. In looking at the willingness of individuals to honor their paroles at any cost, and at two governments at war willing (for a time) to release prisoners on the strength of nothing more than their word of honor not to fight, we see a world far removed from ours. Acknowledging and respecting the unique characteristics of that world remains the best defense against those whose visions of the past require them to believe in a Confederacy defended by battalions of black soldiers, fighting against a racist Lincoln who seeks to prolong their slavery.

---

[69] General Orders No. 191, May 7, 1864, *OR,* ser. 2, vol. 7, p. 126

SERVING PRESIDENT LINCOLN: THE PUBLIC CAREER OF JOHN G. NICOLAY[1]

John R. Sellers

It is not entirely clear why Abraham Lincoln retained John George Nicolay, the young lawyer-clerk who handled his correspondence during the 1860 campaign, as his private secretary in the White House. Reflecting on the appointment thirty years later, Henry C. Whitney, Lincoln's lawyer-friend and fellow traveler on the Eighth Judicial Circuit, characterized Nicolay rather critically as only "a good mechanical, routine clerk" and suggested that this "nobody" owed his appointment to the president-elect's desire to avoid offending one or the other of two better qualified candidates—William O. Stoddard and Benjamin F. James.[2] It is doubtful that Lincoln shared Whitney's sober opinion of Nicolay, but he must have been aware that the reticent clerk he had chosen to accompany him to Washington lacked the refinement and culture, the savoir-faire, expected of appointees to such exalted positions. The decision made, however, Lincoln stood by his harried and often maligned secretary, never once suggesting that Nicolay resign.

Nicolay's principal asset to Lincoln may have been an absolute loyalty. There was never a hint that he might violate the president's trust. Also, Nicolay could be counted upon to represent the commander in chief accurately in delicate political situations. He may not have gotten

---

[1] This essay is based primarily on letters between John G. Nicolay and Therena Bates, 1861–1865, in the Nicolay Papers, Library of Congress.

[2] Henry C. Whitney to William H. Herndon, 23 June 1887, *Herndon's Informants: Letters, Interviews, and Statements about Abraham Lincoln,* Douglas L. ed. Wilson and Rodney O. Davis (Urbana: University of Illinois Press, 1998) 619.

along well with Mary Todd Lincoln, but few people did, at least not for long. Communications between Nicolay and Mary Todd Lincoln became especially strained over such things as the guest list to White House entertainment, seating arrangements at important diplomatic functions, staffing, and miscellaneous expenditures for White House furnishing and decorations.

Unfortunately, Nicolay quickly came to detest the daily stream of office-seekers and supplicants requesting the ritual five-minute audience with President Lincoln. His visible disdain for many callers gained him the unenviable reputation of "the bulldog in the anteroom." Rumors circulated far and wide about his sour and crusty disposition, and inevitably some influential people sought to have him dismissed. Lincoln, although aware of the problem, maintained a seeming indifference. If he raised the issue with Nicolay, he did so in private.

The image of Nicolay so adoringly drafted by his daughter Helen in her 1949 biography, *Lincoln's Secretary*,[3] is quite different from this brief characterization. In all fairness, it should be noted that Helen reached maturity when her father's professional star was at its zenith and that she had been forced to assume the role of an amanuensis when Nicolay's eyes began to fail. Both father and daughter seem to have been blinded by the same light, only in different ways. Nicolay's eyes lost the ability to adjust to light, forcing him to work in near darkness, while Helen, basking in the reflected light of her illustrious father, lost all objectivity.

This is not to imply that Nicolay did not work hard in the White House. He received and reviewed all incoming mail. Particularly delicate or significant missives were referred to the Tycoon, as he and John Hay playfully referred to the president, and he answered or drafted answers to items of secondary importance. Particularly routine inquiries or requests went to assistant secretary John Hay, or in Hay's absence, to William O. Stoddard, Edward D. Neale, and others. Nicolay also delivered verbal or written messages to Congress, and he tried to gauge the way the political winds were blowing both in Washington and the nation at large.

---

[3] Helen Nicolay, *Lincoln's Secretary: A Biography of John G. Nicolay* (New York: Longman's Green, 1949).

Obviously, there were days when the secretary had to drag his exhausted body into bed in the wee hours of the morning, but his claim to have had little time for personal affairs rings false. In reality, Nicolay attended most of the important social events in Washington. Certainly no one can fault the secretary for indulging in such pleasures. Additionally, Nicolay deserves nothing but praise for the time he spent on his one private pleasure–his biweekly letter to his fiancée, Miss Therena Bates of Pittsfield, Illinois, and it is indeed unfortunate that the result of this exchange of pleasantries with the woman he eventually would marry should provide one of the few unflattering glimpses of the secretary.

Nicolay's correspondence with Miss Bates began in early June 1860, shortly after he entered the employment of then candidate Abraham Lincoln. It ended five years and 292 letters later as the stricken secretary sorted and packed the papers of the Lincoln Presidency, or what now constitutes the Robert Todd Lincoln Family Papers in the Library of Congress. Nicolay wrote his love letters, if such they can be called, mostly on "Executive Mansion" stationary, the exceptions being the few missives he penned while on vacation or on political trips. He adopted a program of two letters a week, which translates into one letter every three or four days. Nicolay usually wrote Therena on Wednesdays and Sundays, but often he was so overwhelmed with work that his mid-week letters had to be delayed a day or two and amounted to no more than brief notes, hastily scribbled in time for the morning mail. For Nicolay, however, maintaining the routine was as important as the substance of the letter itself. Once, when he could not think of a plausible excuse for failing to fulfill his literary commitment to Therena, he attributed the neglect to an unfortunate concatenation or chain of unfortuitous circumstances. Any scolding from Therena brought forth an assurance that he would not let the omission grow into a habit. Hence, the longest gaps in this exchange appear understandably in the heat of the 1864 presidential campaign and in winter 1863, which Therena spent in Washington. On the whole, Nicolay inked his amours with remarkable consistency. Regrettably, Therena, an extremely shy and private person, insisted that all of her letters be destroyed. Nicolay grudgingly complied, but for some unexplained reason, Therena kept the letters she received.

Despite exercising one's imagination to the fullest, Nicolay's letters to Therena scarcely qualify as love letters. "Your George," as he dispassionately ended each missive, was as close to an expression of affection as he could bring himself. Such emotional reserve is perhaps best illustrated in the following excerpt from a letter Nicolay sent to Therena just after president Lincoln's first inauguration:

> If I had not been for years educating myself to be a mere bundle of quiet and dignified imperturbability—that was never even to be surprised or betrayed into an emotion, I should sit down tonight and write you a real love-letter—full of all the pathos and passion of which young men[,] or rather boys[,] in their foolish phrensy [sic?] of their first love are guilty.... I have often told you what I again reiterate—that you are the only woman on earth to whom I turn in entire confidence—in whom I have an unshaken faith. You must not[,] therefore[,] be surprised, Therena, that when I become disgusted with all the glaring faults, the hollowness and heartlessness of the great crowd of people of both sexes whom I meet and see, an almost irresistible longing comes over me to go back to the one shrine where I can yet go to worship truth and devotion. You know that I do not cheat myself into the belief that you are perfect—or even near it. Nevertheless[,] it is a relief to have and express such faith as I have in you—even if I must do it through the stiff and formal medium of writing, and at the distance of thousands of miles.[4]

Nicolay had been in Washington just six months when he wrote Therena, "This being here where I can overlook the whole war and never be in it—always threatened with danger and never meeting it—constantly worked to death, and yet doing nothing, I assure you grows exceedingly irksome." It would be a mistake, however, to assume from such complaints that the secretary preferred an active role in the war to the relative safety of Washington. He may have been a brave man.

---

[4] Nicolay to Therena, 17 March 1861, Nicolay Papers, LC.

At least he did not flee the city as did many prominent citizens after the Battle of First Bull Run when a Confederate attack seemed imminent. Yet Nicolay was more a student of war than a warrior. He harbored no illusions about the glories of battle. When the opportunity to be actively involved in the conflict presented itself in the form of a draft notice in late 1864, the secretary immediately claimed poor health and hired a substitute, one Hiram Child, a black man, for the then enormous sum of $550. Therena received assurances that he was actually in good health and had acted as he had only to avoid any appearance of impropriety. Child died in battle a few months later.

Without doubt, Nicolay's health was good, except perhaps for the hint of a future problem with his eyes. That very summer he had had the exhilarating experience of hunting buffalo from horseback in both the Nebraska Territory and the Colorado Territory. His real interest in war was in touring the scenes of recent battles. Nicolay jumped at the chance to visit Pittsburg Landing in the aftermath of the Battle of Shiloh, and he spent four long days mentally reconstructing the movement of Union and Confederate troops in and around Fredericksburg following General Ambrose Burnside's costly attack of December 1862.

One of the most puzzling, and perhaps damning, aspect of Nicolay's White House service was his habit of going on extended summer vacations at the height of each campaign season. These trips put the secretary completely out of touch with authorities in Washington for days and weeks at a time. Anticipating criticism of a seeming indifference to the war, Nicolay informed Therena that he was only trying to avoid the heat and inevitable fevers that plagued Washington each summer, but he later admitted that he was more likely to lose his temper than his health if he remained in the White House. The following lighthearted aside to Therena reveals the manner in which Nicolay actually viewed the threat to his health from the insect world:

> My usual trouble in this room, (my office) is from what the world is sometimes please to call *"big bugs"*—(oftener humbugs)—but at this present writing (ten o'clock P.M. Sunday night) the thing is quite reversed, and *little bugs* are the pest. The gas lights over my desk are burning brightly and the windows of

the room are open, and all bugdom outside seems to have organized a storming party to take the gas light, in numbers which seem to exceed the contending hosts at Richmond. The air is swarming with them, they are on the ceiling, the walls, and the furniture in countless numbers, they are buzzing about the room, and butting their heads against the window panes. They are on my clothes, in my hair, and on the sheet I am writing on. They are all here, the plebeian masses, as well as the great and distinguished members of the oldest and largest patrician families—the Millers, the Roaches, the Whites, the Blacks, yea even the wary diplomatic foreigners from the Musquito Kingdom. They hold a high carnival, or rather a perfect Saturnalia. Intoxicated and maddened and blinded by the bright gas-light, they dance, and rush and fly about in wild gyrations, until they are drawn into the dazzling but fatal heat of the gas-flame, when they fall to the floor, burned and maimed and mangled to the death, to be swept out into the dust and rubbish by the servant in the morning.[5]

Much to Nicolay's dismay, his 1861 vacation in Newport, Rhode Island, was delayed by a condition his doctor described as "billious." The ailment kept him in Washington throughout the First Manassas or Bull Run Campaign. Three powerful purgatives taken almost simultaneously to rid his body of the diagnosed "excess bile" put the secretary in a conflicted state described to Therena as something between muscular lassitude and nervous animation. Nicolay recovered as soon as he stopped taking the prescribed medicines, and, shortly thereafter, departed for Newport.

It would be safe to assume that Nicolay chose Newport as the site of his first White House vacation largely on the recommendation of John Hay. Hay was a graduate of Brown University in Providence, and having spent many leisurely hours in this seaside resort, could attest to the abundance of beautiful young ladies that frequented its beaches each summer.

---

[5] Nicolay to Therena, 20 July 1862, Nicolay Papers, LC.

The trip lasted only three weeks, but the so-called quiet time Nicolay reported to Therena included four or more evening dances, a clam bake, a trip to Providence, dinner aboard the USS *Constitution*, a reception, a tea party, beach walks, concerts, promenades, and evening carriage rides, all in the company of one or more of the fairer sex. Nicolay's letters to John Hay, who remained in Washington, told the real story.

The three succeeding summers found Nicolay in the Minnesota Territory for two months, the Colorado Territory for three months, and Kansas. All three trips were paid for by the United States government. Nicolay was well acquainted with William P. Dole, commissioner of Indian affairs, and doubtless he used his influence with the commissioner to secure successive appointments as secretary to a commissions organized to negotiate treaties with the Indians. Nicolay performed little work for the commissions. Most of his time was spent in hunting or sightseeing. He did carry the funds for the Colorado Indian commission, but it is difficult to imagine that such a task required the personal attention of the president's private secretary.

Also troubling about Nicolay is the casual attitude he displayed toward Therena when he was away from Washington. Even though these two lovers were seldom together, on his 1863 vacation Nicolay scheduled no more than a day or two in Pittsfield out of the sixty to ninety days he was away from Washington. He stopped briefly at Pittsfield en route to the Minnesota Territory in summer 1862, but two or three days later he was writing John Hay from his room at St. Paul's International Hotel about the pleasant babble of female voices in an adjoining room that he hoped to investigate.

If part of Nicolay's purpose in abandoning the capital each summer was to escape the dangers of disease and war, he was only half successful. The trip to Minnesota put him in the middle of a Sioux uprising that left 500 white settlers dead. At one point the commissioners were surrounded by a small band of armed and excited Chippewas led by Chief Hole-in-the-Day. The affair so frightened Nicolay that he wrote John Hay, "I still think it is about an even chance whose scalp will be in chancery first, yours or mine. Pray have the rebels removed from their close proximity to *la Maison Blanche* before I get there. I shall need a quiet retreat in which to recover from my Indian scare." The Arapaho war party that threatened Nicolay on his 1864 vacation forced him to abandon his plan to explore Kansas, where he was speculating in land. Democratic newspapers may have taken unfair advantage of the secretary by suggesting his record-setting transcontinental trip eastward showed a lack of courage, but Nicolay's Washington friends also chided him for giving ground so rapidly to the Arapahos.

Nicolay was on yet another junket, an ocean cruise aboard the gunboat *Santiago de Cuba*, on 14 April 1865, the day President Lincoln was shot. Gustavus V. Fox, assistant secretary of the navy, had arranged the trip for ten or twelve close friends, male and female. The female guests had attracted Nicolay's attention. The voyage included stops at Havana, Cuba; Savannah, Georgia; and Charleston and Hilton Head, South Carolina. Foremost on the agenda was the raising of the Union flag over Fort Sumter on 13 April 1865. Although the voyage put Nicolay out of communication with the White House at what proved to be a critical time, there was nothing the secretary could have done to save President Lincoln. No one expected an assassination attempt. Nicolay heard the tragic news the night of 16 April when the *Santiago de Cuba* reached Cape Henry and took on board a harbor pilot to guide the vessel into Hampton Roads. Naturally, he was devastated. In a letter to Therena written the following day he lamented:

It was so unexpected, so sudden and so horrible even to think of, much less to realize, that we *couldn't* believe it, and therefore remained in hope that it would prove one of the thousand groundless exaggerations which the war has brought forth during the past four years. Alas, when we reached Point Lookout at daylight this morning, the mournful reports of the minute guns that were being fired, and the flags at half-mast left us no ground for further hope. I went on shore with the boat to forward our telegrams, and there found a Washington paper of Saturday, giving us all the painful details[6]

---

[6] Nicolay to Therena, 17 April 1865, Nicolay Papers, LC.

To Nicolay's credit, he was circumspect with Therena on political affairs and on daily life in the Lincoln household. Although he was not a true political insider, he thought of himself as a "high government official," and he attempted to act the part. Certainly, he knew far more than he shared with Therena. Behind-the-back remarks about Mary Todd Lincoln were few despite the budgetary and social tug of war that went on between the secretary and the first lady, and only once did Nicolay reveal details on the improprieties of White House servants.

Nicolay was openly critical of Cabinet Secretaries Simon Cameron and Salmon P. Chase; the former he accused of incompetence, and the latter of political duplicity. Such criticisms were well deserved. Under Cameron, the War Department essentially ran itself, and the Treasury Department under Chase was a hotbed of political intrigue, fueled largely by the secretary himself. Nicolay habitually referred to Treasury Department employees close to Chase as "the treasury rats."

Nicolay was perhaps least guarded in his correspondence with Therena when writing about high-ranking officers in the Union Army. It is difficult to say to what degree the opinions he expressed represented his independent judgment. Certainly he was aware of President Lincoln's frequent disappointment with the top military brass. Especially anathema to Nicolay were Generals John Fremont, Irvin McDowell, John Pope, George B. McClellan, Ambrose Burnside, Joseph Hooker, and Fitz-John Porter. To Nicolay, the generals were either asleep on the job, ignorant, or afraid to fight. Not even the United States Congress escaped the secretary's wrath. Many senators and most congressmen were rascals, particularly Peace Democrats. Obviously, the secretary lacked President Lincoln's generous and forgiving spirit.

Perhaps what renders Nicolay especially vulnerable in any character analysis is the use of his position in the White House to advance the careers of friends and acquaintances. For example, Nicolay obtained military commissions and quick promotions for two Pittsfield men. One was Therena's brother, Dorus Austin Bates, nicknamed Major. Nicolay openly admitted that neither man he helped was qualified for his appointment, but he excused the deed by claiming that he had acted consistently with what was happening throughout the Union Army. Rationalizing further, Nicolay assured Therena that both men would soon learn their duties. In this same vein, Nicolay also managed to get one of his nephews discharged from the army and placed in the Agriculture Department, explaining to Therena, "I hope to make something of him by and by, but for the present he needs instruction more than anything else."

Disenchanted with their work in the White House, Nicolay and Hay both used their influence with the president and Secretary Seward to secure much coveted diplomatic posts in Europe. Nicolay wanted to bring up the subject with Lincoln in summer 1864 but realized the president would not welcome the distraction in the middle of his reelection campaign. However, in early 1865, Nicolay was confirmed as American Consul at Paris, France, at twice his existing salary. Hay was assigned to Paris as Secretary of Legation, and later to Vienna, Austria, in a similar capacity. Not surprisingly, each man clung tenaciously to his European post as long as possible. Hay, in particular, treated the assignment as one long vacation.

As often happens in such situations, Nicolay and Hay became accustomed to political preferment and showed little remorse at squeezing every cent they could out of the government. When John Hay was finally replaced in Vienna by a political neophyte, Nicolay advised him as follows:

> Here you are at a turn in your lane. I have been hoping all along that the *status quo* would be maintained a while longer, so that we might take the boat-ride up the Nile next winter. That, I suppose now we shall have to rub off the slate. What is your program? Of course you will stay in Vienna until Watts comes. He may be a leisurely man and spend a month or two in getting ready and awaiting his instructions. Stay quietly at your post until he presents his writ of ejectment in person. Take all the chances of sun-stroke and cholera and ice-bergs [meaning, travel all over Europe]. Get a friend to quietly suggest to him [Watts] a season of preliminary German practice at Wiesbaden, or persuade him that his best route to Vienna is *via* Constantinople.... At all events take time. That old saw about the

forelock is all well enough, but sometimes a good grip on the hind lock is not to be despised[7]

Nicolay was not a religious man in the traditional sense, although the same could be said of President Lincoln. Neither man attended church in Washington with any regularity. Lincoln, however, possessed an undefined spirituality completely lacking in Nicolay. Therena seems to have sensed this, and being an intelligent woman, tactfully raised the issue with Nicolay by asking for his advice on what she should believe. Nicolay responded, perhaps not as Therena expected or hoped, but in a way that opened a window into her suitor's mind.

While acknowledging foolishness of braving public opinion unnecessarily, as well as the benefits of swimming with the religious current, Nicolay at first dismissed Therena's concerns with the a rather flippant remark about the air of Washington not stimulating his church-going inclinations. However, a short while later, stimulated in part by the untimely death of twelve-year-old Willie Lincoln, the secretary outlined his religious views. It may have been the longest letter he sent Therena, and it is well worth repeating:

> You are entirely right in your conclusion that I desire you to follow your own good judgment and discretion in your religious views and actions. It is, in my opinion, entirely an independent and individual duty and responsibility. I will, however, take the liberty to caution you, that while you act independently of me in these matters, it is equally your duty to act independently (in forming your opinions) *of all other persons and coteries*. You should permit, for example, neither myself, nor the Pope, nor Mr. Carter to be your religious director. While avoiding Scylla, be not wrecked on Charybdis. Be very sure that your faith is not merely the magnetism or sympathetic impulse of personal surroundings and contacts. Particularly beware that you do not yield to religious dictation and domination, which comes under the plausible guise of suggestion, advice, or instruction, whether from persons or books. Listen to all

---

[7] Nicolay to Hay, Paris, 9 August 1868, Nicolay Papers, LC.

suggestion, hear all advice, and receive all instruction, merely as so much *argument*: let nothing but your own mind and heart make up and render the *final judgment.*

On one point prepare yourself to be disenchanted and disappointed: I mean in the amount of support and strength you will be able to give to or receive from, the Church. Sad as the experience may be, you will find the *average* religious ideal of church-members to be very low. Bitter as the conviction may prove, you will find that the boundary of the church, as well as the world outside, encircles all of human folly and weakness. You will find that the plane occupied by church members and that upon which the wordings stand, are deplorably near the same level.

The Christian army never wins victories by battalions. It is individual strength, courage, heroism, that achieves its successes. Therefore be self-reliant—adopt your own faith, and achieve your own works.

The multitudes will ever dance in the valley around the golden calf of Superstition; it is only those who, like Moses, climb *alone* up the mount of sacrifice, through the clouds of creed, the thunders of Bigotry and the lightnings of Doubt, who shall see Divinity face to face with spiritual eyes and receive the true commandments.[8]

Doubtless it would be safe to say that most Civil War scholars will not recognize Nicolay in this brief character sketch, one he unintentionally created. All too often the secretary has been looked upon almost as if he were a shadow image of Abraham Lincoln. Certainly that is the picture Helen Nicolay hoped to perpetuate. In many ways, Nicolay was just the opposite of Lincoln. He was an arrogant, conceited, and elitist, neither seeking nor welcoming the company of common people. He was unforgiving toward military and political failures, and he was extremely vindictive toward the South. He completely misjudged the secession movement and continued to doubt the South's ability to

---

[8] Nicolay to Therena, 23 February 1862, Nicolay Papers, LC

conduct a protracted war. Moreover, Nicolay was not as close to Lincoln as is generally believed. He was younger by almost a quarter of a century, and temperamentally the reverse of the man he most admired. He sided with Lincoln on most of the important political and social issues of the day, such as the expansion of slavery into the western territories, the inviolability of the Federal Union, and emancipation. Most important, however, is the fact that Nicolay recognized the unusual qualities in Abraham Lincoln and made him his lifelong study.

LINCOLN SPINS THE PRESS

Michael Burlingame

In the mid-nineteenth century there was no such office as presidential press secretary, but Lincoln sought to influence public opinion through journalism written by his personal secretaries, John Hay, John G. Nicolay, and William O. Stoddard. Each of these young men penned anonymous or pseudonymous dispatches that resembled today's op-ed pieces.[1] These contributions to the press reveal an aspect of the Lincoln administration that has been insufficiently appreciated, namely, his politically shrewd attempt to mold public opinion through favorable reporting and commentary in newspapers.

It should come as no surprise that as president Lincoln would try to influence press opinion. During the quarter century before his presidency, Lincoln had contributed hundreds of anonymous and pseudonymous pieces to the Springfield *Illinois State Journal*.[2] In 1857

---

[1] Michael Burlingame ed., *Lincoln's Journalist: John Hay's Anonymous Writings for the Press, 1860–1864* (Carbondale: Southern Illinois University Press, 1998); Michael Burlingame, ed., *With Lincoln in the White House: Letters, Memoranda, and Other Writings of John G. Nicolay, 1860–1865* (Carbondale: Southern Illinois University Press, 2000); and Michael Burlingame, ed., *Dispatches from Lincoln's White House: the Anonymous Journalism of Presidential Secretary William O. Stoddard, 1861–1864* (Lincoln: University of Nebraska Press, 2002).

[2] See, for example, his editorial dated 12 December 1860, in Roy P. Basler, ed., *Collected Works of Lincoln*, 9 vols. (New Brunswick NJ: Rutgers University Press, 1953–1955), 4:150. See also Glenn H. Seymour, "'Conservative'—Another Lincoln Pseudonym?" *Journal of the Illinois State Historical Society* 29 (July 1936): 135–50; "Lincoln—Author of Letters by a Conservative,*" Bulletin of the Abraham Lincoln Association* 50 (December 1937): 8–9. J. G. Randall thought that Seymour's thesis "is ingeniously presented, and the reasoning seems pretty sound.... The main arguments for Lincoln's authorship seem to be his connection with the Journal and the test of literary

he drafted an agreement stipulating that he and six others would contribute to a $500 fund "to be used in giving circulation, in Southern and Middle Illinois, to the newspaper published at St. Louis, Missouri, and called 'The Missouri Democrat.'"[3] In 1859 he secretly purchased the Springfield *Illinois Staats-Zeitung,* which was to support the Republican cause.[4] In 1861 he appointed many Republican journalists to important offices.[5] The following year Lincoln urged John W. Forney to establish the *Daily Morning Chronicle* in Washington to support the administration.[6]

The anonymous writings by Hay, Nicolay, and Stoddard may well reflect the thinking of the president, or at least what he wanted the public to think. In a discussion of writings by Lincoln's two main secretaries,

---

style. The letters do seem to have a kind of Lincoln tang." Randall to Arthur C. Cole, n.p., 20 March 1936, copy, J. G. Randall Papers, Library of Congress. William E. Barton contended that, during the secession crisis, "It is practically certain that the Illinois State Journal gave forth editorial utterances which had Lincoln's approval, and some of them may have come from his own pen." Barton, *The Life of Abraham Lincoln* 2 vols. (Indianapolis: Bobbs-Merrill, 1925) 2:2. See also William Herndon, interview by James H. Matheny, November 1866, in *Herndon's Informants: Letters, Interviews, and Statements about Abraham Lincoln,* ed. Douglas L. Wilson and Rodney O. Davis, (Urbana: University of Illinois Press, 1998), 431; Simeon Francis to Anson G. Henry, n.p., 14 July 1855, Henry Papers, Illinois State Historical Library, Springfield; Andy Van Meter, *Always My Friend: A History of the State Journal-Register* (Springfield IL: Copley Press, 1981), 48–49, 67–68; Audus Waton Shipton, "Lincoln's Association with the Journal: An Address Delivered by A. W. Shipton, Publisher of the Illinois State Journal, Springfield, Illinois, at a conference of newspaper publishers and executives, at Coronado, California, September 27, 1939" (pamphlet, 1939); Paul M. Angle, ed., *Herndon's Lincoln* (Cleveland: World, 1942), 184, 197, 296–97; Robert S. Harper, *Lincoln and the Press* (New York: McGraw Hill, 1951), 2, 14–15; William Henry Bailhache, memorandum, San Diego, 14 January 1898, Ida M. Tarbell Papers, Allegheny College; statement of Col. J. D. Roper, 22 October 1897, enclosed in J. McCan Davis to Ida M. Tarbell, Ida M. Tarbell Papers, Allegheny College; Albert J. Beveridge, *Abraham Lincoln, 1809–1858,* 2 vols. (Boston: Houghton Mifflin, 1928), 1:171n, 183, 205n; William E. Barton, "Abraham Lincoln, Newspaper Man," typescript, and "Lincoln Editorials," handwritten memo, Springfield, 28 December 1928, Barton Papers, University of Chicago.

[3]Dated 3 June 1857, in Basler, *Collected Works of Lincoln,* 2:410.

[4]Basler, *Collected Works of Lincoln,* 3:383.

[5]Harper, *Lincoln and the Press,* 76; Harry J. Carman and Reinhold H. Luthin, *Lincoln and the Patronage* (New York: Columbia University Press, 1943) 121–29.

[6]Carman and Luthin, *Lincoln and the Patronage,* 121.

one scholar observed: "Hay and Nicolay seem generally to have adopted Lincoln's opinions as their own; and it may be surmised that the observations in their Letters, Diary, and Notes, were not far out of line with what Lincoln thought at the time, even when they do not quote him directly."[7] The same may be said of Stoddard, who, like Nicolay and Hay, was a young man who revered his boss extravagantly.

Although Stoddard (1835–1925) achieved renown as the author of more than seventy children's books, he is best remembered as "Lincoln's third secretary,"[8] in which capacity he submitted 120 weekly dispatches to the New York *Examiner* under the pseudonym "Illinois." From May 1861 to summer 1864, "Illinois" regularly described and commented on events in Washington and on military, diplomatic, economic, and political developments.

These documents shed both direct and indirect light on Lincoln. Stoddard occasionally described the president's activities and mood. On 8 July 1861, for example, he reported that "President Lincoln, thus far, bears his load of responsibility wonderfully well. He is a little thinner and paler than on the day of his inauguration, and at times, wears a wearied and harassed look, but is the same kind and cordial man as ever, with now and then a relapse into the humorous pleasantry, which in old times formed so marked a feature in his character." Three months later, Stoddard filed a gloomier report: "For a few weeks the President has been looking pale and careworn, as if the perpetual wear-and-tear of the load which presses upon him were becoming too much even for his iron frame and elastic mind."[9]

One source of presidential strain was the torrent of requests from people who regarded him as an all-powerful sovereign who could single-

---

[7] Henry B. Van Hoesen, "Lincoln and Hay," Books at Brown 18 (1960): 155–56.

[8] Reminiscences of William O. Stoddard, Jr., in Edgar DeWitt Jones, "Lincoln's Other Secretary and His Son," typescript, 5, Edgar DeWitt Jones Papers, Detroit Public Library. The material in this section is taken in part from the editor's introduction to Stoddard's Inside the White House in *War Times: Memoirs and Reports of Lincoln's Secretary*, ed. Michael Burlingame (Lincoln: University of Nebraska Press, 2000), vii–xxi.

[9] Washington correspondence, 7 October 1861, New York Examiner, 10 October 1861.

handedly solve their every problem. "Not a day passes," Stoddard wrote on 14 October 1861, "but appeals are made to the Executive for action, on his part, that would be all but impossible if he were an absolute monarch, and many honest people doubtless feel themselves aggrieved that the President does not exercise, in their behalf, prerogatives which any crowned head of Europe would hesitate to assume."

A week later, Stoddard had more cheering news to relate:

> Our worthy Chief Magistrate is in excellent spirits, and looks much better than he did a fortnight since. He is gathering his strength for the labor and excitement of the coming Congress. I am told that he enters into the plans and arrangements of the campaign in all their varied details with the keenest zest, and that the military chiefs have been indebted to his strong and practical good sense for more than one valuable hint and suggestion.

One of the most painful blows Lincoln absorbed during the war was the death of his son Willie, on 20 February 1862. A month later, Stoddard observed that the president "has recovered much of his old equanimity and cheerfulness; and certainly no one who saw his constant and eager application to his arduous duties, would imagine for a moment that the man carried so large a load of private grief, in addition to the cares of a nation."[10]

Like John Hay, Stoddard believed that Lincoln was the indispensable man without whose guidance the nation would cease to exist.[11] On 21 April 1862, he asked his readers:

---

[10] Washington correspondence, 24 March 1862, New York Examiner, 27 March 1862.

[11] In summer 1863 Hay reported to Nicolay that Lincoln:

> Is in fine whack. I have rarely seen him more serene & busy. He is managing this war, the draft, foreign relations, and planning a reconstruction of the Union, all at once. I never knew with what tyrannous authority he rules the Cabinet, till now. The most important things he decides & there is no cavil. I am growing more and more firmly convinced that the good of the country absolutely demands that he should be kept where he is till this thing is over. There is no

Did you ever try to realize the idea of losing our good Chief Magistrate? Perhaps not, but suppose you try, and then look around you in imagination for the man whom you could trust, and whom the people would trust, to take the reins from *his* dead hand. The fact is, that at present the country has entire confidence in no one else, and we might almost say, "after him the deluge," in view of our present condition.

Six months later Stoddard speculated about Lincoln's place in history:

The President is the same thoughtful, careful, kindly, hard-working man as ever, seeming to labor to make good, by the labors of his own brain and hand, all the shortcomings of his myriad subordinates. What his fame will be when all this confused lava of events, now red and molten in the fire of the Present, shall have been cooled in the rigid mould of time, none can tell; but his history will be false to all that is good and true, if his effigy be not that of a great, wise and patriotic statesman.[12]

On 21 July 1862 Stoddard analyzed the source of Lincoln's power:

The President is almost a mystery. Men no longer query whether such or such a General or statesman directs his actions, but "what will he do with" this statesman or that General. He is the most perfect *representative* of the purely American character now in public life—perhaps the most perfect that ever has existed. This is why the mutual understanding between him and

---

man in the country, so wise so gentle and so firm. I believe the hand of God placed him where he is.

Hay to John G. Nicolay, Washington, 7 August 1863, Michael Burlingame, ed., *At Lincoln's Side: John Hay's Civil War Correspondence and Selected Writings* (Carbondale: Southern Illinois University Press, 2000) 49.

[12] Washington correspondence, 17 November 1862, New York Examiner, 20 November 1862.

the people is so perfect. This it is which enables him to exercise powers which would never by any possibility be entrusted to another man, though his equal in other respects. The people know that they can trust their great chief, and so they bid him "see to it that the Republic suffers no detriment," and put in his hands untold treasure and uncounted lives, and the temporary disposal of their time-honored rights. The *habeas corpus* act is suspended—"Lincoln would not do it if it was not needed." The press is muzzled—"Good for him! why don't the old man shut off the *Herald* and the *Tribune*?" Favorite generals are superseded, favorite measures curtailed or disapproved, prejudices rubbed or snubbed, but the President is the stronger for it all.

The president's selflessness contributed to his popularity, Stoddard maintained:

Among the great civilians of the day, the greatest and the strongest, our good Chief Magistrate, is great and strong chiefly because the people have perfect faith in him that he has no ambition, no selfish lust of power, nor any hope for the future unconnected with the welfare of his country. Destroy this faith, and the power of the President would disappear, or would at best sink to the level of his Cabinet officers.[13]

Stoddard's unfavorable assessment of Wendell Phillips may offer a clue to the identity of the unnamed "well-known abolitionist and orator" whom Lincoln called "a thistle" and about whom he exclaimed: "I don't see why God lets him live!"[14] On 18 August 1862 Stoddard asked:

---

[13] Washington correspondence, 2 November 1863, New York Examiner, 5 November 1863.

[14] John Eaton, Grant, *Lincoln and the Freedmen* (New York: Longmans, Green, 1907), 184.

Have you noticed Wendell Phillips's late speeches? He has more fully than ever before defined the true position of himself and friends. He is no longer the apostle of the great reform, even in his own assertion, but seems voluntarily to take his true place once more as a mere vulgar agitator and sensation spouter. The Government was right when he was voted too insignificant for a cell in Fort Warren. Perhaps, however, his present desperate exertions *may* procure for him some sort of cheap and second class martyrdom. Pardon this bit of personality, Mr. Editor, but we who are near the centre of this great and practical fight, see that it is in truth a "good fight of faith," and we are sick and angry with the bleating crowd of fault-finders who help in no one thing, but do their uttermost to clog the chariot wheels of the army which we consider the "host of the Lord." We, as a nation, are just beginning to see and know the true greatness and sublimity of our strange and mighty war, and we are angry alike with those who scoff and those who hinder.

Stoddard's solicitude for the president's well-being appeared in a report he filed in September 1862:

A few days since the President's horse ran away with him during a morning ride, scared by the cheering of a marching regiment, and for a short time the Commander-in-Chief was in danger of serious accident. Thanks, however, to his long limbs and strong arms, he succeeded in retaining his place in the saddle, and in calming his furious and plunging Bucephalus, with no other injury than a slightly sprained ankle. However, we were suddenly shocked into an appreciation, momentarily, of how deep an interest we all had in the safety of our wise Chief Magistrate. Strong men turned to each other with an involuntary shudder. "If he *had* been thrown and killed!" After that, indeed, even the most hopeful could discern little beside clouds and thick darkness.[15]

Patronage matters absorbed an undue amount of Lincoln's time and energy, according to Stoddard, who on 6 April 1863 denounced the:

> Same unceasing throng in the ante-rooms of the President's house, bent on dragging him "for a few minutes only," away from his labors of state to attend to private requests, often selfish, often frivolous, sometimes corrupt or improper, and *not* so often worthy of the precious time and strength thus wasted. The President belongs to the nation—it is seldom that the affairs of any one man cannot be righted, save by bringing to his aid the delegated power of a whole people. No man, however, will see this, when his eyes are veiled by his interest. But who can doubt that our worthy and wise Chief Magistrate would do better, to bring to the grand yet delicate questions which must be finally decided by him alone, a mind unwearied by listening to private griefs or wishes, and unexhausted by pouring out his too ready sympathies upon misfortunes which, powerful as he is, he cannot remedy.

Stoddard's best-known reminiscence of Lincoln is a description of the president's reaction to the crushing Union defeat at Fredericksburg:

> If the same battle were to be fought over again, every day, through a week of days, with the same relative results, the army under Lee would be wiped out to its last man, the Army of the Potomac would still be a mighty host, the war would be over, the Confederacy gone, and peace would be won at a smaller cost of life than it will be if the week of lost battles must be dragged out through yet another year of camps and marches, and of deaths in hospitals rather than upon the field. No general yet found can

---

[15] Washington correspondence, ca. 14 September 1862, New York Examiner, 18 September 1862.

face the arithmetic, but the end of the war will be at hand when he shall be discovered.[16]

Some historians regard Stoddard's account skeptically,[17] but his dispatch of 18 April 1864 lends credence to that recollection:

There are two phases of military doctrine afloat here now-a-days—both of which may be set down as correct, but only one of which can be put into practice. The first, sound enough, with an "if," is that the rebellion is growing rapidly weaker with the very efforts, desperate, exhausting, which it is making to maintain its military establishment. So are we, but we can stand it twenty years longer than they can. So if we did not strike another heavy blow, but acted on the defensive and Fabian policy, merely consolidating and perfecting our occupation of the regions we now hold, and driving in the smaller armies of the rebels, they must soon go under. All very true, but our people have not faith enough to wait, they *must* go in and finish the business. The other creed, the faith of Lincoln and Grant, is that every great battle, even if it is a drawn one, is a defeat to the rebels in its necessary consequences. A battle in which thirty thousand men a side were put *hors du combat*, killed, wounded and missing, but in which neither party could claim a victory, would, nevertheless, drive Lee back to the Lynchburg line, and place Richmond almost at our mercy. Such a thing is horrible to contemplate, but great and desperate battles must and will come.[18]

---

[16] Stoddard, Inside the White House, ed. Burlingame, 101.

[17] "One could wish that this remarkable quotation came from a more reliable source." Don E. Fehrenbacher and Virginia Fehrenbacher, eds., *Recollected Words of Abraham Lincoln* (Stanford: Stanford University Press, 1996) 426.

[18] Lending further support to Stoddard's reminiscence is John Hay's recollection that on the gloomy morning following the First Battle of Bull Run, "when many thought seriously of the end," Lincoln "said, with some impatience, 'There is nothing in this except the lives lost and the lives which must be lost to make it good.' There was probably no one who regretted bloodshed and disaster more than he, and no one who

A legendary punster, Lincoln was perhaps the author of the following play on words that Stoddard described in 1861: "This reminds me of the answer made a short time since to the remark that the editor of the now defunct *States and Union* was a 'very penetrating man.' 'That may be,' was the reply, 'but his paper is a *penny-traitor*.'"[19]

Stoddard paid special attention to blacks in Washington and in the army. In May 1862 he declared shortly after Congress emancipated the slaves of the capital:

> It is the firm belief of your correspondent, from what he has seen and heard among the blacks, that this seemingly small seed, sown here in this District, will yet bear the most important fruit in every one of the border slave States. It seems to me that I can see the gradual entering of a new idea into the darkened minds of the downtrodden race—they begin, the best of them, to feel and cherish the notion of their *nationality*, and the development of the consequent emotions and ideas must follow. I have studied them much for a long time, and, except in isolated instances, have never noticed this before. They have all looked at their condition in a narrow and selfish way, each man for his own hand. There is no stronger civilizing influence, outside of the Christian religion, than a well-directed national feeling, because it leads men to work in unison for the accomplishment of whatever aims they may propose.

Stoddard added that:

> The blacks refuse to regard themselves as *Africans*. This, too, is a new idea, and I cannot help thinking it an advance. They insist that they are Americans, while at the same time they appreciate the disadvantages under which they labor here, and

---

estimated the consequences of defeat more lightly." Hay, "The Heroic Age in Washington," 1871, Burlingame, ed., At Lincoln's Side, 126.

[19] Washington correspondence, 12 May 1861, *New York Examiner*, 16 May 1861.

earnestly desire to find a new and undisputed theatre *on this Continent* for the *locus* of their future nationality. No doubt there is some sense in the idea of civilizing and Christianizing Africa by their means, but we must first civilize and Christianize our missionaries, or we shall be sending the blind to lead the blind, with a full knowledge of what and how deep a ditch awaits their fall.[20]

The following Thanksgiving, Stoddard described a dinner given to freedmen at a "contraband" camp:

The occasion was duly employed by several gentlemen to urge upon them the advantage of the President's favorite scheme of emigration, and seemingly with a very fair degree of success. It was a strange spectacle, that great crowd of black men, fresh from bondage, now, for the first time, beginning to taste of and comprehend that sweet thing called "Liberty"; men, women, and children, who had all their lives listened to orders only, with force to make obedience certain, gathering around their best and wisest friends, and hearkening to the mild voice of persuasion, urging them to their own good.

According to Stoddard, the "crowd contained a large number of thoughtful and intelligent faces, and not a few that lit up with a sudden gleam when, in reply to a remark by Senator [Samuel C.] Pomeroy, a stalwart negro answered, '*I'd fight!* '"[21]

When blacks did start to fight as members of the Union army, they at first suffered discrimination. But as Stoddard reported in May 1863:

It is surprising to see how rapidly men are losing their silly prejudices against the use of black soldiers. I mean in the army. Of course the demagogues of the North are almost as loud as

---

[20] Washington correspondence, n.d., *New York Examiner*, 8 May 1862.
[21] Washington correspondence, 1 December, *New York Examiner*, 4 December 1862.

ever, but among the men in the field, the prevailing sentiment is getting to be, in the rough language of the soldiers, "If the niggers will fight, why, let 'em fight—they're as good as rebels, any day." There is reason to believe, too, that the military feeling is on the increase among the blacks themselves. The resurrection of a manhood buried so long and so deeply must needs be slow, and too many of them have been unable even to hear the call of the trumpet, but the race will yet rise to a newness of life, such as God gives in time to all the nations that are oppressed and cast down.[22]

In July 1863 Stoddard commented on the psychological effect that army service had upon blacks:

This arming the negroes is a great thing in many ways. It is my deliberate opinion, that it will yet solve, in the right way, too, the oft-repeated question—"What shall we do with the South, and with the negroes, after the war is over?" We are educating a new race of freemen, who will take care of the South and of themselves too. Even if they labor under white employers, which is most probable, they will not, and they cannot return to their servile condition, for "the sword ennobles

In 1864 Stoddard sarcastically commented on the record black troops had compiled on the field of battle:

It is found not to be such good fun to fight them as was originally supposed. These "spiritless brutes"—"crushed by long servitude and plantation toil"—"peaceful by nature, and destitute of all the elements of the soldier"—have somehow been waked up to a terribly aggressive military manhood. Can it be possible that the mere idea of liberty for themselves and their children makes these fellows so good at the bayonet? Can it be that *they*, the degraded, the downtrodden, the mere "cattle" of so much

---

[22] Washington correspondence, n.d., *New York Examiner*, 18 May 1863.

legislation and of so much commerce—that *they* can feel any generous enthusiasm for a Government and a people who are doing so much for them? Of course not! The white man monopolizes all these finer and better feelings, and the negro I was talking with the other day was only a parrot. I will tell you a part of what he said. It was at Barnum's Hotel, Baltimore. Noticing that I was wonderfully well waited on by several darkie friends, I began a chat with one of them. "Oh, yes, massa, we knows you: we *heerd* you at de contraband camp; we knows who *you* is." In this he was referring to some humble efforts of mine a year or so ago. "Oh, yes, we is all here *now*, but we is going out to help Grant pretty soon. Most all de rest of us has gone. We knows very well what it all means, and *you see if de black man can't fight for dose men as be fighting for him.*" The good fellow's face had been all smiles till this last, which closed the conversation, and then it darkened into an expression of the sternest resolution, and the black face wore an expression that would have added a dignity to the purest Caucasian lineaments.

Stoddard concluded that:

The men who have all their lives carried napkins are not thereby unfitted to carry the bayonet. And herein is a great political secret. Herein lies the ability of the United States to carry on this war indefinitely, and should we *not* succeed in breaking the strength of the rebellion before January next, there is that vitality, that force, in the President's policy of employing the black men, that will at the worst go far to make up all losses, and that must eventually set the seal of success upon his efforts to save the nation. It must be a bitter pill to the proud aristocrats of Virginia and the Carolinas to weigh their lives in the fearful balances of war against those of men who were once their property. There will be a great deal of that weighing done before this year is over.[23]

---

[23] Washington correspondence, 20 June 1864, *New York Examiner*, 23 June 1864.

Though the president may have encouraged Stoddard to write for the *Examiner*, the idea was originally suggested by the editor of the paper, Edward Bright, Jr., the young secretary's uncle. As Stoddard later recalled, "I was glad to do so and the success which I attained led to my subsequent staff connection with the *Examiner* during many years."[24] The New York *Examiner* was a Baptist weekly founded in 1826 at Utica. At first known as the *Baptist Register*, over time it changed its name to the *New York Baptist Register*, then the *New York Recorder and Register*; from 1855 to 1865 it was published in New York City as the New York *Examiner*. Stoddard, who was a devout Baptist who taught Sunday school and led church meetings, also submitted material for publication to the New York *Tribune*.[25]

It is not certain that Lincoln suggested that Stoddard, Nicolay, or Hay write for the press, but it seems unlikely that they did so without his knowledge and approval. He may have discussed with them either directly or indirectly what they wrote. In any event, their journalism offers new evidence illustrating Lincoln's political shrewdness. As he famously said, "Our government rests in public opinion. Whoever can change public opinion can change the government."[26] Everyone knows how Lincoln tried to affect public opinion with his state papers; few realize how he actively sought to achieve the same end more covertly through the anonymous journalism of his private secretaries.

---

[24] Stoddard, typescript memoirs, 1:312, Detroit Public Library.

[25] A Washington correspondent told the managing editor of the Tribune that "Stoddard wants his papers if you do not publish: has no other copy." Adams S. Hill to Sydney Howard Gay, [Washington], n.d., Gay Papers, Columbia University.

[26] Basler, *Collected Works of Lincoln*, 2:385

LINCOLN AND THE GREELEY LETTER: AN EXPOSITION

Phillip Shaw Paludan

He is part of our culture, an icon used to advertise everything from life insurance to hamburgers. Lincoln is a cultural force outside the literate or educated world. Harry T's, a bar in Lawrence, Kansas, includes in its ads for lunch specials a picture of Lincoln in the Lincoln Memorial, reminding us that not all lunch specials are created equal.

In a more sinister vein, Lincoln is used to justify positions he would abhor. My aunt in California recently sent me something called "Abraham Lincoln's Warning." It quotes Lincoln as a bigot warning against Catholics who want to "destroy our (public) schools and prepare a reign of anarchy here as they have done in Ireland, in Spain and wherever there are people that want to be free."[1]

Now of course Lincoln never said this. In fact, he was angry at the anti-Catholic bigotry of his age that manifested itself in the Know Nothing movement. He told his friend Joshua Speed:

> I am not a Know Nothing. That is certain. How could I be? How can any one who abhors the oppression of negroes, be in favor of degrading classes of white people? Our progress in degeneracy appears to me to be pretty rapid. As a nation we began by declaring that *"all men are created equal."* We now

---

[1] "Abraham Lincoln's Warning". One page sheet said to be "Copied from Knighthood of Catholicism by W. J. Burbank, State Treasurer of Iowa...Lincoln was finally assassinated (sic) April 15, 1865 by Roman Catholics." In possession of author.

practically read it *"all men are created equal, except negroes."*
When the Know Nothings get control it will read "all men are
created equal, except negroes, *and foreigners, and catholics"*
When it comes to this I should prefer emigrating to some country
where they make no pretense of loving liberty—to Russia, for
instance, where despotism can be taken pure, and without the
base alloy of hypocrisy.[2]

Lincoln's ideas can be misrepresented honestly, by mistake, not
intention. I want to focus on one of those mistakes, an important mistake
because it leads to serious misunderstanding about Lincoln's position on
race, slavery, Union, and the rule of law.

If there is one document that is more often quoted than any other in
the argument, debate, or conversation about Lincoln, it is the letter that
Lincoln wrote on 22 August 1862 to Horace Greeley, editor of the New
York *Tribune*—the most widely read newspaper in the nation. On 19
August Greeley wrote an editorial addressed to Lincoln urging the
president to emancipate the slaves. The editorial began with several
accusations that the president was paying too much attention to "certain
fossil politicians hailing from the border states" by not freeing the slaves
for fear of losing border state support. "On the face of this wide earth,
Mr. President, there is not one disinterested, determined, intelligent
champion of the Union cause who does not feel that all attempts to put
down the Rebellion and at the same time uphold its inciting cause are
preposterous and futile.... what an immense majority of the Loyal
Millions of your countrymen require of you is a frank, declared,
unqualified, ungrudging execution of the laws of the land." To Greeley
that meant that Lincoln free the slaves.[3]

Lincoln's reply was this:

---

[2] Lincoln to Joshua Speed, 24 August 1855, *Collected Works of Abraham Lincoln*,
9 vols., ed. Roy P. Basler (New Brunswick NJ: Rutgers University Press, 1953)
2:320–323.

[3] Greeley quoted in Basler, *Collected Works*, 5:389.

Dear Sir...I have just read yours of the 19th addressed to myself through the New York Tribune. If there be in it any statements or assumptions of fact, which I may know to be erroneous, I do not now know and here, controvert them. If there be in it any inferences which I may believe to be falsely drawn, I do not now and here, argue against them. If there be perceptable in it an impatient and dictatorial tone, I waive it in deference to an old friend, whose heart I have always supposed to be right.

As to the policy I "seem to be pursuing" as you say, I have not meant to leave anyone in doubt.

I would save the Union. I would save it the shortest way under the Constitution. The sooner the national authority can be restored; the nearer the Union will be to the "Union as it was." If there be those who would not save the union unless they could at the same time save slavery I do not agree with them. If there be those who would not save the union unless they could at the same time destroy slavery, I do not agree with them. My paramount object in this struggle is to save the Union, and is not either to save or destroy slavery. If I could save the Union without freeing any slave I would do it, and if I could save it by freeing some and leaving others alone I would also do that. What I do about slavery and the colored race, I do because I believe it helps to save the Union; and what I forebear, I forebear because I do not believe it would help to save the Union. I shall do less whenever I shall believe what I am doing hurts the cause, and I shall do more whenever I shall believe doing more will help the cause. I shall try to correct errors when shown to be errors; and I shall adopt new views so fast as they shall appear to be true views.

I have stated my purpose according to my view of official duty; and I intend no modification of my oft-expressed personal wish that all men every where could be free. Yours, A. Lincoln.[4]

---

[4] Ibid., 388–89.

Scholars and many members of the general public see in Lincoln's answer a commitment to saving the Union that overcomes Lincoln's emancipation instincts. They translate the words to mean that the president was not firmly committed to ending slavery and that he did so only because he had to. It is part of a general view of Lincoln as the "reluctant Emancipator" and of an environment in which "it was evidently in an unhappy frame of mind in which Lincoln resorted to the Emancipation Proclamation," as Richard Hofstadter put it. Hofstadter also remarked that the Emancipation Proclamation issued on 1 January 1863 had "all the moral grandeur of a bill of lading."[5]

Lincoln was not a reluctant emancipator. He was a cautious emancipator because he knew that he had to have popular support for any act he took against slavery. But he was moving toward emancipation quite aggressively. His answer to Greeley needs to be seen in the light of certain facts.

First, Lincoln had decided to emancipate the slaves almost a month before he answered Greeley. He had decided to do so around 20 July 1862 and told his cabinet of his decision on the 22 July. Second, Lincoln knew very well that his answer would appear in the widely circulated *Tribune* and would be picked up and reprinted in newspapers throughout the nation. He knew that the letter was a chance to persuade as well as explain. There were several audiences out there, and he appealed to most of them. The president was careful not to insult the editor of the nation's most widely read newspaper. Greeley had attacked him aggressively, but Lincoln was not defensive. He referred to the editor as "an old friend, whose heart I have always supposed to be right." He knew that Democrats as well as Republicans were watching—he used a slogan of the Democratic party to reach out to them. They claimed to be for "the Union as it was." Lincoln told them that "the Union as it was" would benefit from his policy. Lincoln also knew that society had few people who favored racial equality. It was a racist world. The same people who picked up the *Tribune* in New York went off to see the minstrel shows that were the most popular form of entertainment in the country. These

[5] Richard Hofstadter, *The American Political Tradition and the Men who Made It* (NY: Knopf, 1989) 130–31.

shows (whose actors were always whites in blackface) degraded and insulted black Americans to amuse their audiences.[6]

Lincoln knew that to advocate emancipation on grounds that helped blacks more than whites made him vulnerable to the race card—a ducat played consistently by the Democrats of his age. (Someone once noted that so long as the slavery question was about slavery the Republicans had an advantage, but if the issue became race the Democrats forged ahead.) Lincoln needed to place the emancipation of blacks in a package that whites would accept. The Union was the almost universal ideal of northerners; everything that anyone did in the course of fighting the war was going to be to save the Union. Lincoln was preaching to the choir here, but it was a big choir, and he had to rally and reassure them that the very dramatic act of freeing other people's slaves would be in service of the very conservative goal of saving their union.

The conservative view of the Greeley letter also fumbles by contrasting the ideals of saving the Union and emancipating the slaves. The two goals were not alternatives, but were intimately connected. Lincoln wanted to save the Union and to free the slaves. When he spoke of saving the Union, he was talking about a certain kind of union—a union where slavery was not safe. Lincoln's union, seen in its most conservative sense, was one in which Congress could outlaw slavery in the territories and where free states would emerge from those free territories and send to Congress representatives and senators who were hostile to slavery. These congressmen would create an environment of freedom that could draw border slave states into a free soil orbit—as white southerners feared was happening to Kentucky—and persuade slave owners to sell their slaves into the deeper South, expanding the arena of free soil and linking slave border states into the free labor, free soil, free men environment of the North. Runaway slaves would feel an even stronger magnet and that pull would destabilize stay-at-home slaves, the economy, and the world they created.[7]

---

[6] On minstrel show popularity and racism, see Eric Lott, *Love and Theft: Blackface Minstrelsy* (NY: Oxford, 1995); David Roedigger, *The Wages of Whiteness* (NY, Verso, 1995).

[7] William Freehling, *The South vs. the South: How Anti-Confederate Southerners Shaped the Course of the Civil War* (NY: Oxford University, 2001) chapter 2.

All of this was possible in Lincoln's union, without any direct attack on slavery in the slave states. The white Deep South and parts of upper Dixie saw this nightmare coming to life. That is why they seceded. If Lincoln and his soldiers held the Union together, slavery was imperiled. If Lincoln saved the Union without directly freeing a single slave, he would still threaten slavery. He would place slavery in the course of ultimate extinction, as he said.

I think Lincoln would have been happiest if emancipation had come over the long course of ultimate extinction. As late as December 1862, with the emancipation clock already ticking (he had issued the preliminary proclamation in September 1862), Lincoln proposed an emancipation plan that would have allowed states to be compensated for the slaves they surrendered and would have allowed states to take until 1900 to do so. He would also have encouraged, though not compelled, emancipated blacks to leave the country. He argued passionately for this plan.[8]

In our modern environment of "Freedom Now" this proposal has angered some writers as it angered abolitionists of the time, but Lincoln felt the upheaval that emancipation would bring and knew the awesome and complex power of slavery in the South and in the nation. He knew that freedom was a beginning and that it would operate in an environment where whites held much power. Learning to live together in freedom required more than freedom now and devil take the hindmost. Once emancipation began he spoke of letting blacks and whites "gradually live themselves out of their old relation to each other, and both come out better prepared for the new." Lincoln understood that changing the nation's race relations would take a long time. He may have let this understanding slow down his move toward emancipation, but when he acted, less than a month after offering this gradual plan, he acted aggressively and sweepingly, issuing the proclamation he had threatened in September.[9]

Even here, as Lincoln emancipates, some writers diminish Lincoln's contribution to emancipation. The proclamation freed only slaves in

---

[8] Basler, *Collected Works*, 5:527–37.
[9] Ibid., 6:247.

areas still in rebellion as of 1 January 1863. As recently as 2000 a respectable collection of essays on the war repeated a common canard that the proclamation "freed only those slaves over whom the proclamation could have no immediate influence." This repeated a slap of the London *Times* that scolded Lincoln for freeing the slaves he could not touch while leaving in chains those within his hands.[10]

This ignores Lincoln's commitment to the Constitution and his sensitivity to the constitutional limitations of his office. His letter to Greeley expressed his "view of official duty" in contrast to his "oft-expressed *personal* wish that all men everywhere could be free."

Lincoln freed the slaves in the only place he could legally touch them—in areas subject to his power as commander in chief of the armed forces. He could not free slaves in loyal slave states; the Constitution didn't allow that. Neither Congress nor the president had constitutional authority to attack slavery directly in the loyal states. Lincoln could act only under his war powers, as commander in chief in time of war and in places at war against the government. Congress acted against slavery also only where its legal mandate reached—the territories, and the District of Columbia—and in the making of rules for the military especially. Lawmakers were sufficiently respectful of constitutional limitations, and they refused to turn the rebel states into territories and so expand their authority over them.

In short, it is not true that Lincoln freed the slaves only where he could not touch them. Lincoln had taken what he called "the most solemn oath" to "faithfully execute the Office of President of the United States, and will, to the best of my ability, preserve, protect and defend the Constitution of the United States." He freed the slaves in the only place that his oath of office to protect and defend the Constitution of the United States allowed him to free them.

A significant inference of the argument that Lincoln freed slaves where he couldn't reach them is that few slaves were freed by the proclamation. That inference is wrong. How many slaves did the

---

[10] Richard Carwardine, "Abraham Lincoln, the Presidency and the Mobilization of Union Sentiment," *The American Civil War: Explorations and Reconsiderations*, ed. Susan Mary Grant and Brian Holden Reid (Harrow, England: Longman, 2000) 71.

proclamation free? As of 1 January 1863—the day the proclamation became official—2.9 million of the approximately 4 million slaves in the South would be free—82 percent of the slaves in the Confederacy, 74 percent of the slaves in the nation. That was just a beginning. The proclamation was part of a wider antislavery offensive. Lincoln was also contemplating a constitutional amendment freeing all the slaves and asking at the same time that border slave states free their own slaves and be compensated for it.

Furthermore Lincoln was supporting a less obvious revolution that was going on in besieged Dixie. Various generals—John Phelps in Louisiana, David Hunter in South Carolina, Jim Lane in Kansas—were enlisting blacks to perform labor around their encampments but also were teaching them military skills. Hunter's activities are especially illuminating. As early as April 1862 Hunter wrote to Secretary of War Stanton requesting 50,000 muskets and 50,000 pairs of scarlet pantaloons with the goal of arming "such loyal men as I can find in the country." Hunter's next move obscured the importance of those muskets. On 9 May 1862 he publicly announced that he was freeing all the slaves in the Sea Islands of South Carolina. Lincoln countermanded that announcement, but he did nothing to stop Hunter from recruiting black allies. Lincoln allowed generals to enlist black soldiers even as he stopped generals from freeing black slaves. In late August 1862, even as he was explaining to Greeley the need to go slow, the president let Stanton authorize General Rufus Saxton to arm and equip 5,000 black soldiers in South Carolina. It was the beginning of a process that would display black manhood and create powerful claims on equal citizenship for approximately 200,000 black sailors and soldiers.[11]

As war rolled on, black soldiers joined Union ranks. The Emancipation Proclamation of January 1863 called for former slaves to join the army. By January 1863, therefore, Lincoln was at the center of emancipation on several fronts—constitutional amendment, military service, pushing loyal slave states to free their slaves, and general

---

[11] For more extensive discussion see Phillip Shaw Paludan, *The Presidency of Abraham Lincoln* (Lawrence: University Press of Kansas, 1994) 152–53.

emancipation by proclamation. This doesn't seem like reluctance to emancipate.

Of course the Emancipation Proclamation only proclaimed emancipation. But the Declaration of Independence only declared independence. Both documents were promises, pledges. They would have to be kept. If the declarers and the proclaimers won their wars the United States would be an independent nation, and it would be inescapably "dedicated to the proposition that all men [all people], are created equal." Almost the instant it was announced, the proclamation unleashed emancipation. Restive slaves heard the proclamation and kept escaping to Union lines even as Union soldiers marching south expanded freedom's domain with every step. The Greeley letter was essentially a piece of propaganda, an exercise in persuasion. Lincoln did speak of his personal wish that every man be free, but he was not only telling the public what his personal feelings were. The Greeley letter was not a statement of philosophy that reflected only Lincoln's personal private feelings. Lincoln knew he wrote for an audience, and he emphasized those parts of his personal philosophy that he thought would bring the most northerners to his cause.

Lincoln consciously shaped public opinion. He was intently aware that the public was watching him and listening to what he said. He believed, as he said, that "public sentiment is everything. With public sentiment, nothing can fail; without it nothing can succeed."[12] For an allegedly modest man Lincoln spent a huge amount of time being painted and having life masks made. He let the painter Francis Carpenter stay in the White House for five months while Carpenter painted a picture of the first reading of the Emancipation Proclamation. When finished, the portrait was not hidden away by a private collector. It traveled throughout the North and showed to an eager and fascinated public a noble portrait of a great event led by the Great Emancipator. Lincoln was

---

[12] Basler, *Collected Works*, 2:89, 255–56; Phillip Paludan, *"The Better Angels of Our Nature": Lincoln, Propaganda and Public Opinion in the North during the Civil War* (Gerald McMurtry Lecture, Fort Wayne, Indiana, 1992).

serving more than art when he let Carpenter produce that portrait. The president was constantly alert to chances to shape the public mind.[13]

Predominantly Lincoln used the written word as his main instrument of persuasion. Other than his inaugural speeches, he gave very few major speeches while in the White House (he did give nearly 100 short public talks and wrote 4 annual messages), but he wrote several letters that were designed and carefully crafted to mold the public mind. The president wrote these letters with the intention that they have the best possible impact when read, as most of them were designed to be, to larger audiences. Invited to address Republicans in Springfield in late summer 1863, Lincoln declined making the trip but he told his secretary John Hay that he would write a letter, and "it will be a rather good letter." When he sent the letter to his friend James Conkling he sent along these instructions, "You are one of the best public readers. I have but one suggestion. Read it very slowly." Conkling did so, and the letter was picked up in the Northern press and spread widely. One observer noted "It will be on the lips and hearts of hundreds of thousands this day." When the president wrote a letter in June 1863 defending his suspensions of habeas corpus he had that letter printed and then sent it out on the frank of a private secretary, and made sure that a copy got sent to the Loyal Publication society which would then reprint 10,000 copies. Ultimately nearly half a million copies of the letter were circulated. Lincoln's letters didn't just go into some private mailbox.

Lincoln did not speak alone. He mobilized the Northern institutions in behalf of his goals. He helped to found and organize the Union League—a propaganda organization that sent millions of copies of pro-Union—Republican party—pamphlets throughout the North. His friends like Conkling were officers in state branches; his personal secretary William Stoddard was the corresponding secretary for the organizing DC branch of the league. Lincoln cultivated religious organizations so

---

[13] Harold Holzer, *Lincoln Seen and Heard* (Lawrence: University Press of Kansas, 2000) 12–13, 22–24.

effectively that Methodists, for one, became almost synonymous with loyalty.[14]

Lincoln was a propagandist. The role of the president is to shape, not just respond to, public opinion. There is a very important distinction between positive and negative propaganda. Negative propaganda calls upon people's fears and hatreds. It has a little considered but vitally important result. When leaders call on our dark side they legitimize it; they affirm it. They say in effect that we are a people whose fears and hatreds should be appealed to. Our leaders tell us who they think we are by the way they speak to us. They thus help create their society and their nation. Whenever a politician speaks to us we must always ask, "Who do you think I am?" The answer should be: someone better. The health of the polity probably demands that it be someone better.

President Lincoln practiced positive propaganda. He never called the Confederacy or Jeff Davis the enemy. He never played a race card. He reached out to political enemies and adversaries. He did not make politics personal; for Lincoln the political was not the personal. He admonished one politician, "You have more of that feeling of personal resentment than I. Perhaps I have too little of it; but I never thought it paid. A Man has no time to spend half his life in quarrels. If any man ceases to attack me I never remember the past against him."[15]

The best-known example of this tolerance is the case of Senator Charles Sumner who helped to stop Lincoln's reconstruction program in Louisiana. But Lincoln chose Sumner to escort Mary Lincoln into the inaugural ball in March 1865. His favorite saying, according to John Hay, was "I believe in short statutes of limitations in politics." His speeches assumed an audience capable of reason, commitment, and sacrifice in reaching the best goals of the nation; the Gettysburg Address is perhaps the best example of this trait, but other speeches reflect similar values. An 1840s Whig newspaper described this kind of speaking:

---

[14] Carwardine, "Abraham Lincoln, the Presidency," *The American Civil War*, 68–97; Paludan, *Presidency of Abraham Lincoln*, 222–26.

[15] As quoted in Paludan, *Presidency*, 292.

Put the case that the same multitude were addressed by two
orators, and on the same question and occasion: that the first of
these orators considered in his mind that the people he addressed
were to be controlled by several passions.... The orator may be
fairly said to have no faith in the people; he rather believes that
they are creatures of passion, and subject to none but base and
selfish impulses. But now a second orator arises, a Chatham, a
Webster, a Pericles, a Clay; his generous spirit expands itself
through the vast auditory, and he believes that he is addressing a
company of high spirited men, citizens.... When he says "fellow
citizens," they believe him, and at once, from a tumultuous herd
they are converted into men...their thoughts and feeling rise to an
heroical height, beyond that of common men or common times.
The second orator "had faith in the people"; he addressed the
better part of each man's nature, supposing it to be in him—and
it *was* in him.[16]

Lincoln's essentially non-partisan style was sound politics. It
enabled him to build a coalition together to fight the war, a coalition that
included War Democrats and both conservative and radical Republicans.
It allowed him to negotiate with Congress on Reconstruction and kept
him open to the need to make changes in his cabinet that would appeal to
more radical opponents—he fired his postmaster general, Montgomery
Blair, to appease radicals in the 1864 election. He put the most radical of
his cabinet members, Salmon Chase, on the Supreme Court in 1864 in
another move that pleased them. Despite sharp contrast that endured over

---

[16] As quoted in Thomas Brown, *Politics and Statesmanship: Essays on the
American Whig Party* (NY: Columbia, 1985) 10–11; on politics in mid nineteenth
century see Robert Kelley, *The Cultural Pattern in American Politics* (NY: Oxford,
1969). On Whigs see Michael Holt, *The Rise and Fall of the American Whig Party* (NY:
Oxford, 1999) and sources cited there. Writing after the Lincoln Douglas debates the pro-
Republican [Springfield] Illinois *Journal* (14 November 1858, p. 1) observed that
Lincoln's speeches "are stamped with the impress of a sincerity and candor which
appeals at once to the higher and noble faculties of the mind, and wins over the better
feelings and affections of our nature.... They, in effect, are in advance of the age...and
thus contain those elements which ... [carry] them beyond the present and makes them
useful and beautiful in the future."

Reconstruction policy, Lincoln kept the lines of negotiation open. There is reason to believe that Lincoln was moving in a more radical direction when he died, though that point is debatable. But whichever way he was moving, Lincoln's effectiveness is best revealed by what happened when his successor, Andrew Johnson, took over the presidency. Johnson took politics personally, publicly called congressmen names, refused to compromise on Reconstruction measures, and became the first president to be impeached.

Hanging over Lincoln's response to Greeley is a charge that the president was actually a dictator, whose words of respect for and limitations under the Constitution were simply shams. In fact, in 1979 Don Fehrenbacher observed that Lincoln had been described as a dictator by more historians than any other president. Some authors have condemned Lincoln for this outreach of authority. Political scientist Dwight Anderson says that Lincoln "arrogated to himself virtually dictatorial power." The two authors of the popular novels about Lincoln, Gore Vidal and William Safire, both agree on Lincoln's dictatorial power. Vidal has Secretary of State Seward musing that Lincoln "had been able to make himself absolute dictator without letting anyone suspect that he was anything more than a joking, timid backwoods lawyer."

Mark Neely's Pulitzer Prize-winning book *The Fate of Liberty* has done much to discredit that idea. Lincoln arrested precious few people for dissent; most of those arrested were taken as the army advanced into enemy territory, especially in border states. In his overall record there is little to choose between Jefferson Davis and Lincoln—a point proven in another Neely book, *Southern Rights.*[17]

If criticizing Lincoln as a violator of the Constitution has lost momentum, a new book sees Lincoln's allegedly extralegal acts as positive, freeing the nation from a dead hand of conservative constitutionalism and moving the nation to equality. A recent book by

---

[17] Mark E. Neely, Jr., *Southern Rights: Political Prisoners and the Myth of Confederate Constitutionalism* (Charlottesville: University of Virginia, 1999); Neely, *The Fate of Liberty: Abraham Lincoln and Civil Liberties* (NY: Oxford, 1991). I follow Neely's historiography in his epilogue in this latter work.

law professor George Fletcher insists that Lincoln's suspension of the writ shows that he sought to be free of a constitutional system under which equality had been denied. "Lincoln's posture toward the 1787 Constitution was less than reverent," Fletcher says. He accepts Chief Justice Roger Taney's argument that Lincoln's suspension defied the constitutional requirement that only Congress had the power to suspend. The president exercised "extraconstitutional executive power," Fletcher says, in suspending the writ. As is the case with many other authors Fletcher then quotes Lincoln himself apparently casting off constitutional anchors. In his 4 July 1861 address Lincoln asks, "Are all the laws but one to go unexecuted, and the government itself go to pieces lest that one be violated?" The inference is clear: Lincoln violated one law in order to save the government and confessed to doing so. like other authors Fletcher omits the rest of Lincoln's argument: "But it was not believed that any law was violated," the president says and then goes on to argue that since the Constitution doesn't say which branch of government has power to suspend, that the president has constitutional authority to suspend the writ "when in cases of invasion or rebellion the public safety may require it."[18]

Fletcher leaps from Lincoln's admission to make the astonishing claim that "the constitution of 1787 lay suspended in the fires of battle." Fletcher's goal is admirable: to persuade readers that the Civil War created what he calls "Our Secret Constitution." That constitution empowers the national government to protect equality and expand democracy. But Fletcher's Lincoln is a Lincoln that never was.

Throughout his life Lincoln was a respecter of the Constitution and of the rule of law. These feelings were deep within him. When Lincoln was sixteen, a companion, Matthew Gentry, went insane and the experience provoked a poem that began:

---

[18] George Fletcher, *Our Secret Constitution* (NY: Oxford, 2001); Basler, *Collected Works*, 4:430.

But here's an object more of dread
'Than ought the grave contains—
A human form with reason fled,
While wretched life remains.

The poem went on through twelve stanzas describing Gentry as, "Once of genius bright,—a fortune favored child now locked in mental night...maiming himself, trying to kill his mother...a howling crazy man...shrieking and writhing...with burning eyeballs and manic laughter...begging swearing weeping praying." More ominous is the fact that Lincoln is drawn to Gentry, stealing away at night to listen to the plaintive mournful songs of the madman, staying out until sunrise, hovering nearby, nearby the madness.

Douglas Wilson recently observed that fear of madness lead Lincoln to cultivate reason and mental discipline. David Donald notes that "one of Lincoln's deepest concerns was the overthrow of reason." I couldn't agree more. This fear, in a man conscious that he was subject to the power of fate, worked its way into his political philosophy.[19]

The first major address that we have of Lincoln's, "The Lyceum Address," is a paean to having "respect for the laws...become the political religion of the nation." His temperance address extols a "happy day when ...mind, all conquering mind, shall live and move the monarch of the world." His chosen profession was law, and he practiced it for a quarter of a century. As the "Law Practice of Abraham Lincoln" DVD materials demonstrate so well, he spent more hours of his life practicing law than he did any other thing. He tried over 5,000 cases, made his

---

[19] Douglas Wilson, "Young Man Lincoln," *The Lincoln Enigma: The Changing Faces of an American Icon*, ed. Gabor Boritt (NY: Oxford, 2001) 30–35; David Donald, *Lincoln* (NY: Simon and Schuster, 1995) 118; Basler, *Collected Works*, 1:368–370. The Lyceum address has been analyzed by scholars who see Lincoln's own ambition in his discussion of the dangers of dictators in America. Michael Burlingame, *The Inner World of Abraham Lincoln* (Urbana: University of Illinois, 1994) 253–34, on the other hand, argues that Lincoln was attacking Stephan Douglas and Andrew Jackson; thus separating Lincoln's politics and his personal concerns. I think that Lincoln was thinking both in political terms and in the context of his personal fears that people of genius might lose self control and overturn reason just as dictators overthrew the rule of law politically.

fortune, and created much of his vision of society and community in the company of lawyers.[20]

His debates with Douglas predominantly concerned constitutional questions and argument over the intentions of the framers of the Constitution and the Declaration of Independence. His First Inaugural and especially his 4 July 1861 speech were constitutional arguments. His justifications for emancipation were replete with arguments about the constitutionality of his actions and the limitations on his ideals that the Constitution dictated.

This picture of Lincoln the constitutionalist provides a necessary balance to a widespread idea that Lincoln was more dedicated to the egalitarian ideas of the Declaration than to the constitutional system. Indeed, in the hands of Garry Wills the Declaration becomes the eternal light that guided Lincoln to the abiding truth. Wills has Lincoln use the Gettysburg Address as a means to transform the nation's understanding of equality and the national obligation to preserve it.[21]

In an age of "Freedom Now" the temptation to play the Lincoln card in behalf of equality is understandable—predictable—and perhaps instinctive. Lincoln served the cause of equality, no doubt about that. The crucial question with Lincoln is almost always a process question—how did he achieve his goals? How did he want the nation to achieve its goals? Lincoln achieved equality not by ignoring or casting aside the Constitution. Rather, he served equality by linking it to the constitutional system as a whole, by using his people's passionate devotion to the Constitution to inspire them to accept equality.

The Gettysburg Address shows how he connected the Declaration's ideals of equality with the Constitution. The address opens by noting that the new nation was created in 1776 dedicated to the proposition that all men are created equal. But how are we to achieve that ideal? Lincoln's last line tells us that "government of the people, by the people and for the people shall not perish from the earth." The Constitution, the foundation

---

[20] *The Law Practice of Abraham Lincoln: The Complete Documentary Edition,* 3 vols., DVD, ed. Martha Benner, Cullom Davis et al. (Urbana: University of Illinois, 2000).

[21] Gary Wills, *Lincoln at Gettysburg* (NY: Simon and Schuster, 1992).

of our government, is the means to achieve the Declaration's equality ideal.

Why is this point important? Is it just a scholar's point? Well, we do have to be careful about scholars. As Mark Twain warns us, "The work of many scholars has already thrown much darkness on this subject and it is likely if they keep working we shall soon know nothing at all." The interconnection between the Constitution and the Declaration is important to the nation as a whole, to its self-understanding, and to its aspirations. The Constitution provides our respect for the rule of law, the process by which we achieve our goals, our ideals. If we just insist on our goals and our ideals, we may lose faith in our means. People have attacked the Constitution as a pro-slavery document and have seen it as part of "institutional racism." Some insist that we must strike for our ideals and see institutions as the enemy. "Be a rebel," a hundred ads and movies tell us. "Question authority," thousands bumper stickers echo. Surely a little rebellion is in the American soul. But also resting there, and more in the spirit of Lincoln, is respect for law, for it is our law, made at its best to secure equality. In this nation, as Senator Christopher Dodd, among others, has observed, our means are our ends. Respect for our rule of law is fundamental to maintaining respect for orderly change. Lincoln's major contribution was to show that the Constitution was an antislavery document, that the Dred Scott decision was bad constitutional law, that popular sovereignty without respect for equality was a snare and a delusion and that the rule of law was the basis for equal justice. The government created by the Constitution was the means to securing a nation where all people were equal. That was the message of the Gettysburg Address, it is a message from Lincoln we need to keep in mind, part of his positive propaganda, or if you prefer, his friendly persuasion.

We can summarize this Lincoln by seeing him as the great African-American reformer Frederick Douglass saw him. People who note Lincoln's caution in emancipating often speak of him as "the White Man's President." That is the message of Lerone Bennett's attack on Lincoln.[22] The view appears to be substantiated by an 1876 address by

---

[22] Lerone Bennett, *Forced into Glory* (Chicago: Johnson Publishing, 2000).

Douglass—blacks were "only his stepchildren" the ex-slave said. Lincoln was "emphatically the white man's president." That judgment satisfies the Lerone Bennetts of the nation.

What isn't considered as carefully as it might be is that the only hope for the slaves, for black America, was for Lincoln to be the "White Man's President." Imagine the political consequences if Lincoln had run as "the Black Man's President" in an America that, in most states North and South, blacks could not vote. If Lincoln had run as William Lloyd Garrison, or even Frederick Douglass, he would never have been President Lincoln, Congressman Lincoln, Assemblyman Lincoln, or Dog Catcher Lincoln for that matter.

Douglass recognized Lincoln's role. He was being descriptive, not scolding. Douglass in fact had given two speeches within six months of the assassination in which he referred to Lincoln as "emphatically the BLACK MAN'S president." But when Douglass spoke in 1876 he was not bitter at Lincoln for failing to be the exemplar of equality for blacks. Douglass was arguing that even a white man, enmeshed in his duties as president of a predominantly white nation, could reach out and make black people his stepchildren and could include them in the family that was the nation. Lincoln himself had been a stepchild and as such was treated with such love that he always spoke lovingly of his stepmother. Whether Lincoln's commitment to the former slaves rested on a picture in his mind of that relationship is speculative, but we do know that Douglass and Sojourner Truth both remarked on the kindness and respect with which Lincoln treated them. Truth wrote in November 1864, "I was never treated with more kindness and cordiality than I was by the great and good man Abraham Lincoln." Douglass said, "In all my interviews with Mr. Lincoln I was impressed with his entire freedom from popular prejudice against the colored race. He was the first great man that I talked with in the United States freely, who in no single instance reminded me of the difference between himself and myself, of the difference of color."[23]

---

[23] Truth quoted in Carleton Mabee, "Sojourner Truth and President Lincoln," *New England Quarterly* 61 (December 1988) 521; Douglass in Allen Thornedyke, ed.

Lucas Morel pointed out that Douglass gave his 1876 speech from a platform that included President Grant and other major white leaders. He was not trying to assess Lincoln's role in posterity. Douglass was trying to show these powerful white leaders that even though their main constituency was white, they could, like Lincoln, reach out and protect black Americans as stepchildren at least. Given the fact that an election was under way in which Southern black voters were being shot, hanged, mutilated, and otherwise terrorized, most black Americans would have been delighted to gain the protection as the stepchildren of which Douglass spoke. Douglass provided an assessment of Lincoln's action that rings true. Lincoln had to have the support of the majority white population. Douglass proclaimed:

Had he put the abolition of slavery before the salvation of the Union he would have inevitably driven from him a powerful class of the American people and rendered resistance to rebellion impossible. Viewed from the genuine abolition ground.... Mr. Lincoln seemed tardy, cold, dull and indifferent; but measuring him by the sentiment of his country, a sentiment he was bound as a statesman to consult, he was swift, zealous, radical and determined.[24]

That statement wraps up the message of Lincoln's letter to Greeley, his role as emancipator and his role as a positive propagandist. It is the best way to remember him: operating within the political constitutional system, proving that that system could bring forth the equality promised

---

Reminiscences of Abraham Lincoln by Distinguished Men of His Time (NY: North American Review, 1886) 193.

[24] *Life and Times of Frederick Douglass. Written by Himself.* (Reprinted from 1892 edition by Collier Books, London, 1962) 489. See chapter 7, Lucas Morel, "America's First Black President? Lincoln's Legacy of Political Transcendence," in this volume.

in 1776, and calling on the people to live up to the better angels of their nature. We need to remember that things like that are within us, the people whose government this is.

LINCOLN'S PARDONS AND
WHAT THEY MEAN

William Lee Miller

So there I was scribbling away about Lincoln's pardons, explaining to anyone who would listen that this is an important presidential power and that in the same paragraph (Article II, section II, paragraph 1) that makes the president commander in chief, the Constitution grants to him—or imposes upon him if you will—the power "to grant reprieves and pardons for offenses against the United States, except in cases of impeachment."

The pardon may wipe away all punishment or it may commute or reduce punishment.

The pardon may be unconditional or it may have conditions attached.

By a "reprieve" a president may suspend punishment, by a "pardon" remit punishment. Lincoln was told by his attorney general that "a reprieve does not annul the sentence…it only prolongs the time."[1]

And most important: the president's power to expunge or diminish punishment is unlimited. It is a constitutionally granted power that rests with the president exclusively and personally.

Faced with an enormous stack of cases early in his presidency, Lincoln asked Judge Advocate General Joseph Holt whether the power could be delegated, and the answer came back: No. This power is his

---

[1]See note in Roy Basler, ed. *Collected Works of Abraham Lincoln*, 9 vols. (New Brunswick NJ: Rutgers University Press, 1953) 5:129. This note is in reference to Lincoln's 4 February 1862 Stay of Execution for Nathaniel Gordon.

alone, at his sole discretion. There he (and some day, she) sits, with the papers of a particular case in front of him, with the fate and often the life of a convicted person resting on his decision. It is a point at which a president's moral understanding is revealed with a rare clarity.

He may make the decision to pardon for his own reasons, whatever they may be. The pardoning power of presidents (and of governors of American states as well—and of kings and queens in the days of the royal pardon) is a point in the formal system at which the particular characteristics of a singular case on the one side, and the moral understanding of a single individual on the other, can determine the result.

It is interesting that the American Founders, heirs of the tradition of republicanism, who wanted to limit royal dispensations by which kings could single out individuals for favor or disfavor, should include this power for their new chief executive.

But they did. They provided that for all offenses "against the United States"—that is, against federal law—the president's power to expunge or diminish punishment is unlimited.

I was explaining all of this to anyone who would listen—when suddenly late in January 2001 I did not need to explain the pardon power any longer. But the furor over the Clinton pardons, and the retaliatory exhuming of dubious pardons by other recent presidents, skewed the treatment of the subject too much toward the misuse of presidential pardons. Lincoln's admirable use of it served justice and mercy—but a discriminating mercy.

While he too would have appeals for clemency for ordinary peacetime crimes, he uniquely would also deal, with malice toward none, with enemies who were not enemies in a war that was not a war against a state that was not a state—rebels.

The little American army was suddenly swollen by an enormous influx of civilians. A raw private found guilty of "desertion" or "insubordination" or "willful disobedience" or "using threatening language toward his superior officer" or "sleeping on post" and sentenced—this would get your attention—to be "shot to death with musketry."

But this total civilian with the power to pardon would stop the execution with a telegram, get the papers on the case, and commute the punishment, asking: What possible injury can this lad work upon the cause of this great Union? I say let him go.

He would say: "Let him fight instead of being shot."

The pardon power as applied to "Offenses against the United States" means against federal law—including courts-martial in the armed forces of the United States.

A court-martial would order some private (as it usually was) to be shot for "desertion" (as it usually was) or for "cowardice and absence without leave" (23 June 1863) or for "mutiny" (26 June 1863 and again on 18 July 1863 or 21 July, a sergeant, hanged for mutiny) or for "violence to a superior officer" or for "disobedience and insubordination" (26 June 1863, a busy day) or for "striking and using threatening language toward his superior officer" (28 April 1863) or for "willful disobedience of orders" (9 July 1864) or for "sleeping on post" (26 June 1863 and again on 26 April 1864) but—to repeat—again and again for "desertion."[2]

The president, again and again, would stop the execution with a telegram. He would read the papers on the case and commute the punishment to something else.

In September 1862 he appointed to the newly created position of Judge Advocate General Joseph Holt, a Union-supporting Kentuckian who had served in Buchanan's cabinet. Holt with his staff soon had a primary duty receiving and making recommendations on these courts-martial. On appointed days he would come over to the executive mansion and sit with Lincoln and one of the secretaries and go through and decide the cases.

Lincoln's evolving practice of commuting the death sentences of sleeping sentinels and leg cases and homesick Union soldiers was warmly received by some of the broad public in the North. In 1863 a government clerk took the story of one of those sleeping sentinels and

---

[2] All of the pardons referred to here are in the *Collected Works of Abraham Lincoln*, at the date cited.

produced a famous popular sentimental poem, which has many things wrong, but was not without some basis in fact. A Vermont farm boy volunteered, and then, sensibly accustomed to sleeping when it was dark, fell asleep one night while on sentry duty. He was therefore sentenced to be shot.

Then (according to the legend and the poem), Lincoln intervened and pardoned him, and the soldier went on to fight and die bravely in battle, with praise for the president on his lips.

The poem's account of the presidential intervention, which occurs, of course, just at the last minute "before the fatal volley sounds," goes like this:

> Then suddenly was heard the noise of steeds and wheels
> approach,
> And, rolling through a cloud of dust, appeared a stately
> coach.
> On, past the guards, and through the field, its rapid
> course was bent,
> Till, halting, 'mid the lines was seen the nation's
> President!

That the president himself would come roaring up in his coach, at the last minute, with a pardon in his hand, is a particularly wonderful feature of this poem.

The painter Frances Carpenter, who painted "First Reading of the Emancipation Proclamation," worked on his painting right in the Lincoln White House in early 1864 and was able therefore to produce a valuable little book with the subtitle "Six Months at the White House." He gave a sample of the president's pardoning, of the sort that became legend. A poor woman from Philadelphia had been waiting with a baby in her arms for several days to see the president. Her husband had furnished a substitute for the army, but sometime afterward, in a state of intoxication, was induced to enlist. Upon reaching the post assigned his regiment, he deserted, thinking the government was not entitled to his services. Returning home, he was arrested, tried, convicted, and sentenced to be shot. The sentence was to be executed on a Saturday. On the previous

Monday his wife left her home with her baby, to endeavor to see the president.

Carpenter got this tale from an old White House retainer named Daniel. Said Daniel:

> She had been waiting here three days, and there was no chance for her to get in. Late in the afternoon of the third day, the President was going through the passage to his private room to get a cup of tea. On the way he heard the baby cry. He instantly went back to his office and rang the bell. "Daniel," said he, "Is there a woman with a baby in the anteroom?" I said there was, and if he would allow me to say it, it was a case he ought to see; for it was a matter of life and death. Said he, "Send her to me at once." She went in, told her story, and the President pardoned her husband.
>
> As the woman came from his presence, her eyes were lifted and her lips moving in prayer, the tears streaming down her cheeks. Said Daniel, "I went up to her, and pulling her shawl, said Madam, it was the baby that did it."[3]

The Critics

Not everybody applauded these presidential pardons, and the criticisms did not come solely from the military. Attorney General Edwards Bates is quoted as saying that Mr. Lincoln was almost an ideal man, lacking only one thing: "I have sometimes told him...that he was unfit to be entrusted with the power. Why, if a man comes to him with a touching story his judgement is almost certain to be affected by it. Should the applicant be a *woman,* a wife, a mother, or a sister,—in nine cases out of ten, her tears, if nothing else, are sure to prevail."[4] The pardon clerk working in the Justice Department under Attorney General Bates wrote that "my chief, Attorney Bates, soon discovered that my most important

---

[3] Frances B. Carpenter, *The Inner Life of Abraham Lincoln: Six Months in the White House* (Lincoln: University of Nebraska Press, 1995) 130–33.

[4] Carpenter, *The Inner Life of Abraham Lincoln,* 68–69.

duty was to keep all but the most deserving cases from coming before the kind Mr. Lincoln at all, since there was nothing harder for him to do than to put aside a prisoner's application and he could not resist it when it was urged by a pleading wife and a weeping child."

Secretary of State Salmon Chase is quoted as having made a particularly pungent statement of the alleged result of Lincoln's tenderness: "Such kindness [meaning the pardons] to the criminal [!] is cruelty to the army, for it encourages the bad to leave the brave and patriotic unsupported."

Many generals (though not all) were even more severe. General Butler said his victory took so long because "pusillanimity and want of executive force in government." General Daniel Taylor said: "If we attempt to shoot a deserter, you pardon him and our army is without discipline." Colonel Theodore Lyman in General Meade's army of the Potomac said: "All this [great outrages in the rear] proceeds from one thing—the uncertainty of the death penalty through the false merciful policy of the President." In one case, Lincoln pardoned a deserter at a wife's request only to have the soldier desert once more. General John A. Dix, Department of the East, attached the following comment to the papers of this case: "Respectfully forwarded the request that the attention of the President...may be called to the case for the purpose of suggesting that his interposition, on the ex parte representations of interested persons, in cases of military crime, is almost always hazardous" (2 May 1864).

There is a legend—unsubstantiated—that General Sherman, on being asked how he carried out courts-martial in light of Lincoln's pardons, answered: "I shot them first." But we do know what Sherman wrote in a letter to Judge Advocate General Holt in April 1864: "Forty or fifty executions now would in the next twelve months save ten thousand lives."

Although most Lincoln biographers warm to the tender-hearted president, not all do. William Barton, the former preacher, writing in the 1920s, put it harshly and added the suggestion that Lincoln may have been fooled: "Lincoln had little time to investigate and it is to be feared that in some cases the alleged widow had rented the black clothes for the occasion, and had help in inventing the fiction about her family...Lincoln was very easily imposed upon...in the long run it had been better for the discipline of the army if he had kept his hands off." Working on a Lincoln book, I went through, counted, and analyzed the pardons in Lincoln's collected papers—168 in which he wrote something—and then noted that there were 661 more that were brought to him in great batches in 1864. There were days when Holt would come over with huge stacks of pardon cases, so many as to drive the editors of Lincoln's collected papers, who print everything—even two word notes on the back of an envelope—into counting instead of printing: "February 9, 1864, 63 court martial cases reviewed by Lincoln on this date." On 11 February 1864, there were forty-six more. On 14 April 1864, there were sixty-seven cases; on 21 April 1864, seventy-two cases; and so on.

I learned then the retired psychiatrist Thomas Lowry and his wife Beverly were going into the archives—sorting through the records of 80,000 Union Army courts-martial—a feat never attempted before. Thomas Lowry wittily remarked that the Civil War was not fought for the benefit of researchers, but they did find a great many pardons and among those were the Lincoln pardons for which there is no comment in the collected papers. The Lowrys have produced a book, *Don't Shoot that Boy!: Abraham Lincoln and Military Justice.*[5] From these two sources—the collected papers and the Lowry's book—it is possible to make some informed generalizations about Lincoln use of the pardon power, primarily with respect to the Union Army.

Ten Conclusions about Lincoln
1. He understood the necessity of order, government, and the discipline of a functioning army. He was no revolutionary, no anarchist, or pacifist, and he understood the necessary role of coercion in law and government.

Moreover, this inexperienced newcomer from the West would prove, to the surprise of many, to have what Seward would call "Executive Force"—the ability to make painful decisions. He did not

---

[5] Thomas P. Lowry, *Don't shoot that Boy!: Abraham Lincoln and Military Justice* (Mason City IA: Savas Pub. Co., 1999.)

procrastinate, he did not flinch, and he did make great decisions in a time of the terrible scourge of a destructive war. Furthermore, no one cared more about the effective functioning of the Union armies or was more resolute in prosecuting the war than he.

He wanted effective military action by the Union armies even more, it would seem, than McClellan, and Meade after Gettysburg, and most of his other generals—until he found Grant.

He wanted an effective Union army and Union victories for high reasons and not so high reasons. As he would say in the first inaugural, he would take a solemn oath, registered in heaven, to defend the Union. As he would say in the second inaugural, it was the victories of those Union armies "upon which all else chiefly depends." Indeed, his own reelection in 1864 had depended on it.

Moreover Lincoln did understand the problem of desertions; he would make one of his memorable metaphors about the difficulty of moving armies when where are multiple desertions: "It is like shoveling fleas, trying to get an army intact from here to there." He knew the general's argument and would state it often: "Some of my generals complain that I impair discipline by my frequent pardons and reprieves." In one of his most famous public letters, to a meeting of Union Democrats in June 1863, he defended this and similar actions: "Must I shoot a simple-minded soldier boy who deserts, while I must not touch a hair of the wily agitator who induces him to desert?"

I want to call attention to the sentences preceding that famous one: "I understand the meeting, whose resolution I am considering to be in favor of suppressing the Rebellion by military force—by armies. Long experience has shown that armies cannot be maintained unless desertions shall be punished by the severe penalty of death. The case requires, and the law and the Constitution sanction, this punishment." So Lincoln himself said, in that context, then his sentence about the simple-minded soldier boy and the wily agitator. All this is to say he did not issue his pardons from a soft sentiment that failed to understand what the argument was or what the issue was.

2. He did not pardon everyone.

Lincoln did not pardon bounty-jumpers, those entrepreneurial scoundrels who would enlist, get the bounty, desert, enlist again under a new name, in attempt to get themselves another bounty.

He did not pardon a soldier, however tearful his wife's plea, who deserted three times—who was incorrigible. He did not, as a rule, pardon soldiers convicted of acts that would be crimes if committed by civilians—larceny, murder, and particularly rape.

Many of Lincoln's acts of clemency in capital cases in the Union Army were not outright pardons but were commutations of the sentence. Dry Tortugas, the bleak prison camp in undeveloped Florida to which great numbers were pardoned and where unshot deserters were sent, was not exactly a picnic area.

Although he was generous to ordinary Confederate soldiers and civilians, he approved execution of every one of the Confederate recruiters who was caught—who came North to entice men in the rebel army.

Moreover, Lincoln was not always swayed by tearful appeal or eminent references. For example, two famous cases, not of union soldiers: A slave trader from Maine, Nathaniel Gordon, had been sentenced to death in November 1861 by a New York circuit court judge. President Lincoln was presented with the petitions of, as he put it, "a large number of respectable citizens" who "earnestly sought [him] to commute the said sentence of said Nathaniel Gordon to a term of imprisonment for life."[6]

But Lincoln wrote, "I felt it to be my duty to refuse." What he did do was to postpone the execution for two weeks because Nathaniel Gordon needed time to make the necessary preparation for "the awful change that awaits him." He was executed on 21 February 1862, the first and only slave trader ever to be executed for that crime under American law.

There was an even greater outpouring of petitions, telegrams, and appeals from respectable citizens in 1863 on behalf of a distinguished citizen of Norfolk, Virginia, named Dr. David M. Wright. Highly

---

[6] Stay of Execution for Nathaniel Gordon, 4 February 1862.

regarded by his fellow citizens and a man of certain eminence and reputation, he had been standing with the crowd on 11 July 1863 looking on at a stunning sight: a company of black soldiers from the Union army marching up the street of his Southern city. There were jeers and taunts from the crowd. The commanding officer, marching at the head of the "colored" troops, was a Lieutenant Anson Sanborn. Some exchange between Sanborn and Wright led to a verbal altercation, and Wright drew a pistol and shot and killed the twenty-year-old Sanborn.

Wright was sentenced by a military commission to be hanged. Now came the petitions, telegrams, personal appeals to the president, not only from the South but from the North—Dr. Wright was well connected—and a plea that Wright's wife might see the president in his behalf. No, it was useless.

"The subject is a painful one, but the case is settled," wrote Lincoln. On the day that Wright was finally to be hanged—more than three months after his sentencing—there was still hope that a presidential pardon would come, but there was no last minute telegram in this case and on 23 October 1863, Dr. Wright was executed.

Lincoln was not always the most lenient figure; he did approve severe punishments—his was a discriminating mercy.

3. He took care; he paid attention to the particular case.

One is impressed with the picture of the swamped wartime president going through these appeals, one by one. Perhaps the most striking case is not from the Union army or from the war directly but from an Indian uprising in Minnesota in summer 1862. Frustrated by a thousand mistreatments, the Sioux went on a rampage. Violence spread throughout southwestern Minnesota and produced a racially charged frenzy in the white population of the upper Midwest.

The president in Washington, preoccupied with the war, made the mistake of sending General John Pope, the defeated general from Second Bull Run, to command the troops that would quell the outbreak. General Pope's scarcely statesmanlike response to this assignment included saying that the Sioux were to be treated "as maniacs or as wild beasts."[7] This remark is typical of others quoted by historian David Nichols from white leaders in the area.

The rebellion was quelled. A military commission was established that sentenced 303 Sioux warriors to be executed for killings and "outrages," by which the commission meant rapes. Those proposed executions had to be submitted to this still rather new president in Washington, with his power to pardon. And so what did he do? He promptly directed the angry authorities in Minnesota to execute no one without further word from him.

General Pope, a Minnesota senator, and the Minnesota governor all told him that the people of the state were so infuriated that if the Sioux were not all executed legally, they would be killed illegally. Lincoln resisted and ordered that the complete records of the trial be sent to him. Learning from his Judge Advocate General that presidential powers could not be delegated, he personally—in the midst of Civil War pressures and woes—went through the records one by one, of the convicted Sioux, and sorted out those who were guilty of serious crimes. He was shocked by what he found.

The "trials" had become shorter and shorter, averaging less than fifteen minutes each. Indians who honestly admitted their involvement in battles had condemned themselves. Acceptance of normally inadmissible hearsay evidence and the denial of due process and counsel were commonplace. Indians who had peaceably surrendered, having been told they would be safe, were then convicted on the slimmest basis; if one admitted to firing a gun, that was enough for a sentence of death.[8]

Lincoln worked through the transcripts for a month, sorting out those who were guilty of serious crimes. The number kept shrinking. Only 2 were clearly guilty of rape, and only 39 out of the 303 condemned by the military were guilty of killing innocent farmers.

---

[7] David A. Nichols, *Lincoln and the Indians: Civil War Policy and Politics* (Columbia: University of Missouri Press, 1978) 87. Nichol's work is a definitive study of this episode, and I rely on it throughout this section.

[8] Nichols, *Lincoln and the Indians,* 94–118 *passim.*

Biographer David Herbert Donald presents the touching picture of Lincoln conscientiously going over each individual case, and then when he had sorted out the thirty-nine, carefully writing out in his own hand the names and telling the telegraph operator to be particularly careful because a slight error with these unfamiliar names might lead to the executing of the wrong man.

On the day after Christmas in 1862 the thirty-nine Sioux were hanged in Mankato, Minnesota. It was the largest mass execution in American history, but there were 265 Sioux who were still alive because the conscientious president stopped the process and went through the cases one by one.

There was much resentment in Minnesota for his radical reduction in the number of condemned men, for Lincoln's multiple pardons. In the 1864 election the Republicans did less well than before in Minnesota. A Minnesota senator, and a former governor, said that Lincoln would have had a larger majority in Minnesota if he had hanged more. Lincoln responded: "I could not afford to hang men for votes."[9]

Do you imagine that William Tecumseh Sherman would be scrupulous about the facts in each case, about the particulars of the justice (let alone mercy) of the executions—forty or fifty of them!—that will have, in his view, so salutary an effect? For his purpose, to scare troops into discipline, it does not matter with what care each case is considered, or whether the particular decision is just. Lincoln did care.

4. As a politician he was aware of the larger public context of the war.

He went against political advantage in the Minnesota Indian case and in other cases, but his political sense figured in his decision-making.

The war was fought by a people with a meager military tradition, indeed with roots in a tradition of radical Whigs that was hostile to the very idea of a standing, professional army. The little army of 17,000 professionals, stripped of many of its best leaders by defections to the Confederates, was suddenly swollen by this enormous influx of civilians, first of 75,000 volunteers, signing on for ninety days in the first flush of

---

[9] Nichols, *Lincoln and the Indians,* 18.

idealistic zeal, and then as the war ground on, of conscripts drawn by the coercion of state power from the farm and the shop and the street by the hundreds of thousands. The nation was to have its first experience of a modern popular army drawn from the whole people.

The military code of conduct that this transformed army inherited reflected the disciplining severities of a long European professional military tradition, including summary execution by a firing squad. The generals and some of the civilians thought that the whole point was neither justice nor mercy to an individual but solely collective good of the army—order, discipline—which then served the collective good of the Union. You had to have some shootings of deserters to make soldiers stay in the army and fight. So they said.

Lincoln—the politician in a people's war for a government of, by, and for the people—broadened the picture. These soldiers were not the rootless professionals of past armies whose whole life was the army; these were boys from villages with friends, fathers, mothers, sweethearts, people who knew them—and congressmen who represented them. As a politician Lincoln was certainly more aware of a larger consequence of shooting these boys—out in the public where their mothers and sweethearts and friends would all know it—than the generals needed to be. And he noticed this significant point: even his critics, when they knew the boy in question, made specific (perhaps embarrassed) requests for pardons. That should tell us something.

Gideon Welles, the secretary of the navy, criticized his chief's excessive leniency in his diary more than once, including this entry for Saturday, 24 December 1864: "Called on the president to commute the sentence of a person condemned to be hung. He at once assented. Is always disposed to mitigate punishment. Sometimes this is a weakness." But, we may note, significantly, Welles here criticizes the president for doing in general what this instance he, Welles, himself had just asked him to do!

Henry Wilson tells a tale of a particular pardon, and of Lincoln's significant response:

I remember talking early one Sabbath morning with a wounded Irish officer who came to Washington to say that a soldier who had been sentenced to be shot in a day or two for desertion had fought bravely by his side in battle. I told him that we had come to ask him to pardon the poor soldier. After a few moments reflection he said, "My officers tell me the good of the service demands the enforcement of the Law, but it makes my heart ache to have the poor boys shot. I will pardon him, and then you will all join in blaming me for it. You all censure me for granting pardons, and yet you all ask me to do so."

5. He had the self-confidence to make his own decisions.

There is a famous quotation from John Hay, Lincoln's secretary in the White House, about Lincoln's intellectual self-confidence, which was enormously frustrating to men who were vastly more learned—notably Charles Sumner and Salmon Chase. I suggest that *this* was closely related to that what I may call moral self-confidence on Lincoln's part: he did believe he could make judgments about right and wrong and justice and mercy that went against his generals, and sometimes his advisers including Holt.

His military experience was confined to a few weeks in the Illinois militia fighting mosquitoes and making raids on the wild onions. Nevertheless he stood up to the generals and everyone else, and decided.

Fairly early, he began not to take for granted the appropriateness of all military definitions and military decisions based upon them.

On 25 October 1862 he decided the case of Private Conrad Zachringer of Company A, 12th Missouri Volunteers. According to the record, Private Zachringer "caused, and excited mutiny by taking hold of First Lieutenant Mittman, then officer of the day, by the throat" (thereby violating the Seventh Article of War), "did strike First Lieutenant Englemann, and throwed him on the ground" (thereby violating the Ninth Article of War), "did refuse to obey" (thereby violating the Twenty-seventh Article of War). Despite his plea "that he was drunk and knew nothing," he had been found guilty on all charges by a court-martial in Helena, Arkansas, and sentenced to be shot—"to be shot to death with musketry," as the General Court-Martial Orders sometimes sternly put it.

Lincoln perceived that despite all the elaborate paraphernalia of military law, what the offense amounted to was a drunken binge. His order of 25 October 1862 said, The prisoner's offense in this case, being to some extent the result of sudden passion, and not of premeditation, the sentence of death is mitigated to imprisonment for one year, commencing on this day, and to be dishonorably discharged from the service, with loss of pay and emoluments.

Some further Lincoln orders:

10 April 1862, General George G. Meade: "What possible injury can this lad work upon the cause of this great Union? I say let him go."

8 November 1862. "I suppose the case within was, at least technically, a desertion. In consideration of his after conduct, let the boy, James W. Walters, be pardoned."

18 July 1863, is forthright enough: "Let him fight instead of being shot."

Again: "better to have this young man for three years, than to shoot him."[10]

"Do not execute sentence upon young Perry from Wisconsin for sleeping at his post until case is reviewed."

"This young man is but 16 years old. I know his father well. He is a fine boy, but overcome with fatigue and sleep has incurred the dreadful penalty of death. Please telegraph Genl Thomas to suspend execution."[11]

6. He removed the tendency to favor officers.

In the *Life of Billy Yank,* Bell Irvin Wiley notes a marked slanting in favor of officers.

> Not only did officers guilty of serious offenses such as cowardice, desertion and theft frequently escape punishment by resigning, but in instances where they were brought to trial they often got off much more lightly then enlisted men charged with the same breeches of discipline. Since the making of arrests and the preferring of charges were exclusive officer functions,

---

[10] Order concerning Lewis H. Cox, alias John M. Dillon, 18 September 1863.

[11] To Maj. Gen. George H. Thomas, 26 April 1864.

commissioned personnel sometimes were inclined to consider themselves a mutual protective association.

Lincoln reversed or at least qualified that.

By way of illustration, a story of successive days in June 1863. On 23 June Lincoln dealt with the case of a Private James G. Lyon, 5th Vermont Volunteers, who was found guilty of "cowardice and absence without leave" and sentenced to be shot. On the next day, 24 June, he dealt with the case of Captain William P. Eagan of the 23d Kentucky Volunteers, who had also been found guilty of "cowardice" but who was sentenced only to dishonorable dismissal. Lincoln commuted the sentence of Private Lyon to imprisonment at hard labor, but upheld the dismissal of Captain Eagan.

The Lowrys write: "Hundreds of Union soldiers were shot by firing squads. If a Union Officer stood before a firing squad, we have not seen the record. Officers could resign, soldiers could not." Civil war scholar and editor of the Grant papers John Y. Simon wrote, "In that avalanche of cases, not a single officer was condemned to death." Mark Neely notes that Lincoln was notably tougher on officers than on enlisted men: "of 59 convictions involving officers in the last half of 1863, 14 were given more severe punishments by the president than by their courts-martial."

7. *He developed his own clear principle against shooting youngsters.*

Lincoln put it quite clear in a wire to General Meade on 8 October 1863: "I am unwilling for any boy under eighteen to be shot." The father of the boy in that case "affirms that he is yet under sixteen." This youngster—"boy" as Lincoln would often say—had been scheduled "to be shot to-morrow, as a deserter." We could make a long list of pardons that Lincoln granted to a "boy" or to a "lad" who was seventeen, sixteen, fifteen, or "very young."

Again and again he would telegraph something like "If there is any reason to believe that this boy was under eighteen when he deserted, suspend his execution until further order." No matter what your martial law claims that he has done, if he is under eighteen, don't shoot him.

"I am appealed to in behalf of John Murphy, to be shot tomorrow. His mother says he is but seventeen." On 3 January 1863: Let this woman have her boy out of Old Capital Prison: "hadn't we better spank this boy and send him back to Kansas?"

8. With malice toward none: he had developed a principled avoidance of hatred, grudges, revenge, and malice.

Avoidance of malice was not just the phrase in the second inaugural; it was a developed pattern of behavior and explicit principle that one can see emerging in the years just before he becomes president, and then further when he is in office, about which he used that word more than once.

As we have seen in the case of the Minnesota Sioux, Lincoln had an inclination to be very careful in the presence of passionate ill-wishing. Explicitly, an ethic that repudiated malice avoided, in his phrase, "planting thorns," and not holding grudges. To Stanton toward the end of the war he would write, "the government can properly have no motive for revenge, no purpose merely for punishment's sake." One of his great sentences that adds something to the second inaugural Lincoln wrote to a Louisiana Unionist in 1862: "I shall do nothing in malice. What I deal with is too vast for malicious dealing."

Lincoln disciplined himself of that extra, added desire to harm, to get back, to retaliate, to hurt someone as we have been hurt—to take out our frustrations—to make large collective condemnations. But of course there was more: not only with malice toward none but...

9. With charity for all: the most notable feature of his pardoning was his sympathetic identification with the accused.

His charity was a discriminating mercy, but it was mercy all the same. The testimony is overwhelming that Lincoln, man and boy, had an unusually intense sympathy with suffering of his fellow creatures: for lost cats, mired down hogs, birds fallen out of the nest, turtles with hot coals placed on their backs by his youthful playmates. Lincoln's sympathy extended also, as is not always the case with animal-lovers, to his fellow human beings: to the old Indian who went into his Blackhawk War camp and was set upon by his militia mates; the woman he encountered in court whose drunken husband beat her; the coffle of slaves he saw on the boat in the Ohio, chained together like fish on a line; the farm boy who was going to be shot for falling asleep on sentry duty. Leonard Swett, Lincoln's longtime friend and associate, wrote to the President's former law partner Herndon not long after the assassination: "I remember one day being in his room when he was sitting at his table a large pile of papers before him. After a pleasant talk, he turned quite abruptly and said, 'Get out of the way, Swett; to morrow is butcher-day, and I must go through these papers and see if I cannot find some excuse to let these poor fellows off.'"

Some variation on the word "butcher," as here in "butcher-day," referring to the executions would seem to have been a regular anguished usage of Lincoln's. His explanation of one of his pardons from 7 January 1864 could hardly be more direct: "I am trying to evade the butchering business lately."

Among the excuses he would find, in addition to youth, would be "unsoundness of mind" and other debilitating ailments: "so diseased as to be unfit for Military duty."[12] He also used the excuse of the hardship and poverty of the family: "[The mother] says she is destitute."[13] Also he used the unfairness for trickery in mustering, particularly of Germans, particularly in New York. Once Lincoln telegraphed: "Boy discharged and mustering officer rebuked. A. Lincoln."[14]

Of course there were his famous "leg cases" drawing on a joke that he had used long before to illustrate a different point: a man's (or a boy's) head and heart may be steadfast, but he may be afflicted with cowardly legs, that carry him willy-nilly away from battle. Captain Harry S Truman of the 129th Field Artillery from Missouri, a reader (despite his mother's opinion) of books about Lincoln, on his way overseas in World War I, would write to his girlfriend Bess Wallace back in Missouri that he hoped he would not prove to be one of the "leg cases."

Perhaps a characteristic Lincolnian reason for granting your pardon would be telling your story particularly well. The president sent this 3

---

[12] To Edwin M. Stanton, 29 May 1862.
[13] To Edwin M. Stanton, 2 September 1863.
[14] To Joseph Holt, 10 February 1864

November 1863 inquiry to General Meade: "Samuel Wellers, private in Co. B 49th. Penn Vols. Writes that he is to be shot for desertion on the 6th. His own story is rather a bad one, and yet he tells it so frankly, that I am some what interested in him." Then he asked, in hope, about this frank storyteller: "Has he been a good soldier, except the desertion?" And of course, "About how old is he?"

This is not the only time that telling one's story well had an effect on the lover of good storytelling, Abraham Lincoln. On 1 July 1864 he issued an order for the release of a Confederate prisoner that read: "This man being so well vouched, and talking so much better than any other I have heard, let him take the oath…and be discharged."

The story is told of a convicted deserter who, as the case was presented to Lincoln, had no sweetheart, parents, wife, sister, children, or congressman to plead for him—perhaps the thought was that the president would not be inhibited by weeping intercessors from the letting the execution stand. Lincoln is said, in this perhaps apocryphal but morally significant story, to have responded: "If he has no friend, I'll be his friend," and signed a reprieve.

But Lincoln's actions were not simply unmerited mercy. It was also the case that:

10. Finally, his charity redefined justice.

Justice and charity can be set over against each other. Justice is a balancing, an equilibrium: this properly matches that; the scales are properly balanced; the punishment fits the crime; each is given what is deserved, what is merited.

Charity does not ask about merit, or balance, and may rise into the wonderful but dangerous realm of forgiveness and grace. On the other hand, charity may have an effect upon what justice is seen to be—mercy may season justice—or more than that, may overthrow or transcend but enlarge our sense of what is just.

Our empathetic identification may furnish the materials not for a violation of, but for a better understanding of, what is just.

That is what happens repeatedly in history.

How does it come about that child labor, punishment by the rack and whip and the branding iron, the African slave trade, human slavery

itself, the total submission of women to men, the systematic denial of
education to the poor, the use of torture as an instrument of state policy,
all of which were once widely accepted as just—as what is
deserved—are now as widely repudiated, and seen to be unjust?

Lincoln thought about and identified with the situation of raw
recruits from out of a moral conviction that rejected the radical
disproportion of the sentence of death in the typical case. He looked at
"justice"—what is "due"—with the eyes of charity, and saw that, at least
in this new case of a mass army drawn from the whole people, the
received formulae of military practice had to be reformulated.

What we, using Lincoln's word, and that of the King James Bible,
are calling "charity," beginning in sympathetic identification, developing
into a general moral principle, led to a redefinition of what is just and
unjust. I interpret Lincoln's clemency to Union soldiers in this way: not
that his charity ignored or contradicted or "rose above" "justice," but that
it redefined what is just.

Lincoln's long time friend Leonard Swett wrote to Herndon that:

> He (Lincoln) had very great kindness of heart. His mind
> was full of tender sensibilities; he was extremely humane, yet
> while these attributes were fully developed in his character and
> unless intercepted by his judgment controlled him, they never
> did control him contrary to his judgments. He would strain a
> point to be kind, but he never strained to breaking. Most of men
> of much kindly feeling are controlled by this sentiment against
> their judgment, or rather that sentiment beclouds their Judgment.
> It was never so with him. He would be just as kind and generous
> as his judgment would let him be—no more.

Lincoln's fundamental generosity did not violate or ignore or
"becloud" his "judgment," to use Swett's term. But that "judgment" itself
was reshaped by the charitable insight into a general principle.

One can see this developing in the case of deserters in his exchanges
with generals. On 31 March 1863, General Joseph Hooker, discerning—
significantly—from individual case after individual case what he
understood the president's policy to be, had sent, apparently in one batch,

fifty-five cases of soldiers sentenced to be shot for desertion, recommending that they be pardoned. Lincoln proceeded to write on the envelope containing these records of fifty-five: "Pardoned A. LINCOLN."

In a telegram to General Meade on 26 December 1863, Lincoln made the standard order, "do not execute" a particular private until further order, and added this significant request: "whenever it shall be quite convenient I shall be glad to have a conference with you about this class of cases."

Already on 10 March 1863, he issued a proclamation granting a general amnesty to all soldiers then absent without leave (AWOL three days and you are considered a deserter) if they would report back to their unit by 1 April.

On 26 February 1864, General Butler rather grumpily wired Lincoln, in response to a presidential telegram suspending an execution of one private, that "the president is informed that no death sentence will be executed in this department for desertion without his assent—as I understand it to be his policy not to have such executions."

It was indeed his policy. On that same day the war department issued General Order No. 76, on the topic, Sentence of Deserters, changing, by presidential order, the sentencing of the whole class of deserters, "mitigating" the punishment of those condemned to death by court-martial to imprisonment at Dry Tortugas, and empowering commanding generals to restore to duty those whom they judged appropriate.

I infer two developments, interwoven. On the one side the beleaguered but conscientious president was in danger of being overwhelmed by the sheer numbers. On the other his merciful interpretation of case after case had led him to a general conviction about the justice of the pattern of what the army classified as desertion.

His implicit conclusion was that rather than shooting to death with musketry men—or boys—the commanding general could decide either to let him fight instead of being shot, or to send him to the Florida prison camp.

But in any case, Don't Shoot that Boy.

AMERICA'S FIRST BLACK PRESIDENT?

LINCOLN'S LEGACY OF POLITICAL TRANSCENDENCE

Lucas E. Morel

A few years ago, the author Toni Morrison described former president Bill Clinton as "our first black President." In an essay for the *New Yorker*, she explained, somewhat tongue-in-cheek, that "white skin notwithstanding," Clinton was "blacker than any actual black person who could ever be elected in our children's lifetime."[1] Although she did note

---

[1] The relevant excerpt reads as follows:

> African-American men seemed to understand it right away. Years ago, in the middle of the Whitewater investigation, one heard the first murmurs: white skin notwithstanding, this is our first black President. Blacker than any actual black person who could ever be elected in our children's lifetime. After all, Clinton displays almost every trope of blackness: single-parent household, born poor, working-class, saxophone-playing, McDonald's-and-junk-food-loving boy from Arkansas. And when virtually all the African-American Clinton appointees began, one by one, to disappear, when the President's body, his privacy, his unpoliced sexuality became the focus of the persecution, when he was metaphorically seized and bodysearched, who could gainsay these black men who knew whereof they spoke? The message was clear: "No matter how smart you are, how hard you work, how much coin you earn for us, we will put you in your place or put you out of the place you have somehow, albeit with our permission, achieved. You will be fired from your job, sent away in disgrace, and—who knows?—maybe sentenced and jailed to boot. In short, unless you do as we say (i.e., assimilate at once), your expletives belong to us.

his African-American appointees, her major point of associating Clinton with black America was his upbringing in a poor, single-parent household, among other things, not unlike the image held by many Americans when they think of the black underclass today. Perhaps not so tongue-in-cheek, we might ask ourselves when studying a president known as the Great Emancipator, couldn't Abraham Lincoln be considered America's first black president?

Leaving aside Lerone Bennett's resurrected claim that Abraham Lincoln was a racist,[2] whose opinion of Father Abraham might we do well to consider as a way of informing our own judgment of this nation's sixteenth president? For this purpose, let me propose Lincoln's only contemporary rival in rhetorical brilliance and argument, Frederick Douglass. As an escaped slave, abolitionist orator, and editor, this "other" Douglass in Lincoln's life was uniquely situated to review the public career of Abraham Lincoln as the foremost representative and spokesman for America's most persecuted and oppressed minority.

Whether as a stump speaker and newspaper editor for the burgeoning abolitionist movement or as the occasional but perceptive visitor to President Lincoln, Douglass took many opportunities to review and comment on the progress of the Lincoln administration in securing freedom for black Americans. I will focus on Frederick Douglass's most famous commentary on the statesmanship of Abraham Lincoln, his "Oration in Memory of Abraham Lincoln," delivered at the unveiling of the Freedmen's Monument in Lincoln Park, Washington, DC, on 14 April 1876.

The date was picked to commemorate the eleventh anniversary of Lincoln's assassination, as well as the fourteenth anniversary of the emancipation of slaves in the nation's capital.[3] On the speaker's platform

---

Toni Morrison, "The Talk of the Town," *New Yorker* (5 October 1998) 32.

[2] Lerone Bennett, Jr., *Forced into Glory: Abraham Lincoln's White Dream* (Chicago: Johnson Publishing Company, 2000). For a critique of Bennett's book, see Lucas E. Morel, "Forced into Gory Lincoln Revisionism," *Claremont Review of Books* (Fall 2000) S12–S13.

[3] The assassination of Abraham Lincoln took place the night of 14 April 1865, and he died of a mortal head wound the following morning at 7:22 A.M. David Herbert

sat the former Union general—now president—Ulysses S. Grant, his cabinet, justices of the Supreme Court, and members of both houses of Congress. In fact, Congress had declared a holiday for the District of Columbia and even appropriated money and designated a site for erecting the monument.[4] With the nation's "movers and shakers" in attendance, Douglass had a national forum like no other he had experienced throughout his many days as an indefatigable abolitionist speaker.[5]

Two months after Lincoln's death, Douglass was invited to participate in another commemoration of the departed president in the nation's capital. Then living in Rochester, New York, he declined the invitation to celebrate the Fourth of July with the Colored People's Educational Monument Association because of the short notice. In his reply, he said he would be with them "in spirit and purpose" and exhorted the organization to make "the immediate, complete, and universal enfranchisement of the colored people of the whole country" the message of the hour.[6] However, when invited to become an officer of the Educational Monument Association the following month, he declined with a fervor and argument that helps place his 1876 speech in bolder relief.

Donald, *Lincoln* (New York: Simon & Schuster, 1995) 599. Congress abolished slavery in the District of Columbia on 16 April 1862. See Lincoln's "Message to Congress" (16 April 1862), *Collected Works of Abraham Lincoln*, 9 vols., ed. Roy P. Basler (New Brunswick NJ: Rutgers University Press, 1955) 5:192. Owners were compensated up to three hundred dollars per slave and Congress authorized $100,000 for voluntary colonization of the freed slaves to Haiti or Liberia. Charles M. Christian, *Black Saga: The African-American Experience* (Washington, DC: Civitas/Counterpoint, 1999) 191–92.

[4] Merrill D. Peterson, *Lincoln in American Memory* (New York: Oxford University Press, 1994) 55–60.

[5] An indication of the seriousness with which Douglass approached his speech on 16 April 1876, might be inferred from his lecture schedule the months immediately preceding the unveiling of the Freedmen's Monument. In February 1876, as in December 1875, he spoke almost every day, whereas in March he spoke only once until his 16 April oration. See John W. Blassingame and John R. McKivigan, eds., *The Frederick Douglass Papers*, 5 vols. (New Haven: Yale University Press, 1992) 4:xxxiii–xxxiv.

[6] "To Messrs. William Syphan and John E. Cook" (1 July 1865), *The Life and Writings of Frederick Douglass,* 5 vols., ed. Philip S. Foner (New York: International Publishers Co., Inc., 1975) 4:169. (Hereinafter cited as *Life and Writings*.)

The National Lincoln Monument Association, as the organization was also called, was chartered in May of 1865 to honor Lincoln's efforts on behalf of black Americans with a monument. The actual monument was to be a college exclusively for blacks.[7] Douglass, of course, was all for educating blacks, but he did not like the idea of combining a monument to Lincoln with a school for blacks only—especially one built with money raised primarily from whites. He called the idea "an offence against good taste" and "calculated to place the colored people in an undesirable and discreditable position before the country."[8]

This last point reflected Douglass's longstanding belief that for black Americans to receive equal treatment by government they not be viewed or treated with condescension or contempt by whites. Because the money would be raised from whites as well as blacks, but for the benefit of blacks alone, Douglass thought the idea looked too self-serving. Moreover, for blacks to rely on whites to fund a monument as an expression of black gratitude toward Lincoln would only perpetuate the notion of blacks as a dependent class of American citizens. "We should bury our own dead and build our own monuments," Douglass explained, "and all monuments which we would build to the memory of our friends, if we would not invite the continued contempt of the white race upon our heads."[9] Simply put, for the freedmen to begin their new life as free Americans, Douglass believed they could not be seen as charity cases—a position of inferior status ill suited for those claiming equal citizenship.[10]

---

[7] The Preamble to the Constitution of the Educational Monument Association reads (in part) that their Colored People's National Monument will be "a seat of learning...for the education of the children of Freemen and Freedmen, and their descendants forever; and to be called the National Lincoln Monument Institute." http://lcweb2.loc.gov/cgi-bin/query/r?ammem/murray:@field(FLD001+91898189+):@@@REF

[8] "To W.J. Wilson" (8 August 1865), *Life and Writings*, 4:171.

[9] *Life and Writings*, 4:172.

[10] Douglass said as much at the Colored Convention of 1853: "[O]ur object is not to excite pity for ourselves, but to command respect for our cause, and to obtain justice for our people." "The Claims of Our Common Cause" (July 1853), *Life and Writings*, 2:255. See also "The Color Question" (5 July 1875), *The Frederick Douglass Papers*, 4:419–22, where Douglass argues for a black "declaration of independence" from white benevolent societies that exploit the needs of blacks for their own monetary gain.

In addition, Douglass could never support any institution that would remain exclusively black (or white, for that matter); this only bolsters racial prejudice. "Hence," Douglass argued, "I am not for building up permanent separate institutions for colored people of any kind." Said institutions undermine the foremost lesson Americans needed to learn in the aftermath of the Civil War: "Equal Manhood means Equal Rights."[11] By paraphrasing the central principle of the Declaration of Independence, Douglass sought to give color prejudice no foothold in any endeavor to improve the condition of blacks in America.

Douglass was equally aghast at the thought of raising money in the name of Lincoln so soon after the president's death. As he put it, "I am not so enterprising as to think of turning the nation's veneration for our martyred President into a means of advantage to the colored people, and, of sending around the hat to a mourning public." Douglass thought the idea was "derogatory to the character of the colored people of the United States."[12] A monument to Lincoln? Yes. A college open to blacks? Absolutely. But a "monument-college" for blacks with white funding as essential for its success? Count Douglass out.[13]

---

[11] "To W.J. Wilson" (8 August 1865), *Life and Writings*, 4:172. Cf. "The Douglass Institute" (29 September 1865), *Life and Writings*, 4:178–79, 182, where Douglass defends black institutions as a temporary expedient in the face of color prejudice.

[12] *Life and Writings*, 4:173. With emphasis, Douglass concluded: "*It looks to me like an attempt to wash the black man's face in the nation's tears for Abraham Lincoln!*"

[13] Early in his public career, Douglass exhorted blacks to organize with whites wherever they could, "and where you cannot, get up societies among yourselves, but without exclusiveness." He quickly acknowledged, though, that organizations and institutions exclusively for blacks might be a temporary expedient in the face of a color prejudice that limited educational opportunities for black Americans: "It will be a long time before we gain all our rights; and although it may seem to conflict with our views of human brotherhood, we shall undoubtedly for many years be compelled to have institutions of a complexional character, in order to attain this very idea of human brotherhood." "An Address to the Colored People of the United States" (29 September 1848), *Life and Writings*, 1:333. He reiterated this opinion, "in a modified degree," when speaking seventeen years later at the dedication of a Baltimore school for blacks named after him: "The latent contempt and prejudice towards our race,...not only justify for the present such associate effort on our part, but make it eminently necessary." "The Douglass Institute" (29 September 1865), *Life and Writings*, 4:179. See also William S. McFeely, *Frederick Douglass* (New York: W.W. Norton & Company, Inc., 1991) 243–45. In 1889 Douglass spoke emphatically against "the cultivation of race pride,"

With the passing of just over a decade and Reconstruction on the wane, Douglass was all the more insistent that black Americans receive due protection of their rights as citizens. He took the occasion of a monument to Lincoln, conceived and funded primarily by black Americans, to keep their concerns at the top of America's political agenda.

On 14 April 1876 a black and white procession marched its way to Lincoln Park, where they heard a prayer and a reading of the Emancipation Proclamation before President Grant pulled the cord to unveil the monument titled "Emancipation." Almost $17,000 had been raised from black Americans, mostly former soldiers, to construct the 12-foot-tall "Emancipation Group," as it was called.[14] Set upon a 10-foot pedestal paid for with a $3,000 appropriation from Congress, it depicted Lincoln with his right hand clasping the Emancipation Proclamation and left hand extended over a kneeling slave, rising from his broken chains.[15] With the infamous Hayes-Tilden Compromise less than a year away, resulting in the removal of federal troops from the former rebel states, the crouching freedman, frozen in time, would prove to be terribly prophetic.

The kneeling posture of the freed slave was said to have disturbed Douglass. As one in attendance later recalled, "He was very clear and emphatic in saying that he did not like the attitude: it showed the Negro on his knees, when a more manly attitude would have been more

---

including exclusively black associations, as "a positive evil" if viewed as "an essential element of success in our relations to the white race." Douglass thought that racial separation would lead to black isolation from the majority-white society, which would have all the more reason not to associate with blacks. "The Nation's Problem" (16 April 1889), *Frederick Douglass: Selected Speeches and Writings*, ed. Philip S. Foner and Yuval Taylor (Chicago: Lawrence Hill Books, 1999) 730, 732. (Hereinafter cited as *Selected Speeches and Writings*.)

[14] Freeman Henry Morris Murray, *Emancipation and the Freed in American Sculpture: A Study in Interpretation* (Freeport NY: Books for Libraries Press, 1972, orig. publ. 1916) 26–32, 198–202. The monument, erected by the Western Sanitary Commission, bears the name, "Freedom's Memorial."

[15] For an account of the monument's origin and a description of its unveiling, see *Lincoln in American Memory*, 55–60, and Benjamin Quarles, *Frederick Douglass* (Washington, DC: Associated Publishers, Inc., 1948) 276–77.

indicative of freedom."[16] But he delivered his address without commenting on the statue's design. After all, the unveiling of a monument depicting the liberator of black slaves on the anniversary of his death would seem like the last occasion to mount a headlong criticism of the one they have gathered to commemorate. How churlish to erect a monument, only to proceed rhetorically to tear it down! And so it is startling how much Douglass does give a candid assessment of Lincoln as the emancipator of black Americans.

Douglass draws the color line[17] at the outset of his speech by mentioning that "[w]ise and thoughtful men of our race," meaning the black race, in future will mark the occasion of the unveiling of the Freedmen's Memorial Monument "with a sense of manly pride and complacency."[18] This perspective of Douglass's, as a former slave and advocate of the equal rights of black Americans, is crucial for understanding why he later says that Lincoln was not entirely "either our man or our model."[19] On the one hand, he congratulates black Americans for the idea and fulfillment of commemorating Lincoln's contributions to their collective welfare. This is something of which they can be proud and marks their progress in doing for themselves and not relying on the beneficence of others.

On the other hand, he wants the nation to know how blacks, in particular, view Lincoln. Apparently, their erecting a monument to

---

[16] Murray, *Emancipation and the Freed in American Sculpture*, 198–99. For an account of how the monument's freed slave was modeled after Archer Alexander, "the last fugitive slave captured under civil law in Missouri," see William G. Eliot, *The Story of Archer Alexander: From Slavery to Freedom, March 30, 1863* (Boston: Cupples, Upham and Company, 1885) 13–15, http://docsouth.unc.edu/eliot/eliot.html. (Electronic edition; property of the University of North Carolina at Chapel Hill.).

[17] The "color line" is more commonly associated with W. E. B. Du Bois's use of the term in his famous book of essays, *The Souls of Black Folk*: "The problem of the Twentieth Century is the problem of the color-line." *The Souls of Black Folk*, ed. Henry Louis Gates, Jr., and Terri Hume Oliver (New York: W. W. Norton & Company, Inc., 1999) 17, 5, and 5 n. 1. Douglass, however, used the term as early as 1881; see "The Color Line" (June 1881), *Life and Writings*, 4:342–352, and "Address to the People of the United States" (24 September 1883), *Life and Writings*, 4:373–92.

[18] "Oration in Memory of Abraham Lincoln" (14 April 1876), *Life and Writings*, 4:309.

[19] *Life and Writings*, 4:312.

Lincoln is not self-explanatory. To present Lincoln as the Great Emancipator, as the statue clearly does, only tells half the story of his relationship to black America. For the rest of the story, we need Frederick Douglass. The speech, in short, is a balancing act of three aims: congratulating black Americans for their achievement, an expression of thanks to "the first martyr President of the United States,"[20] and presenting a more robust and candid assessment of Lincoln's achievement on behalf of black Americans. It is their monument, and so they (through Douglass) have chosen to give their version of Lincoln's contribution to their progress as an American people.

Douglass notes that the location of the memorial, the nation's capital, draws the nation's attention to the event, especially given the dignitaries present. Moreover, with the future of Reconstruction in jeopardy, Douglass intends the commemoration of Lincoln to keep alive his words and deeds in the hearts and minds of his audience and the "loyal and true men all over this country."[21] In so doing, black Americans would have a better chance to secure their rights and privileges as American citizens. At bottom, Douglass is proud of this achievement of black Americans to become an active part of the nation's self-understanding and history.

Douglass then notes how the unveiling of the monument "in peace today is a compliment and a credit to American civilization." In contrast with "the spirit of slavery and barbarism," the occasion displays the "glorious change" that has transpired among "white fellow-citizens" and, as a result, among black Americans. Douglass hopes the day will be but one milestone in a series of milestones marking the path to "still greater national enlightenment and progress in the future" for blacks in the United States.[22] Whites, as well as blacks, therefore receive Douglass's praise for making the day's event possible.

He then announces the reason for their assembly: to express the appreciation of black Americans for the services rendered to them by the now departed president, Abraham Lincoln. The act of expressing thanks

---

[20] *Life and Writings*, 4:311.
[21] *Life and Writings*, 4:309.
[22] *Life and Writings*, 4:310.

was one Douglass did not take lightly; he thought it reflected a distinctly human quality that would ennoble black Americans in the eyes of their white fellow-citizens. Two years before, Douglass gave a eulogy for Massachusetts Senator Charles Sumner—a longtime advocate for black Americans—at a memorial service arranged by Washington's leading black citizens. One of seven eulogists that evening, Douglass noted, "We do well to be here this evening; these meetings do us credit, which no other meetings have ever done us." The influential New York *Tribune* had charged blacks with ingratitude for not following Sumner in voting for its editor, Horace Greeley, for president of the United States. But Douglass commented that Sumner "never shared this reproach; he believed that the colored men had sense enough and devotion enough to do what they thought to be right." Douglass closed his eulogy by exhorting his audience to go home and teach their children "the name of Charles Sumner; tell them his utterances, and teach them that they, like him, can make their lives sublime by clinging to principles."[23] For Douglass, blacks organizing a tribute to a man they understood to be their friend was a fitting demonstration of black initiative and humanity. It was one that would find its consummation in the 1876 memorial in honor of Lincoln, who likewise clung to principles that elevated him above the political practice and sentiment of his own times.

Douglass prefaces his formal announcement of the aim of his speech with a reminder that the location of their celebration, the nation's capital, is "the most luminous point of American territory," principally, because it is "where the ablest and best men of the country are sent to devise the policy, enact the laws, and shape the destiny of the Republic." He is ever mindful of how much remains to be done to secure the equality of rights of black Americans—and what better time to hint at this task than in the presence of so many of Washington's political players. What better way to remind the nation's leaders of their duty to all American citizens, including the black population, than with a

---

[23] "Eulogy for Charles Sumner" (16 March 1874), *The Frederick Douglass Papers*, 4:400, 401.

monument to the Union's political savior erected in the backyard of the Capitol building?[24]

After Douglass repeats his praise of the "colored people" for expressing gratitude to "an American great man" for the first time in American history, he hastens to add that he does not mean to suggest that because of their raising of the Freedmen's Memorial Monument that black Americans claim "superior devotion" to the nation's sixteenth president. "We fully comprehend," Douglass observes, "the relation of Abraham Lincoln both to ourselves and to the white people of the United States." Here Douglass shifts from praising the praisers, the blacks who thought of and brought to fruition a monument to Lincoln's memory, to distinguishing the respective debt that white as opposed to black Americans owe to Lincoln. Simply put, Douglass does not want to rob Lincoln's example of its educative effect on white Americans, in whose hands to a great degree rests the fate of black Americans.[25] Given that Lincoln's example is "likely to be commended for honor and imitation long after" his death, Douglass wants white Americans to see the fallen

---

[24] Douglass emphasizes the political authority possessed by many of the distinguished members of his audience by referring to each federal department represented at the unveiling. In so doing, he offers a testimony to the nation of the implicit approbation the federal officeholders give to the black dedication of a monument to Abraham Lincoln:

> in the presence and with the approval of the members of the American House of Representatives, reflecting the general sentiment of the country; that in the presence of that august body, the American Senate, representing the highest intelligence and the calmest judgment of the country; in the presence of the Supreme Court and Chief-Justice of the United States, to whose decisions we all patriotically bow; in the presence and under the steady eye of the honored and trusted President of the United States, with the members of his wise and patriotic Cabinet

"Oration in Memory of Abraham Lincoln" (14 April 1876), *Life and Writings*, 4:311.

[25] Ten years after his 1876 oration on Abraham Lincoln, Douglass would still write, "What the future of the Negro shall be, is a problem in which the white man is the chief factor. The Negro holds only a secondary position. He is the clay, the white man is the Potter." "To W. H. Thomas" (16 July 1886), *Life and Writings*, 4:443.

president as one of them even more so than the savior of black Americans.[26]

In short, for the sake of black Americans as well as white Americans, Lincoln must be viewed as the white man's president *par excellence*—all the more so because Lincoln, despite sharing "the prejudices common to his countrymen towards the colored race," was able to transcend these prejudices to achieve freedom for blacks in America.[27] As Douglass put it less than two months after Lincoln's assassination, "He was the first American President, who thus rose above the prejudices of his times, and country."[28] As a political actor, Lincoln offers to Douglass an example for subsequent white officeholders to follow: a political transcendence above the mere "interests," "associations," and "habits of thought"[29] of fellow whites that freed the enslaved African on American soil.

To illustrate the magnitude of Lincoln's act of political transcendence, Douglass begins by simply identifying Lincoln with the interests of white men, even going so far as to say that Lincoln was "preeminently the white man's president, entirely devoted to the welfare of white men." This language is jarring to the modern ear, given what we know of the friendship between Lincoln and Douglass, as Douglass himself characterized it in his third and final autobiography (published in 1881) and various speeches he delivered after Lincoln's passing.[30] It was

---

[26] "Oration in Memory of Abraham Lincoln" (14 April 1876), *Life and Writings*, 4:311–12.

[27] *Life and Writings*, 4:315.

[28] Speech delivered at Cooper Institute, NY, on (probably) 1 June 1865, Reel 19, Frederick Douglass Manuscripts, Library of Congress (photocopy provided by Michael Burlingame) 23. (Hereinafter cited as "Cooper Institute" [1 June 1865]).

[29] "Oration in Memory of Abraham Lincoln" (14 April 1876), *Life and Writings*, 4:312.

[30] In his Cooper Institute speech of 1 June 1865, Douglass observed of Lincoln that "he was one of the very few white Americans who could converse with a Negro without any thing like condescension, and without in anywise reminding him of the unpopularity of his color" and noted "his kindly disposition toward colored people." "Cooper Institute" (June 1, 1865) 24, 25. Describing his first interview with the president (on 10 August 1863), which he titled "The Black Man at the White House," Douglass wrote, "I was never more quickly or more completely put at ease in the presence of a great man than in that of Abraham Lincoln.... I at once felt myself in the presence of an honest man—one

equally jarring given the occasion for the 1876 address, the unveiling of a monument to Lincoln himself.

Historian Michael Burlingame pointed out that only a month and a half after Lincoln's assassination, Douglass described Lincoln as "emphatically the black man's President: the first to show any respect for their rights as men."[31] Unless we want to charge Douglass with inconsistency on so important a subject as Lincoln's legacy vis-à-vis black Americans, this apparent contradiction needs resolution. Although Douglass changed the word "emphatically" to "preeminently" when shifting from Lincoln's *bona fides* among blacks to that among whites, in both cases he argues for Lincoln's primary concern for members of his own race. Here is the passage containing the reference to Lincoln as "emphatically the black man's President" in full:

> But what was A. Lincoln to the colored people or they to him? As compared with the long line of his predecessors, many of whom were mainly the facile and servile instruments of the slave power, Abraham Lincoln, *while unsurpassed in his devotion to the welfare of the white race*, was also in a sense hitherto without example, emphatically the black man's

---

whom I could love, honor, and trust without reserve or doubt." *Life and Times of Frederick Douglass* in *Frederick Douglass: Autobiographies*, ed. Henry Louis Gates, Jr. (New York: Literary Classics of the United States, Inc., 1994) 785, 786. On 19 August 1864, he was invited to a second meeting with the president to discuss the possibility of organizing a "band of scouts" to proclaim emancipation to slaves behind Confederate lines and encourage more of them to escape into Union lines. Of this meeting, Douglass wrote, "Mr. Lincoln was not only a great President, but a GREAT MAN—too great to be small in anything. In his company I was never in any way reminded of my humble origin, or of my unpopular color." *Life and Times of Frederick Douglass*, 797. Douglass published this third autobiography in 1881. For Douglass's response to Lincoln's proposal for encouraging slaves to escape from behind Confederate lines, see "To Abraham Lincoln" (29 August 1864), *Life and Writings*, 3:405–406.

[31] Michael Burlingame "'Emphatically the Black Man's President': New Light on Abraham Lincoln, Frederick Douglass, and Black Freedom" (address delivered at conference: "War Makes Rattling Good History: Civil War Scholarship in the 21st Century" in Wittenberg, Germany, 29 March 2001). http://www.zusas.uni-halle.de/academics/conferences/burlingame-abstract.htm.

President: the first to show any respect for their rights as men.[32]
(Emphasis added.)

In this June 1865 speech, Douglass strives to justify black fealty to
Lincoln in the face of various attempts to keep black faces out of public
commemorations of Lincoln's death.[33] Thus, he argues for a black
devotion to Lincoln every bit the equal to that of the presently mourning
whites: "No people or class of people in this country, have a better
reason for lamenting the death of Abraham Lincoln, and for desiring to
honor and perpetuate his memory, than have the colored people."[34]

However, in this June 1865 speech, he adds, "We stand even yet,
too near the newly made grave of Abraham Lincoln either for a full
analysis of his character—or for a dispassionate review of his official
life. The wound caused by his death is yet too deep—too fresh, the
sorrow too lasting, and the mind too excited with the scenes of sorrow,
for just criticism or unbiased Eulogy."[35] That assessment would come on
14 April 1876.[36]

In his 1876 address, he confesses that the "race to which we belong
were not the special objects of his consideration. Knowing this, I
concede to you, my white fellow-citizens, a preeminence in this worship

---

[32] "Cooper Institute" (June 1, 1865) 3.

[33] "And yet we are about the only people who have been in any case forbidden to
exhibit our sorrow, or to show our respect for the deceased president publicly. The
attempt to exclude colored people from his funeral procession in New York was one of
the most disgraceful, and sickening manifestations of moral emptiness, ever exhibited by
any nation or people professing to be civilized." "Cooper Institute" (1 June 1865) 2. For a
description of the New York funeral procession that initially barred the inclusion of
blacks, see Peterson, *Lincoln in American Memory*, 18.

[34] "Cooper Institute" (1 June 1865) 2. See also a speech delivered in December
1865, Frederick Douglass Manuscripts, Library of Congress (photocopy provided by
Michael Burlingame) reel 14, p. 12: "Whosoever else have cause to mourn the loss of
Abraham Lincoln, to the colored people of the country, his death is an unspeakable
calamity."

[35] "Cooper Institute" (1 June 1865) 23.

[36] In 1883 Douglass would argue that Lincoln's tenure as president was recent
enough not to "require extended notice of his statesmanship, or of his moral and mental
qualities." "The United States Cannot Remain Half-Slave and Half Free" (16 April 1883),
Life and Writings, 4:368.

at once full and supreme." Lincoln would agree that black Americans did not constitute a "special" concern for him as president because he believed, in keeping with the Declaration of Independence, that no race should receive special protection under a government devoted to the rights of all of the governed. To the extent Lincoln as president seemed to favor whites over blacks, it was merely the prudent consideration of what was possible to accomplish in light of the prevailing sentiments of his day. The consent of the governed, after all, is the operative principle of American self-government. Thus, Lincoln had to take into account the opinions and prejudices of the majority of loyal Americans—that is, white Americans—as he led the nation to address the greatest threat to its existence as a free republic.

At this point in his address, Douglass does not show an appreciation of Lincoln's prudence as the president of a self-governing people. Their consent Lincoln must both receive on election day and earn in between elections in order to effect the highest practical security for the rights of Americans—including blacks—that popular prejudice will allow. This requires more than appealing to their reason, which was the task of his First Inaugural Address. It required an appeal to their self-interest, which reflects their color prejudice as well as their conception of justice.

It is to Douglass's credit, and the signal distinction of his 1876 address, that he acknowledges this understanding of Lincoln's task as president. But at the outset, he gives us his appraisal of Lincoln as the war years began. Importantly, as the speech progresses, so does Douglass's appreciation, or at least his portrayal, of what Lincoln eventually accomplished as president on behalf of enslaved blacks in America.

One cannot forget that the precarious status of the freedmen, especially in the South, was foremost on Douglass's mind. By the time of the 1876 presidential election, only three Southern states would still be governed by Republicans, and even they came under so-called "redeemer" governments when the Democratic Party instituted "home rule" in the wake of the removal of federal troops after Rutherford B. Hayes assumed the presidency. Insofar as white Americans in both the North and the South had grown tired of the "bayonet rule" of federal troops throughout the former Confederate states, Douglass devoted most of his post-bellum speeches to reminding the nation of their responsibility to protect the equal citizenship of blacks as they implemented the Reconstruction amendments. As he put it in December 1863, "[O]ur work will not be done until the colored man is admitted a full member in good and regular standing in the American body politic."[37]

Douglass did not want conventional wisdom to place the Negro on the knee of Abraham Lincoln. This would make Lincoln in a sense America's first black president and hence limit Lincoln's presidential legacy to his tenure in office and not allow for the extension of Lincoln's principles and policies, especially regarding Reconstruction, into subsequent administrations. Douglass had to get whites not only to revere Lincoln but to see him as their guide in knitting the nation back together. The relevance of the Lincoln presidency to subsequent generations of white Americans, in short, was at stake in 1876. Douglass used his 1876 address at the unveiling of the Freedmen's Monument to keep Lincoln's efforts on behalf of blacks at the forefront of the national mind.[38] With the demise of his newspaper in 1874, Douglass turned all the more to the lecture circuit as the principal means of communicating his message to the nation on behalf of black Americans.[39] With the Republican National Convention just two months away and much of the party's leadership sitting on the platform as he spoke, Douglass pressed his advantage as a regular on the Republican speaking tour to preach to a choir he thought might soon forget their verses.[40]

---

[37] "Our Work is not Done" (3–4 December 1863), *Life and Writings*, 3:381.

[38] For Douglass as purveyor of an "emancipationist vision of Civil War memory," see David W. Blight, *Race and Reunion: The Civil War in American Memory* (Cambridge MA: Harvard University Press, 2001) 92–93, 132–34, 303, 315–19.

[39] The editors of the *Frederick Douglass Papers* note that between 1864 and his death in 1895, Douglass delivered approximately eight hundred speeches. See introductions to the *Frederick Douglass Papers*, ed. John W. Blassingame and John R. McKivigan, 4:xv and 5:xiii, respectively.

[40] His close confidante Ottilia Assing remarked in a 30 April 1876 letter to her sister in Europe, "No, Douglass cannot come this summer, for he is completely taken up in the service of the Republican party during the campaign." William S. McFeely, *Frederick Douglass* (New York: W. W. Norton & Company, Inc., 1991) 289. A month before his oration in memory of Abraham Lincoln, he affirmed, "The Republican Party is still the party of justice and freedom. It is, relatively, the black man's party." "The

Douglass, thus, takes a few paragraphs of his memorial to Lincoln to delineate the reasons why Lincoln should not be considered "in the full sense of the word, either our man or our model." He highlights that "during the first years" of Lincoln's administration, he was willing to "deny, postpone, and sacrifice the rights of humanity in the colored people to promote the welfare of the white people of this country."[41] This matter-of-fact observation becomes all the more manifest as Douglass gives examples of Lincoln's presidential actions that did not advance the immediate interests of enslaved blacks prior to the Emancipation Proclamation of 1863 or the immediate interests of the freedmen after emancipation as they took an increasing role in the prosecution of the Union war effort. In particular, Douglass notes that Lincoln "came into the Presidential chair upon one principle alone, namely, opposition to the extension of slavery," which in Douglass's mind was far from a ringing endorsement of abolitionism, simply.[42]

Douglass is correct to surmise that Lincoln did not view his constitutional authority to include the abolition of slavery by mere executive fiat, especially during a time of peace. At his first inauguration as president, Lincoln was painstakingly clear about what he and his party were on record as supporting and hence what he intended to carry out with regards to the slavery question.[43]

Country Has not Heard the Last of P. B. S. Pinchback" (13 March 1876), *The Frederick Douglass Papers*, 4:426. The previous year, Douglass gave a speech in which he observed, "The signs of the times are not all in our favor. There are, even in the Republican party, indications of a disposition to get rid of us." "The Color Question" (5 July 1875), The Frederick Douglass Papers, 4:417.

[41] For a clear, short history of Douglass's rhetorical agitation during Lincoln's presidency, see Christopher N. Breiseth, "Lincoln and Frederick Douglass: Another Debate," *"For a Vast Future Also":* Essays from the Journal of the Abraham Lincoln Association, ed. Thomas F. Schwartz (New York: Fordham University Press, 1999) 69–86.

[42] A month after the presidential election of November 1860, Douglass wrote that Lincoln was not an "Abolition President." He did, however, add that the election "has demonstrated the possibility of electing, if not an Abolitionist, at least an *anti-slavery reputation* to the Presidency of the United States." "The Late Election" (December 1860), *Life and Writings*, 2:527, 528. (Emphasis in original.)

[43] "First Inaugural Address—Final Text" (4 March 1861), *Collected Works*, ed. Basler, 4:262–71.

But in saying of Lincoln that "the Union was more to him than our freedom or our future," Douglass gives short shrift to Lincoln's understanding of constitutional self-government: namely, that a free society requires a limited government, one in which the powers of the rulers must be vested by the ruled and scrutinized in their operation.[44] Lincoln saw union as the immediate goal of the Civil War, but he always understood its preservation as the means of providing an ever-increasing protection of the equal rights of all.[45] So the "future" of the black race in America is encompassed by the near-term preservation of the Union. Without the Union—and a constitutional one, at that—with, instead, a triumphant rebellion of eleven Southern states becoming a confederate nation unto themselves, there would be no future for the enslaved blacks in America, at least no future they could look to with hope for an improvement of their condition. At this point in the speech, Douglass does not interpret Lincoln's reticence on the matter of the "rights of humanity in the colored people" as principled constitutionalism; instead,

---

[44] Lincoln briefly described American self-government in his first inaugural address: "A majority, held in restraint by constitutional checks, and limitations, and always changing easily, with deliberate changes of popular opinions and sentiments, is the only true sovereign of a free people. Whoever rejects it, does, of necessity, fly to anarchy or to despotism.... By the frame of the government under which we live, this same people have wisely given their public servants but little power for mischief; and have, with equal wisdom, provided for the return of that little to their own hands at very short intervals." "First Inaugural Address—Final Text" (4 March 1861), *Collected Works*, ed. Basler, 4:268, 270.

[45] "This is essentially a People's contest. On the side of the Union, it is a struggle for maintaining in the world, that form, and substance of government, whose leading object is, to elevate the condition of men—to lift artificial weights from all shoulders—to clear the paths of laudable pursuit for all—to afford all, an unfettered start, and a fair chance, in the race of life. Yielding to partial, and temporary departures, from necessity, this is the leading object of the government for whose existence we contend." "Message to Congress in Special Session" (4 July 1861), *Collected Works*, ed. Basler, 4:438. As early as 1854, Lincoln spoke of saving the Union by "re-adopt[ing] the Declaration of Independence" and, hence, treating slavery as a necessary evil. Doing so would make the Union "forever worthy of the saving." "Speech at Peoria, Illinois" (16 October 1854), *Collected Works*, ed. Basler, 2:276. See also Lincoln's "Speech in Independence Hall, Philadelphia, Pennsylvania" (22 February 1861), *Collected Works*, ed. Basler, 4:240.

he connects Lincoln's inaction toward American slaves to a natural sympathy with the white race.[46]

Douglass's early depreciation of a constitutional union that would enslave a portion of its population led him to undervalue the lofty status it held in Lincoln's political constellation.[47] Seven years after his 1876 oration, Douglass agreed with Lincoln that preserving the union of the American states was essential to the eventual liberation of the enslaved African in America: "Had the Union been dissolved, the colored people of the South would now be in the hateful chains of slavery."[48] In fact, Douglass would say as much later in his 1876 oration. But at this juncture in the speech, Douglass speaks as the Douglass of old, the Douglass of pure abolitionism. Union in this sense meant a union or constitution devoid of moral purpose.

In describing the significance of the abolition of slavery in the nation's capital, which preceded Lincoln's Preliminary Emancipation Proclamation by five months, Douglass remarked: "It was the first step toward a redeemed and regenerated nation. It imparted a moral and human significance to what at first seemed to the outside world, only a sanguinary war for empire."[49] Indeed, during the Civil War, Douglass repeatedly downplayed the importance of Union, especially as the primary goal of the war effort. On July 4, 1862, Douglass commented on Lincoln's efforts to prosecute the war for the sake of Union, not emancipation: "To my mind that policy is simply and solely to reconstruct the union on the old and corrupting basis of compromise, by which slavery shall retain all the power that it ever had, with the full

---

[46] In his commentary on Lincoln's First Inaugural address, Douglass wrote: "If we held the Constitution, as held by Mr. Lincoln, no earthly power could induce us to swear to support it." "The Inaugural Address" (April 1861), *Life and Writings*, 3:75.

[47] As Alexander Stephens famously described Lincoln's devotion to the American union, "The Union with him in sentiment, rose to the sublimity of a religious mysticism." Quoted in George Anastaplo, *Abraham Lincoln: A Constitutional Biography* (Lanham MD: Rowman & Littlefield Publishers, Inc., 1999) 185.

[48] "The United States Cannot Remain Half-Slave and Half-Free" (16 April 1883), *Life and Writings*, 4:367. Douglass added, "It was not the destruction but the salvation of the Union that saved the slave from slavery and the country to freedom, and the Negro to citizenship."

[49] *Life and Writings*, 4:367.

assurance of gaining more, according to its future necessities."[50] A month after Lincoln's first election to the presidency, Douglass went so far as to say that he himself was "decidedly for a dissolution of the Union!" A departed South would remove federal responsibility for returning fugitive slaves to their Southern masters and undermine the security of the slave system by inviting a more successful attempt to free the slaves, as Douglass put it, "the John Brown way."[51]

Unlike John Brown, arguably Frederick Douglass's greatest moral hero,[52] Abraham Lincoln did not have the luxury of espousing the abolition of slavery outright as part of the presidential authority vested in him by the Constitution or by the votes of the American people. At this point in his speech, Douglass does not come to terms with Lincoln's situation as an incoming president, representing what many deemed a sectional party and facing a nation with seven states already voting themselves out of the Union and others ready to bolt from the Union in the event the new administration acted in any way hostile to Southern interests. It is as if Douglass wants his audience to see Lincoln as abolitionists first saw him, from the perspective of those who had called for "immediate, unconditional emancipation" on the part of one they hoped would be, if not an abolitionist president, at least an anti-slavery one. After Lincoln's nomination in June 1860, Douglass believed him not "yet to be proved a great statesman," but one he hoped would demonstrate a "growth in grace" as his presidency progressed.[53]

---

[50] "The Slaveholders' Rebellion" (4 July 1862), *Life and Writings*, 3:256. One month later, Lincoln would state his war aim with crystalline precision: "My paramount object in this struggle *is* to save the Union, and is *not* either to save or to destroy slavery." "To Horace Greeley" (22 August 1862), *Collected Works*, ed. Basler, 5:388.

[51] "Speech on John Brown" (December 1860), *Life and Writings*, 2:536, 537, 533. In Booker T. Washington's biography of Douglass, he cites Douglass in revolutionary fervor: "Standing outside of the pale of American humanity, denied citizenship,...and longing for the end of bondage for my people, I was ready for any political upheaval that would bring about an end to the existing condition of things." *Frederick Douglass* (New York: Greenwood Press, 1969, orig. publ. 1906) 216.

[52] "History has no better illustration of pure, disinterested benevolence." "John Brown" (30 May 1881), *Selected Speeches and Writings*, 641. See also Waldo E. Martin, Jr., *The Mind of Frederick Douglass* (Chapel Hill: The University of North Carolina Press, 1984) 267–69.

[53] "The Chicago Nominations" (June 1860), *Life and Writings*, 2:484.

In one of the most famous passages of his address, Douglass now refers to white Americans as "the children of Abraham Lincoln," adding that black Americans were "at best only his step-children."[54] This reinforces white identification with Lincoln as one of their own, as Douglass hopes to keep Lincoln's legacy alive among the political forces that would soon shape the civic and political destiny of almost six million black Americans. To no one's surprise, it is at this point that Douglass exhorts the whites in his audience to "multiply his statues," in contrast with the *one* monument produced by black Americans. Even though the occasion for Douglass's address is the unveiling of a monument conceived and paid for by black Americans, Douglass makes sure that their contribution to the national commemoration of Lincoln's legacy does not suggest a greater loyalty on Lincoln's part to black Americans than to his fellow whites. As he put it, "First, midst, and last, you and yours were the objects of his deepest affection and his most earnest solicitude." Therefore, white Americans should see Lincoln as their hero, honor him with words matched by monuments, and most especially—one would infer—follow his political example as they worked to reconstruct the nation after a bitterly fought war among themselves. By extending Lincoln's legacy into their political practice, whites would likewise be helping the newly freed blacks to be more secure in their newfound freedoms.

Of course, Douglass still wants the whites in the audience to appreciate the effort being made that day by blacks to honor Lincoln. He, therefore, concludes this paragraph by justifying the day's commemoration as a black tribute to Lincoln by noting that "while Lincoln saved for you a country, he delivered us from a bondage" much worse than that which "your fathers rose in rebellion to oppose." By juxtaposing the respective debts of black and white Americans to Lincoln, Douglass establishes the foundation for the tributes of both blacks and whites.

However, to say that Lincoln saved "a country" for whites, but merely released blacks from slavery, begs the following question: did

---

[54] "Oration in Memory of Abraham Lincoln" (14 April 1876), *Life and Writings*, 3:312.

Lincoln not save the country for black Americans as well?[55] This remains to be seen, or rather, remains a task for Lincoln's successors to perform throughout the federal government, which is exactly the point of the Douglass's speech and his remaining political agenda. Unless white Americans see that abolition was a necessary but not sufficient condition for securing freedom for black Americans, unless federal—if not state—laws put teeth into the constitutional bite of the Reconstruction amendments, blacks especially in the South would find themselves in a country that still put the interests of whites ahead of blacks.

Douglass goes on to defend the longstanding and principled devotion of black Americans to Lincoln. "The name of Abraham Lincoln," Douglass argues, "was near and dear to our hearts in the darkest and most perilous hours of the Republic." Their faith can be demonstrated by recounting, as he does, the many apparent rebuffs they suffered under Lincoln's scrupulous adherence to the letter of the Constitution. When Lincoln by word or deed fell short of their initial hopes or expectations, the faith of black Americans "was often taxed and strained to the uttermost, but it never failed." As Douglass summed up, "Our hearts believed while they ached and bled." Perhaps because Reconstruction seems less and less of a concern for the party of Lincoln in 1876, Douglass calls to mind this earlier devotion on the part of black Americans—a devotion deriving not from "blind and unreasoning superstition" but from what Douglass calls a "comprehensive view of Abraham Lincoln," which made "reasonable allowance for the circumstances of his position." They believed Lincoln "when shrouded in clouds of darkness, of doubt, and defeat"; they would, by implication, believe the Republican Party while it hesitated regarding the future security for black Americans' rights, especially as the consequence of a new administration the following year. Taking an active, not passive, role in the shaping of their and the collective American destiny, blacks put their faith in Lincoln and will do, Douglass implies, the same for his party if they show a "living and earnest sympathy" for the same movement toward freedom that Lincoln showed as president.

---

[55] Before the end of the war Douglass believed Lincoln had dropped his Whig sympathy for black colonization.

To be sure, Douglass's rhetoric during those wilderness years for black Americans reflected anything but unqualified praise for Lincoln's efforts on the part of blacks. For example, hearing that Lincoln discussed colonization with a Negro delegation in August 1862, Douglass sniffed that Lincoln's proposal reflected "his pride of race and blood, his contempt for Negroes and his canting hypocrisy." He added, "Mr. Lincoln is quite a genuine representative of American prejudice and Negro hatred and far more concerned for the preservation of slavery, and the favor of the Border Slave States, than for any sentiment of magnanimity or principle of justice and humanity."[56] Nevertheless, Lincoln's steadfast conviction that slavery should be contained and not expanded throughout the American frontier placed him, in the minds of blacks, "at the head of a great movement,...which, in the nature of things, must go on until slavery should be utterly and forever abolished in the United States."[57]

Returning to his defense of a distinctly black commemoration of Lincoln, Douglass argues that under Lincoln's "wise and beneficent rule," black Americans rose from slavery to freedom. He repeats the phrase "under his rule" or a variation thereof nine times, as he recounts—as a counterpoise to the previous paragraph's litany of Lincoln's failures—Lincoln's successes in moving blacks toward greater spheres of liberty. Douglass lays out the concrete benefit that came to blacks during Lincoln's presidency in order to demonstrate a unique connection between Lincoln and black America. His list of Lincoln's glories culminates with the Emancipation Proclamation, which Douglass calls "the immortal paper" but which he believes came not quickly but "in the fullness of time" as Lincoln gave Confederates one hundred days

---

[56] "The President and His Speeches" (September 1862), *Life and Writings*, 3:267, 268. See also "The Inaugural Address" (April 1861), "To Hon. Gerrit Smith" (22 December 1861), "The Slaveholders' Rebellion" (4 July 1862), "January First, 1863" (January 1863), "The Commander-in-Chief and His Black Soldiers" (August 1863), and "To an English Correspondent" (16 September 1864), *Life and Writings*, 3:71–80, 184, 242–259, 305–10, 369–72, and 404, respectively.

[57] Douglass wrote that black Americans concluded "the hour and the man of our redemption had somehow met in the person of Abraham Lincoln." "Oration in Memory of Abraham Lincoln" (14 April 1876), *Life and Writings*, 3:313–14.

to preserve slavery in exchange for submitting once again to the Constitution. Unlike many American schoolchildren and perhaps a majority of adults today, Douglass recognized that the proclamation applied only to states or portions thereof still in rebellion against the Union. Nevertheless, he observes that the Emancipation Proclamation, "though special in language, was general in its principles and effect, making slavery forever impossible in the United States."[58]

He concludes the paragraph, "Though we waited long, we saw all this and more." Douglass wants no one to interpret the tardiness of black freedom in America as indicative of passivity or inattentiveness on their part; all along, they watched and judged Lincoln's words and actions to discern progress for the Negro in America. By highlighting this vigilance, Douglass suggests a more active and engaged participation in the political process by blacks than might otherwise be inferred by white Americans. As they witness the freemen take their first steps of social, civil, and political liberty, this implicitly argues for their full inclusion as American citizens.

Douglass now mentions "statesmanship" for the first time in his speech, noting that blacks became more patient with Lincoln once he proved to be "as good as his word" with his final emancipation proclamation on 1 January 1863: "[W]e were thenceforward willing to allow the President all the latitude of time, phraseology, and every honorable device that statesmanship might require for the achievement of a great and beneficent measure of liberty and progress." The unasked question was: Would the Republican Party of 1876 prove as good as their word if they held onto the presidency in the upcoming election?[59]

---

[58] Shortly after Lincoln issued his preliminary Emancipation Proclamation, Douglass called the document "a righteous decree" and "the most important of any to which the President of the United States has ever signed his name." "Emancipation Proclaimed" (October 1862), *Life and Writings*, 3:273, 274. See also Abraham Lincoln, "Preliminary Emancipation Proclamation" (22 September 1862), *Collected Works*, ed. Basler, 5:433–36. For the best exposition of Lincoln's two proclamations of emancipation, see George Anastaplo, "The Emancipation Proclamation," in *Abraham Lincoln: A Constitutional Biography*, 197–227.

[59] In 1876 the Democrats controlled the House of Representatives for the first time since 1860.

For his part, Douglass may have bided his time inwardly in the year that followed Emancipation, but his mouth expressed a fervent impatience with Lincoln's policy to save "that old worn-out, dead and buried Union, which had already become a calamity and a curse."[60] In a speech he delivered thirteen months after Lincoln's Emancipation Proclamation, Douglass castigated the president for continuing to wage war not so much against slavery but for union. Although he called the Emancipation Proclamation "a wise measure," it permitted slaveholding as "the exclusive luxury of loyal men." Douglass simply could not bear the thought of an end to the bloody and costly conflict that would not result in the total abolition of slavery. Moreover, he did not think any union that would survive the conflict could last without a clear, moral basis for that unity. For Douglass, this required a "a new order of social and political relations among the whole people." In short, a "Union without unity" would not produce a true peace: "What we now want is a country—a free country—a country not saddened by the footprints of a single slave—and nowhere cursed by the presence of a slaveholder." Douglass did not think, then, that the president could establish this basis for unity while issuing messages to Congress that reflected the "heartless sentiments" and "moral indifference" of the old union-savers. [61]

Returning to the April 1876 oration, Douglass now calls Lincoln "this great and good man" with a "high mission in the world," before stating that little more can be said to improve our understanding of a man

---

[60] "The Mission of the War" (13 February 1864), *Life and Writings*, 3:396. For Douglass, "no war but an Abolition war; no peace but an Abolition peace; liberty for all, chains for none; the black man a soldier in war, a laborer in peace; a voter at the South as well as at the North; America his permanent home, and all Americans his fellow-countrymen." *Life and Writings*, 3:403. In August 1863 Douglass indicated his impatience with the president when he complained in his *Douglass' Monthly* about black Union soldiers being killed or sold into slavery by the Confederate army with no threat of reprisals from the nation's commander-in-chief: "Having had patience and forbearance with the silence of Mr. Lincoln a few months ago,...the time for this is past.... It is now for every man who has any sense of right and decency, to say nothing of gratitude, to speak out trumpet-tongued in the ears of Mr. Lincoln and his Government and demand from him a declaration of purpose, to hold the rebels to a strict account for every black federal soldier taken as a prisoner." "The Commander-in-Chief and His Black Soldiers" (August 1863), *Life and Writings*, 3:372.

[61] "The Mission of the War" (13 February 1864), *Life and Writings*, 3:396, 394.

who can be known well simply by reading his words.[62] By directing the audience to Lincoln's words, Douglass affirms the importance of those words in guiding the nation to what he called earlier "still greater national enlightenment and progress in the future."

The shorthand version of this theme of Douglass is his criticism of Andrew Johnson as compared with Abraham Lincoln: "He knew him [Lincoln] to be a progressive man—one who did not begin [like President Johnson] as a Moses and end as a Pharaoh."[63] Two years later, he derided President Johnson and the Democratic Party for "feeding the rebel imagination with a prospect of regaining through politics what they lost by the sword."[64]

Douglass now reiterates Lincoln's sympathy toward white fellow countrymen (as distinguished from his solicitude toward blacks) as an essential part of his ability to direct "the loyal American people" to victory in the Civil War and all its attendant achievements—including emancipation. Douglass then defines Lincoln's political priorities: first, save the Union; second, abolish slavery. This is Douglass's clearest admission that despite words and deeds that seemed to put the interests of black Americans second to that of whites (i.e., the Union), Lincoln

---

[62] "Oration in Memory of Abraham Lincoln" (14 April 1876), *Life and Writings*, 4:315.

[63] "The Assassination and Its Lessons" (13 February 1866), *The Frederick Douglass Papers*, 4:112. As military governor of Tennessee, Andrew Johnson responded to a crowd of freedmen in Nashville on 24 October 1864, who had called on him at his capitol residence: "Well, then,...humble and unworthy as I am, if no better shall be found, I will indeed be your Moses, and lead you through the Red Sea of war and bondage, to a fairer future of liberty and peace." "The Moses of the Colored Men" (24 October 1864), cited in David Warren Bowen, *Andrew Johnson and the Negro* (Knoxville: University of Tennessee Press, 1989) 81; see also Hans L. Trefousse, *Andrew Johnson: A Biography* (New York: W. W. Norton & Company, Inc., 1989) 183–84. The previous month, Johnson had suspended the practically defunct slave code and ordered courts to treat slaves as free blacks. See John Cimprich, *Slavery's End in Tennessee, 1861–1865* (University: University of Alabama Press, 1985) 43–45. As president, Johnson repeated his identification with Moses in a meeting he held with a black delegation that included Douglass. See "Interview with President Andrew Johnson" (7 February 1866), *Life and Writings*, 4:185, and David W. Blight, *Frederick Douglass' Civil War: Keeping Faith in Jubilee* (Baton Rouge: Louisiana State University Press, 1989) 190–91.

[64] "The Work Before Us" (27 August 1868), *Life and Writings*, 4:210.

had always—even before the war—seen that slavery would have to go in order for freedom under the American banner to thrive through out the nation. [65] To achieve either union or emancipation, he needed the support of "his loyal fellow-countrymen." This leads to the climax of the speech: "Had he put the abolition of slavery before the salvation of the Union, he would have inevitably driven from him a powerful class of the American people and rendered resistance to rebellion impossible."[66] Here Douglass acknowledges that his own solution for ending the war, which was to make it an "abolition war," would have failed to end either the rebellion or slavery. The task of freeing the American slaves, as well as preserving the Union, was never Lincoln's alone, but one he would need "a powerful class of the American people" to accomplish.[67] In fact, Douglass himself had acknowledged this, at least in principle, as early as December 1863, when he remarked, "But we are not to be saved by the captain, at this time, but by the crew. We are not to be saved by Abraham

---

[65] Douglass repeated this sentiment in his third autobiography, where he praised Lincoln's 1858 "House Divided" speech: "These were not the words of an abolitionist—branded a fanatic, and carried away by an enthusiastic devotion to the Negro—but the calm, cool, deliberate utterance of a statesman, comprehensive enough to take in the welfare of the whole country." *Life and Times of Frederick Douglass,* 737. For the passage Douglass extolled, see "'A House Divided': Speech at Springfield, Illinois" (16 June 1858), *Collected Works,* ed. Basler, 2:461. Douglass also noted that when Lincoln decided to enlist blacks as soldiers, he had to consider means "which would the least shock and offend the popular prejudice against him." *Life and Times of Frederick Douglass,* 777.

[66] "Oration in Memory of Abraham Lincoln" (14 April 1876), *Life and Writings,* 4:316. In December 1863 Douglass wrote of his first meeting with Lincoln, where Lincoln explained his ability to secure the equal protection of black soldiers as hindered by the color prejudice of the country: "[T]he country needed talking up to that point.... He knew that the colored man throughout this country was a despised man, a hated man, and that if he at first came out with such a proclamation, all the hatred which is poured on the head of the Negro race would be visited on his administration. He said that there was preparatory work needed, and that that preparatory work had now been done." "Our Work is not Done" (3–4 December 1863), *Life and Writings,* 3:385.

[67] In his 1881 autobiography, Douglass acknowledged Lincoln's political prudence as exhibited in the guarded language of his Emancipation Proclamation: "While he hated slavery, and really desired its destruction, he always proceeded against it in a manner the least likely to shock or drive from him any who were truly in sympathy with the preservation of the Union, but who were not friendly to emancipation." *Life and Times of Frederick Douglass,* 793.

Lincoln, but by that power behind the throne, greater than the throne itself."[68]

This brings us to the clearest appraisal of the Lincoln presidency in all of Douglass's writings: "Viewed from the genuine abolition ground, Mr. Lincoln seemed tardy, cold, dull, and indifferent; but measuring him by the sentiment of his country, a sentiment he was bound as a statesman to consult, he was swift, zealous, radical, and determined." According to Douglass, part of Lincoln's genius was that even though he was sympathetic toward white Americans first and foremost, he saw the need to extend the principles of the regime to blacks as well as whites. He brought enough of his countrymen with him to save the union and secure emancipation. As Douglass put it in June 1865, "The American people, indebted to themselves for themselves, saw in him [Lincoln] a full length portrait of themselves. In him they saw their better qualities represented, incarnated, and glorified—and as such, they loved him."[69]

It is almost as if Douglass's view of Lincoln and his presidency undergo a refining process as the speech progresses, culminating in the conclusion just cited. Douglass, thus, takes his audience on this historical journey of appreciative critique—or critical appreciation—of Lincoln's statesmanship to show whites, in particular, how blacks acted with civic vigilance despite their lack of full civil and political rights. By tracing the path of Lincoln's political transcendence, a presidential legacy black Americans watched with both anxiety and hope, Douglass demonstrates how one can act on a higher plane than merely the inherited beliefs and prejudices of one's class or race.[70]

Also to Douglass's credit, he presents his and the abolitionists' perspective alongside that of Lincoln and other loyal countrymen at large and concludes that Lincoln's progress toward Union and emancipation

---

[68] "Our Work is not Done" (3–4December 1863), *Life and Writings*, 3:385.

[69] "Cooper Institute" (1 June 1865) 22.

[70] "Put away your race prejudice," was Douglass's constant exhortation to America. "Why is the Negro Lynched?" (1894), *Life and Writings*, 4:523. If the nation chose to "conquer its prejudices," the so-called Negro problem would vanish. "The Nation's Problem" (16 April 1889), *Selected Speeches and Writings*, 728.

was as speedy and sure as "his times" and the "condition of his country" would permit.[71]

In the next paragraph, Douglass repeats his claim that Lincoln "shared the prejudices of his white fellow-countrymen against the Negro," but only to accent his anti-slavery *bona fides*.[72] Douglass quotes Lincoln's second inaugural address to highlight Lincoln's view that justice was served if the Civil War pays in blood and treasure for "two hundred years of bondage."[73] In striking contrast with his earlier observation that Lincoln appeared indifferent to the plight of black slaves in America, Douglass now remarks that the loyalty of the South—while they abided by the Constitution—obligated Lincoln to protect their slaves as president, despite its natural injustice: "because it was so nominated in the bond." Here Douglass truly gets into Lincoln's skin to view slavery from his constitutional standpoint as a non-abolitionist but anti-slavery Republican.

What makes this aspect of Lincoln's public persona so appealing to Douglass is Lincoln's capacity for transcendence, a capacity cultivated by a profound adherence to the principles of the American regime.[74] But for these principles, Lincoln would not have achieved the greatness denoted by his traditional legacy. It is to Lincoln's credit and to the nation's that so deep an understanding and open a sympathy could

---

[71] "Progress…can never be as fast as one would like, because any political progress worthy of free men must take into account the lingering resistance of the ignorant as well as the insistent demands of the just." George Anastaplo, *Human Being and Citizen: Essays on Virtue, Freedom and the Common Good* (Chicago: The Swallow Press, Inc., 1975) 191.

[72] "Oration in Memory of Abraham Lincoln" (14 April 1876), *Life and Writings*, 4:316.

[73] In a December 1865 address, Douglass wrote: "No two papers are in stronger contrast than his first and his last inaugural addresses. The first was intended to reconcile the rebels to the government by argument and persuasion, the second was a recognition of the operation [of] inevitable and universal laws. In this he was willing to let justice have its course." Speech delivered in December 1865, Frederick Douglass Manuscripts, Library of Congress (photocopy provided by Michael Burlingame) reel 14, p. 11.

[74] En route to his first inauguration as president, Lincoln said, "I have never had a feeling politically that did not spring from the sentiments embodied in the Declaration of Independence." "Speech in Independence Hall, Philadelphia, Pennsylvania" (22 February 1861), *Collected Works*, ed. Basler, 4:240.

combine with the truth of human equality to produce what ultimately became a "new birth of freedom" for the regime.[75]

Douglass states that the "honest and comprehensive statesman" will be judged by history or "time" more aright than during his tenure in office. As one of the "great public men," Lincoln was criticized from all sides during his presidency, from abolitionists (like Douglass) to slaveholders. But, Douglass notes, the more sober, deliberate, dispassionate "judgment of the present hour" (i.e., eleven years after Lincoln's death) sees Lincoln as the man best suited to fulfill the dual mission of Union-saving and slave-freeing.[76]

Douglass then cites Lincoln's modest upbringing, natural endowments, and hardy work habits as attributes that endeared him to the American people and gained him their votes and support—a helpful adjunct to his efforts to move the nation forward to greater expansion of freedom than they otherwise would have supported. In fact, the last nine paragraphs of the twenty-four-paragraph speech serve to close the speech in a spirit most consistent with the occasion: namely, lauding the late president's character and achievements. Otherwise, the monument becomes a vain production, demeaning to the blacks that conceived it.

Douglass also observes that Lincoln assumed the presidency—a difficult job in normal circumstances—in the most trying of times, a moment where the national existence was in doubt. Self-preservation was the immediate and abiding task of Lincoln as the incoming president. Duty, truth, and trust were exhibited in his actions and words as he attempted to exercise his presidential authority to prevent disunion.[77]

Douglass concludes that Lincoln "knew the American people better than they knew themselves."[78] That is to say, he knew what they professed to believe and respected them and their principles enough to hold them to it and move them to a greater commitment to and practice of their highest ideals. By appealing to "the better angels of...[their]

---

[75] "Address Delivered at the Dedication of the Cemetery at Gettysburg—Final Text" (19 November 1863), *Collected Works*, ed. Basler, 7:22–23.

[76] "Oration in Memory of Abraham Lincoln" (14 April 1876), *Life and Writings*, 4:317.

[77] *Life and Writings*, 4:318.

[78] *Life and Writings*, 4:318.

nature," as Lincoln put it in that famous last line of his First Inaugural Address,[79] Lincoln appealed to what was most American about them.

Douglass calls the assassination of Lincoln the "crowning crime" of slavery.[80] But ever the optimist, Douglass gleans from the tragedy of Lincoln's assassination renewed hope in the "deeper abhorrence of slavery" and "deeper love of the great liberator" produced among most Americans. The assassination only adds to the devotion of Douglass and his audience to Lincoln, especially because of what he stood for: "fidelity to union and liberty." Here Douglass reminds his audience that to save the Union was to save the foremost instrument of liberty: the Constitution and the principles Lincoln taught were so intrinsic to its success.[81] Douglass was carrying the torch for Lincoln's own project of teaching Americans that to believe in the Union, to believe in the Constitution, was to believe in the principles of human equality and liberty for which it stood. As he said of the martyred president in December 1865, "Dying thus, his name becomes a text from which to preach that liberty, and that human equality, to strike down which he was ruthlessly murdered."[82]

Douglass congratulates "our race," meaning Americans of African descent, for their monument raising in memory of Lincoln, "our friend and liberator." Gratitude expressed by the monument and occasion places black Americans within "the range of human brotherhood," a needful conviction of all Americans or at least a sufficient number that would ensure continued progress on behalf of blacks in America. Douglass renders a history, if not of the Civil War, of Lincoln's presidency as it affected blacks in America, especially slaves—a fitting tribute upon the unveiling of a monument depicting Lincoln as the Great Emancipator. In

---

[79] "First Inaugural Address—Final Text" (4 March 1861), *Collected Works*, ed. Basler, 4:271.

[80] "Oration in Memory of Abraham Lincoln" (14 April 1876), *Life and Writings*, 4:319.

[81] See "Fragment on the Constitution and the Union" (c. January 1861), *Collected Works*, ed. Basler, 4:168–69.

[82] Speech delivered in December 1865, Frederick Douglass Manuscripts, Library of Congress (photocopy provided by Michael Burlingame) reel 14, p. 9.

other words, here's how America should view the Lincoln presidency and thus allow his legacy to inform their political practice.

Douglass takes to heart the fact that Lincoln died as "the first martyr President of the United States," a death caused in great part because of Lincoln's actions on behalf of American slaves. It was important, in Douglass's personal assessment of Lincoln, to discern Lincoln's inner sentiment toward black Americans. It was not enough for him to appreciate the president's actions as they affected blacks; rather, Douglass wanted to know just what Lincoln thought of him and his race. His conclusion can be seen in a letter he wrote to Mrs. Lincoln upon receiving from her one of the president's canes. Referring to it as "an object of sacred interest," Douglass wrote that he would consider it "a token not merely of the kind consideration in which I have reason to know that the president was pleased to hold me personally, but as an indication of his humane interest in the welfare of my whole race."[83]

Just two years after his 1876 oration, Douglass spoke at Union Square, New York, to the Lincoln Post of the Grand Army of the Republic. There he called Lincoln "the best man, truest patriot, and wisest statesman of his time and country."[84] Given the host and venue, this comes as no surprise. But Douglass repeated this high praise of Lincoln five years later in a fiery speech titled "The United States Cannot Remain Half-Slave and Half Free." After observing that Lincoln's name "should never be spoken but with reverence, gratitude, and affection," Douglass called him "the greatest statesman that ever presided over the destinies of this Republic."[85]

Nevertheless, for the self-respect of his black countrymen, Frederick Douglass does not depict their departed president and emancipator as a

---

[83] "To Mrs. Abraham Lincoln" (17 August 1865), *Life and Writings,* 174.

[84] "There was a Right Side in the Late War" (30 May 1878), *Selected Speeches and Writings*, 627.

[85] "The United States Cannot Remain Half-Slave and Half Free" (16 April 1883), *Life and Writings*, 4:368. Douglass took his title from an argument Lincoln presented in his famous "House Divided" speech, where Lincoln accepted the Republican nomination to run for the U.S. Senate against the incumbent, Stephen A. Douglas. See "'A House Divided': Speech at Springfield, Illinois" (June 16, 1858), *Collected Works*, ed. Basler, 2:461–62.

perfect political savior. As Douglass renders him, Lincoln did not make blacks the priority of his administration and, hence, blacks should not pretend that Lincoln did. It would overlook too blithely the many rebuffs they withstood until Lincoln finally did the favor that mattered to that immediate generation. And this Douglass chooses to share with the whites in the audience. By seeing Lincoln as black Americans saw him, in both good times and bad, whites are better able to value the civic engagement of their black fellow-countrymen, which Douglass saw as a helpful step toward greater protection of their rights. Instead of mere recipients of the political crumbs from the white man's constitutional table, to the extent permitted by the majority-white society, black Americans watched Lincoln as president, judged him, and accepted him as he proved himself to them. The implicit lesson is that now, more than a decade after Lincoln's death, white politicians will receive the same vigilance from the nation's black citizens.[86]

Ralph Ellison, a kindred spirit of Frederick Douglass, lends a lyrical aspect to this reflection on Douglass's assessment of Lincoln as the Great Emancipator:

> Sometimes, yes...sometimes the good Lord...I say sometimes the good Lord accepts His own perfection and closes His eyes and goes ahead and takes His own good time and He makes Himself a man. Yes, and sometimes that man gets hold of the idea of what he's supposed to do in this world and he gets an idea of what it is possible for him to do, and that man lets that idea guide him as he grows and struggles and stumbles and sorrows until finally he comes into his own God-given shape and achieves his own individual and lonely place in this world....

---

[86] Speaking to a "Convention of Colored Men" in Kentucky in 1883, Douglass observed, "If the Republican party cannot stand a demand for justice and fair play, it ought to go down. We were men before that party was born, and our manhood is more sacred than any party can be. Parties were made for men, not men for parties." "Address to the People of the United States" (24 September 1883), *Life and Writings*, 4:381.

So let us pray, not for him but for ourselves and for all those whose job it is to fill those great big shoes he left this nation to fill."[87]

[87] Ralph Ellison, *Juneteenth: A Novel*, John F. Callahan, ed. (New York: Random House, 1999) 282, 283

A KING'S CURE, A KING'S STYLE:

LINCOLN, LEADERSHIP, AND THE THIRTEENTH AMENDMENT

Michael Vorenberg

A vicious, disfiguring disease ravaged the cities and countryside of medieval and early modern Europe. It was a strain of tuberculosis that produced in its victims ugly eruptions around the glands of the neck and lower face. Cursed by kings as a scourge of God, it became known to the people as the "king's evil." The educated elite knew it as scrofula. Unlike the bubonic plague, whose physical symptoms were not always obvious and could sometimes be hidden, scrofula's effects were almost always visible because they occurred above the neckline of garments. It was, in a sense, the most public disease, and its only acknowledged cure came through the mystical power believed to reside in the body of the sovereign. Kings were called upon to touch the sores of the afflicted to heal the disease. The king's evil, it seemed, required a king's cure. Reports of the practice began circulating in the early twelfth century in France and, later in the century the "royal touch," as it had become known, seems to have arrived in England.[1]

The practice flourished over the next five hundred years but began to fade with the arrival of the Enlightenment to western Europe; the last

---

[1] Marc Bloch, *The Royal Touch*, trans. J. E. Anderson (1923; Max Leclerc et Cie, Proprietors of Librairie Armand Colin, 1961; rev. ed., New York: Dorset Press, 1989) 11–27.

reported instance of a king applying the royal touch came in May 1825, when Charles X of France touched about 120 sufferers—and was promptly ridiculed by his critics in the popular press. Belief in the healing power of kings persisted, even if the practice of the ritual did not. Forty years after Charles X applied the royal touch, a French priest who had undertaken a history of the royal touch admitted in his book that while he had started the project a skeptic, he had become a "firm believer" in the legitimacy of the king's cure. The year was 1865.[2]

In that same year, on 1 February, an American president also invoked the king's cure. The occasion was a response by Abraham Lincoln to a serenade celebrating the passage by Congress of the Thirteenth Amendment abolishing slavery. Lincoln pronounced the amendment "A king's cure for all the evils."[3] Here was an unusual skirmish in what James McPherson has called Lincoln's "War with Metaphors." McPherson praised the ways Lincoln, unlike his counterpart Jefferson Davis, deployed commonplace words and images to make complex ideas accessible to the common people. But here was Lincoln the champion of democracy drawing a metaphor from, of all things, a monarchy. He had no doubt learned of the royal touch from the popular histories of kings contained in the lesson books, or "readers," that he had committed to memory as a young man.

Kings seemed to be on his mind in those days. At the Hampton Roads peace conference only two days after Lincoln's response to the serenade, one of the Southern envoys who dared to suggest that Lincoln model his reconstruction policy on that of Charles I of England was met with the president's response that all he recollected of Charles I was that he "lost his head in the end."[4] Perhaps Lincoln knew as well that Charles I had done more than any monarch to institutionalize the practice of the royal touch. Under his reign, a mention of the practice was written into

---

[2] Bloch, *The Royal Touch,* 227–28.

[3] Roy P. Basler, ed., *The Collected Works of Abraham Lincoln,* 9 vols. (New Brunswick NJ: Rutgers University Press, 1953–55) 8:254.

[4] Alexander H. Stephens, *A Constitutional View of the Late War Between the States* (Philadelphia: National Publishing Company, 1870) 2:613; see William C. Harris, "The Hampton Roads Peace Conference: A Final Test of Lincoln's Presidential Leadership," *Journal of the Abraham Lincoln Association* 21 (Winter 2000): 31–61.

the *Book of Common Prayer*. In his exile, Londoners afflicted with scrofula beseeched him to return to the city to perform the service. After his execution, his blood was collected by mourners who swore by the healing power of this vestige of the martyred king.[5] Perhaps it was also such knowledge of kings—in this case, the martyrdom of Charles I during the English Civil War—that had set Lincoln to thinking of his own martyrdom during his own country's Civil War.

Just what did Lincoln have in mind when he called the Thirteenth Amendment a "King's Cure"? Did he think of himself as the king who had devised the cure? And what did the amendment cure exactly?

By looking at Lincoln's involvement in the amendment, we can learn much about Lincoln's approach to leadership, especially his role as a *legislative* leader—that is, as a leader who could work with Congress, state lawmakers, and the people themselves to create laws. This is not the way we normally think of Lincoln. Instead, he lasts in our memory mainly as a *war* leader, an executive who did not so much make new law as negotiate around existing law in order to prosecute the war as effectively as possible. Even his best-known act, the Emancipation Proclamation, was not really a new law. Rather, as Lincoln himself so often pointed out, it was a military proclamation that merely lent executive power to an existent congressional law, the Second Confiscation Act; as a wartime measure only, Lincoln said, it might be suspended once the war was over, or it might be overturned by a later Congress or Supreme Court.

We do not think of Lincoln as spending much time pushing legislation through Congress. Both James G. Randall and Harold Hyman observed that there were no laws under Lincoln that we tend to think of as "administration bills," nor were there many presidential vetoes, the Wade-Davis pocket veto being a significant exception.[6] Lincoln thus stood in contrast to the Democrat Andrew Jackson, who openly orchestrated congressional legislation and liberally used the veto, most

---

[5] Bloch, *The Royal Touch*, 207–10.
[6] James G. Randall, "Has the Lincoln Theme Been Exhausted?" *American Historical Review* 41 (1936) 287–88; Harold M. Hyman, "Lincoln and Congress: Why Not Congress and Lincoln?" *Journal of the Illinois State Historical Society* 58 (1975) 57–73.

famously during the Bank War. Lincoln, if we believe David Herbert Donald, may have expanded the wartime powers of the presidency in unprecedented ways, but he still believed that the normal process of lawmaking lay within the exclusive province of Congress; he was the anti-Jackson, the "Whig in the White House."[7]

Yet this model of a president disengaged from Congress simply falls apart when we consider Lincoln's activity on behalf of the Thirteenth Amendment, which was arguably the most significant measure passed by either of the two Civil War congresses. He was neither dictatorial nor detached. Rather, he practiced a form of strategic intervention. He was as willing as Andrew Jackson had been to use the powers of persuasion and patronage to steer legislation through Congress, but, unlike Jackson, he had a modesty that allowed him to understand that in some circumstances his preferred legislation might fare better if he kept his distance. Even when he did intervene in Congress, he kept a long arm's length from the actual manipulations, for he understood, perhaps from the negative example of "King" Andrew Jackson, or perhaps from the even more negative example of King Charles I, that the executive must *seem* to stay aloof of the deliberations of the people's representatives no matter what the extent of his actual intervention.

The nuances of Lincoln's approach to lawmaking are often overlooked in the traditional story of his handling of the Thirteenth Amendment. That story has four major parts. First, after Lincoln issued the final Emancipation Proclamation on 1 January 1863, he decided that Congress should pass and the states should ratify an antislavery amendment that would put emancipation on surer constitutional footing. Second, soon after the Senate passed the amendment, Lincoln tried to give the measure even more momentum by having his party, now named the National Union Party, endorse the amendment in the platform designed by the national convention in June 1864. Third, after winning reelection, Lincoln proclaimed his victory a mandate for the amendment and applied his power in unprecedented ways in the lame-duck session of the House of Representatives, successfully securing the amendment's

---

[7] David Donald, "Abraham Lincoln: A Whig in the White House," *Lincoln Reconsidered* (1956; reprint, New York: Vintage Books, 1961) 187–208.

passage. Fourth, Lincoln pressed for a hasty ratification of the amendment by the states; as part of this process, he encouraged newly formed Union legislatures in ex-Confederate states to ratify the measure, and he pressed Congress to accept these ratifications as legitimate.

Each of these parts of the story requires closer interrogation. First, for almost a year and a half after signing the Emancipation Proclamation, Lincoln showed no signs of wishing to supplement the proclamation with a constitutional amendment abolishing slavery. Only a month before the final proclamation, Lincoln had proposed three constitutional amendments that would have allowed slavery to exist until at least 1900. These amendments, proposed in his annual message to Congress of 1862, assured freedom only to those slaves liberated, as he put it, "by the chances of the war, at any time before the end of the rebellion."[8] The measures encouraged but did not require states to emancipate all other slaves by 1900, they provided compensation to slave owners for the loss of their human property, and they provided funds to colonize the freed people abroad. The amendments represented no new step toward securing legal freedom for all slaves; rather, they represented a revised form of Lincoln's old strategy of using inducements to encourage states to return to the Union. The inducements were the same as they had been since the beginning of the war: federal funds for compensation and colonization, and a promise of non-interference with slavery once the rebellious states had ceased their hostilities.

These measures fared as poorly as Lincoln's earlier proposals for compensated emancipation, which were aimed mainly at the border states. No one in the last session of the Thirty-seventh Congress during the spring of 1863 lobbied for these amendments on the president's behalf. The only bill for gradual emancipation during this congressional session was one promising federal compensation to slave owners from Missouri who freed their slaves. The bill passed in the Senate but died in the House as opponents warned that Congress would never deliver the promised government bonds to slave owners, and even if it did, Union military losses could make the securities worthless. To this objection the president offered the accurate prediction: "You southern men will soon

---

[8] Basler, *Collected Works*, 5:530.

reach the point where bonds will be a more valuable possession than bondsmen. Nothing is more uncertain now than two-legged property."[9]

Lincoln had lost his gradual emancipation program, but he had learned a valuable lesson: proposed emancipation legislation was more sure of success if it came from Congress rather than from the president. The various proposals for gradual or compensated emancipation that had originated in the White House, measures such as the bill for compensated emancipation in Delaware and the constitutional amendments for gradual emancipation, had gone nowhere. The only measures incorporating gradualism or compensation that had had any success in Congress, measures such as the confiscation acts and the act emancipating slaves in Washington, DC, had all originated in Congress.

Perhaps it was because of this lesson taught to him by the thirty-seventh Congress that Lincoln was so slow to propose or endorse a constitutional amendment abolishing slavery immediately. Abolitionist groups such as the Women's Loyal National League had begun petitioning for such an amendment in the summer of 1863, but Lincoln said nothing of these proposals.[10] In his Gettysburg Address in November of 1863, he promised a "new birth of freedom," but he offered no specific proposal that would write this new birth of freedom into law.[11] When the Thirty-eighth Congress convened in December of that year, it immediately began considering proposals for an antislavery amendment.[12] Lincoln's advisors urged him to endorse one of the measures or propose one of his own. He shot back to one advisor, "Is not the question of emancipation doing well enough now?" and to another, "Our own friends have this under consideration now, and will do as much without a Message [from me] as with it."[13] Lincoln had learned

---

[9] James G. Blaine, *Twenty Years of Congress* (Norwich, CT: Henry Bill Publishing Company, 1884) 1:448.

[10] For popular initiatives for an emancipation amendment, see Michael Vorenberg, *Final Freedom: The Civil War, the Abolition of Slavery, and the Thirteenth Amendment* (New York: Cambridge University Press, 2001) chapter 2.

[11] Basler, *Collected Works*, 7:23.

[12] Vorenberg, *Final Freedom*, chapter 2.

[13] William H. Herndon and Jesse W. Weik, *Abraham Lincoln: The True Story of a Great Life* (New York: D. Appleton and Company, 1913) 2:241 (Lincoln was responding in this instance to Leonard Swett); Lincoln to John D. Defrees, 7 February 1864,

from his mistakes during the previous congressional session: he would keep his distance from Capitol Hill.

The president's reluctance to get behind the amendment—at least in public—also represented an ideological preference for achieving major reforms outside of the procedure of constitutional amendments. As a congressman in 1848, Lincoln opposed a constitutional amendment providing for internal improvements. "New provisions," he argued, "would introduce new difficulties, and thus create, and increase appetite for still further change.... [L]et it [the Constitution] stand as it is."[14] He made the same point as president in 1864 to a group of preachers who pleaded with him to back an amendment declaring the existence of God: "The work of amending the Constitution should not be done hastily."[15]

Lincoln did believe in constitutional evolution—that was one of the central points of the Gettysburg Address—but, like many ex-Whigs, he assumed that this evolution would occur mainly through legislative initiatives at the federal level and constitutional change at the state level, not through alterations of the *federal* constitution, which over the past sixty years had become something of an untouchable national icon.[16] Thus his main efforts in 1863 and early 1864 on behalf of turning his emancipation policy into actual law took the form of efforts to change state constitutions, not the federal Constitution. That strategy was made explicit in the December 1863 proclamation on reconstruction, which

---

Collected Works, ed. Basler, 7:172. Isaac N. Arnold, another of Lincoln's friends, seems to have met with silence when he made a similar suggestion; see Arnold to Lincoln, 4 December 1863, Robert Todd Lincoln Collection, Manuscripts Division, Library of Congress, Washington, DC.

[14] Basler, *Collected Works*, 1:488.

[15] Washington *Daily National Intelligencer*, 24 February 1864, 3.

[16] On the Whigs' preference for legal change through legislative initiative as opposed to the Democrats' preference for constitutional amendments, see Michael F. Holt, *The Political Crisis of the 1850s* (1978; New York: W. W. Norton & Company, 1983) 106–109; Perry Miller, *The Life of the Mind in America: From the Revolution to the Civil War* (New York: Harcourt, Brace & World, 1965) chapter 7; and Harold M. Hyman and William M. Wiecek, *Equal Justice Under Law: Constitutional Development, 1835–1875* (New York: Harper & Row, 1982) 3–5. On the sanctification of the national Constitution during the antebellum period, see Michael Kammen, *A Machine That Would Go of Itself: The Constitution in American Culture* (1986; reprint, New York: Vintage Books, 1987) chapters 3–4, especially 101–104.

said nothing of a federal antislavery amendment, and it lay behind Lincoln's work behind the scenes in 1863 and 1864 to promote the drafting of new, antislavery constitutions in Union slave states such as Missouri and Maryland as well as Confederate states like Louisiana and Arkansas.[17]

The first part of the traditional story of Lincoln and the Thirteenth Amendment turns out to be fiction. He did not turn from the Emancipation Proclamation directly to the antislavery amendment. Rather, he allowed Congress to act on its own in creating the amendment, and he turned his efforts instead to the state constitutions.

The second part of the story, in which Lincoln made sure to have his party write the amendment into its national platform in 1864, is no fiction, but the reasons for this strategic intervention by the president have been largely misunderstood by historians. There is no question that Lincoln asked some of his allies to back the amendment at the party's national convention.[18] To Edwin D. Morgan, the chairman of the party, Lincoln proposed that the amendment serve as the so-called "key notes" of Morgan's opening address.[19] Lincoln got his wish. Morgan called for the amendment in his address, and the resolutions committee made it a plank of the platform.[20]

It would be a mistake to believe, as most of the history of this incident seems to imply, that Lincoln's intervention was the most important factor leading the convention to endorse the amendment. In fact, Republicans at the convention would almost certainly have offered an antislavery amendment in the platform even if Lincoln had said nothing. Already the Senate had passed the measure, and the House was poised to continue its debate after the convention. Even before Lincoln's involvement, Republican politicians had received many requests from

---

[17] William C. Harris, *With Charity for All: Lincoln and the Restoration of the Union* (Lexington: The University Press of Kentucky, 1997) 123–228.

[18] See, for example, Noah Brooks, *Washington in Lincoln's Time*, ed. Herbert Mitgang (1895; Athens: University of Georgia Press, 1989) 141–42.

[19] Isaac N. Arnold, *The Life of Abraham Lincoln* (Chicago: Jansen, McClurg and Company, 1885) 357–58.

[20] Donald B. Johnson, *National Party Platforms* (Urbana: University of Illinois Press, 1978) 1:35–36.

their constituents to have the convention back the amendment. Congressman Thaddeus Stevens had been advised by one fellow Pennsylvanian that "the radical men in and out of Congress should make some demonstration which will free Mr. L[incoln] up to some *higher point* and then go to Baltimore and put it in the platform."[21] One week before the convention, a third party calling itself the "Radical Democracy" had met in Cleveland, nominated John C. Frémont for president, and framed a platform that included no fewer than three constitutional amendments, one of which abolished slavery and secured for all men "absolute equality before the law."[22] Delegates at the Republican convention in Baltimore were sure to follow the example set in Cleveland and propose some sort of antislavery amendment.

Lincoln's intervention in his party's national convention was more an act of necessity than choice. He had to make sure that his party did not follow the example set in Cleveland too closely. The Cleveland convention's remarkable proposal for an amendment establishing "absolute equality" was nearly identical to a measure proposed by Senator Charles Sumner and then defeated during the Senate debate of the antislavery amendment. Its egalitarian language no doubt went too far for most Republicans. Lincoln had to intervene to make sure that the convention did not endorse an amendment so explicitly radical that it would further divide his party and prevent him from being able to endorse it. The strategy succeeded: the platform of the Republicans, or so-called National Union Party, included only an amendment abolishing slavery. Lincoln, in his speech accepting the nomination, could endorse the measure, saying "in the joint names of Liberty and Union, let us give it [the amendment] legal form, and practical effect."[23] But the issue of black equality was left in the scrap heap of the Baltimore convention hall, a fact not missed by abolitionists like Wendell Phillips, who spent much of the summer accusing Lincoln of co-opting the radicals'

---

[21] John A. Hiertand to Thaddeus Stevens, 29 May 1864, Thaddeus Stevens papers, Manuscripts Division, Library of Congress, Washington, DC.

[22] Edward McPherson, *The Political History of the United States of America During the Great Rebellion* (1865; reprint, New York: Da Capo Press, 1972) 413.

[23] Basler, *Collected Works*, 7:380.

emancipation amendment and pruning from it the proposal for equal rights.[24]

Phillip's accusation was justified. What was omitted from the Baltimore platform, and from much history since then, was the fact that the antislavery amendment was initially intended by most Republican congressmen not as a stand-alone measure but as one part of a two-tiered plan of reconstruction legislation. The first part, the amendment, would assure freedom to all slaves and through its enforcement clause would give Congress the power to adopt legislation granting civil rights to ex-slaves. The second part was the actual civil rights legislation. For most Republican congressmen, the two pieces were mutually dependent: the antislavery amendment required civil rights legislation to give legal life to black freedom; and civil rights legislation needed the amendment to provide constitutional legitimacy. Lincoln wanted only the first part of the package—the antislavery amendment—to appear in the platform. He wanted the Union united behind emancipation, not divided by black equality.

That strategy became even clearer when he pocket-vetoed the Wade-Davis bill one month after the convention. By that time, the House of Representatives had voted on the amendment and failed to secure the two-thirds majority necessary for its adoption. That meant that the Wade-Davis bill, which included a provision freeing all slaves by statute, was the only bill left in the current congressional session that could free the slaves immediately. But the bill also included provisions granting certain civil rights to ex-slaves, and it included provisions that would have undermined Lincoln's efforts to allow ex-Confederate states to rejoin the Union speedily. It was these reconstruction provisions, even more than the emancipation provision, that turned Lincoln against the bill.

Yet he disingenuously referred mainly to the emancipation issue in his message explaining the pocket-veto. He denied a "constitutional

---

[24] Theodore Tilton to Wendell Phillips, 31 May 1864 (with enclosure from the *Independent*) and 17 July 1864, as well as James Miller McKim to Wendell Phillips, 12 July 1864 and 20 July 1864, all in Wendell Phillips papers, Houghton Library, Harvard University, Cambridge MA. See HL. See James M. McPherson, *The Struggle for Equality: Abolitionists and the Negro in the Civil War and Reconstruction* (Princeton: Princeton University Press, 1964) 275–79.

MICHAEL VORENBERG 163

competency in Congress to abolish slavery in States" and stated his hope and expectation "that a constitutional amendment, abolishing slavery throughout the nation, may be adopted."[25] Lincoln thus plucked from a two-part congressional reconstruction scheme the most politically acceptable piece, the antislavery amendment. Rather than acknowledge the amendment for what it was—a *component* of congressional reconstruction—he framed it as an *alternative* to congressional reconstruction. Lincoln had finally come to embrace the antislavery amendment, but he did so as much out of a desire to sidestep the thorny issue of African-American equality as out of a desire to make emancipation irrevocable. It was a crucial moment in the life of the amendment, one that reveals Lincoln's skills as a legislative leader. Having remained aloof as congressmen created the amendment, he now stepped in to give the measure a public meaning distinct from that given to it by its creators.

The next part of the story of Lincoln's involvement with the Thirteenth Amendment is surely the best known. As traditional history has it, Lincoln almost single-handedly rammed the amendment through the House of Representatives during the final session of the thirty-eighth Congress in the winter of 1864–1865.

There is no question that the president worked to have the amendment adopted by this Congress, but before examining what he actually did, we need to ask a more fundamental question, one that is too often unasked: Why was it so important to Lincoln that this House, the one meeting in December 1864, adopt the amendment, when the next House, which he could call into session as early as three months later, would have the two-thirds Republican majority needed to adopt the measure? Obviously, Lincoln wanted slavery abolished legally and quickly. But also, he wanted the *issue* of slavery taken out of his hands, which is precisely what the amendment would do. Ever since July 1864, when he had written the so-called "To Whom It May Concern" letter, which said that he would enter into peace talks only on the terms of Union *and* emancipation, Lincoln had been hounded by the false charge

---

[25] Basler, *Collected Works*, 7:433–34.

that his insistence on emancipation was the only obstacle to an immediate peace with the Confederates.

In fact, as Lincoln well knew, it was the Confederates' insistence on separation from the Union that kept the war going. The sooner Congress adopted the amendment and sent it to the states for ratification, the sooner Lincoln could take the position that his position on emancipation was irrelevant, for the people were deciding the matter on their own through their elected officials in Congress and in state legislatures. Finally, Lincoln preferred that the passage of the amendment be a bipartisan rather than a Republican effort. Democrats and border-state Unionists who had usually voted against emancipation held about 40% of the seats in the House of Representatives; about a quarter of that group would have to vote for the amendment for it to be adopted by the two-thirds majority. Adoption of the amendment would thus symbolize an end to old party divisions over slavery, and it was precisely this effort to create a larger, lasting Union party that had captivated Lincoln for years.[26] The amendment, then, would be both a rehearsal and a catalyst for the solidification of the new party.

Lincoln was in a delicate position, for while he fully intended to exert his influence to have the amendment adopted sooner rather than later, he knew now, as he had known before, that the measure must appear as an initiative coming from the people rather than from the president. If the measure became known simply as Lincoln's amendment, not only would his opponents vote against it, but it would lose its power as a symbol of bipartisan unity against slavery. He would need the leadership style of a skillful king to obtain his king's cure.

He began by calling for the amendment in his annual message to Congress of 1864, claiming that the recent election was a mandate for the measure. "The voice of the *people* now, for the first time, [is] heard upon the question," he declared.[27] That claim was already misleading, for the amendment had been eclipsed in the 1864 political campaign by the "To

---

[26] Michael F. Holt, "Abraham Lincoln and the Politics of Union," *Abraham Lincoln and the American Political Tradition,* ed. John L. Thomas (Boston: University of Massachusetts Press, 1986) 111–41.

[27] Basler, *Collected Works*, 8:149 (emphasis added).

Whom It May Concern" letter, which seemed to make emancipation a presidential ultimatum—something the amendment did not do.[28]

Lincoln then took careful steps that would leave no political tracks. In separate conversations with at least six congressmen who had voted against the amendment back in June 1864, he expressed his wish to see the amendment adopted. He put no such request in writing, and he offered no explicit promise in return for a congressman's vote.[29] The most conniving thing he seems to have done was, emblematically, something that required inaction rather than action. A shady character named Abel Rathbone Corbin told Lincoln that he could get votes from Missouri congressmen previously opposed to the amendment if Lincoln would hold off on appointing a federal judge to that state. Corbin was a wealthy New York city financier who, after the war, made a name for himself by marrying the sister of President Ulysses Grant and then, with his friend Jay Gould, using his connection to Grant to try to corner the gold market—a clumsy effort leading to the financial panic known as "Black Friday."[30] With the Thirteenth Amendment, he was playing for smaller stakes, promising to secure a few votes in exchange for Lincoln's gratitude—and the later favors gratitude might bring. Corbin asked Lincoln to leave the Missouri judgeship vacant so that Corbin could persuade different Missouri congressmen that the judgeship would be

---

[28] Michael Vorenberg, "The Deformed Child: Slavery and the Election of 1864," *Civil War History* 47 (September 2001): 240–57.

[29] Only four of the congressmen whom Lincoln talked to directly are identified in the sources: James S. Rollins, Austin A. King, Samuel S. Cox, and John Todd Stuart. See Rollins's account in Isaac N. Arnold, *The Life of Abraham Lincoln* (Chicago: Jansen, McClurg, and Company, 1885) 358–59; Cox's account in *Union–Disunion–Reunion: Three Decades of Federal Legislation* (1885; reprint, Freeport NY: Books for Libraries Press, 1970) 310–11; Isaac N. Arnold's account in *The History of Abraham Lincoln and the Overthrow of Slavery* (Chicago: Clarke and Co., 1866) 469; and John B. Alley's account in Allen Thorndike Rice, ed., *Reminiscences of Abraham Lincoln* (New York: North American Review, 1888) 585–86. Also see Michael Vorenberg, *Final Freedom*, chapter 7.

[30] On Corbin, see Mark Wahlgren Summers, *The Era of Good Stealings* (New York: Oxford University Press, 1993) 184–85; Summers, *The Plundering Generation: Corruption and the Crisis of the Union, 1849–1861* (New York: Oxford University Press, 1987) 102–103; and William S. McFeely, *Grant: A Biography* (New York: W. W. Norton and Company, 1981) 319–29.

theirs to name if they voted the right way on the amendment. The judgeship was to be "a serpent hanging up on a pole," Corbin told Lincoln, a prize that all would expect but only one would receive. No evidence exists suggesting that Lincoln took Corbin's plan seriously, though the president did fail to appoint someone to the Missouri post before his death.[31]

Like a good king, Lincoln avoided any action that directly lowered himself into the dirty side of politics. There is no evidence, reliable or unreliable, that Lincoln himself promised any favor to someone in advance of that person's vote for the amendment. The only somewhat incriminating evidence comes from John B. Alley, a Massachusetts congressman who reported years after the event that Lincoln told two unidentified congressmen to procure two votes for the amendment. When the congressmen asked for more specific instructions, Lincoln supposedly responded, "I leave it to you to determine how it shall be done; but remember that I am President of the United States clothed with great power, and I expect you to procure those votes."[32] It is hard to think of a president less likely to say, "I am President of the United States clothed with great power" than Abraham Lincoln. The fact is, he did not have to say this, for everyone already knew it. By endorsing the amendment in his annual message, and by directly confronting certain congressmen, Lincoln sent a clear signal that he would look kindly on opposition members who lent their support to the legislation. The message was certainly received in the House. "The wish or order of the President is very potent," said an opponent of the amendment during the debate. "He can punish and reward."[33]

Instead of making specific promises to potential converts, Lincoln let his lieutenants make the bargains and use his name to seal the deals. That was the arrangement he seemed to have had with the shady Abel

---

[31] Abel Rathbone Corbin to Abraham Lincoln, 8 December 1864, Robert Todd Lincoln Collection, Manuscripts Division, Library of Congress, Washington, DC.

[32] Allen Thorndike Rice, ed., *Reminiscences of Abraham Lincoln* (New York: North American Review, 1888) 585–86.

[33] US Congress, House, *Congressional Globe,* 38th Cong., 2d sess., (9 January 1865) pt. 1, p. 180. Also see ibid. (10 January 1865) 189 (Kasson) 200 (Grinnell) and ibid. (31 January 1865) appendix, 53–54 (Harding).

Corbin, and it was the same arrangement that he seems to have had with the more respectable politicians working on his behalf, most notably Congressman James M. Ashley, the sponsor of the amendment in the House, and William Henry Seward, the secretary of state. Lincoln's name would be used, but the president himself would not know of the specifics.[34] At least a few deals were designed in this fashion, and at least one is well documented. Congressman Anson Herrick, a New York Democrat, received a promise from James Ashley that, if he voted for the amendment, his brother would receive an appointment as a federal revenue assessor. Herrick already had planned to vote for the measure, but he made the deal anyway. After the amendment had been adopted, Herrick went to Lincoln and told him the promise made to him by Ashley; Lincoln responded that "whatever Ashley had promised should be performed," and he sent the recommendation for Herrick's brother to the Senate. Unfortunately for the congressman, Lincoln died after recommending his brother, and when the Senate refused to confirm the appointment, Andrew Johnson turned his back on poor, jilted Herrick.[35]

Although Lincoln trusted the details of the negotiations to others, on at least one occasion he was asked to become directly involved. Ashley told Lincoln that he could get votes for the amendment if the president could get Senator Charles Sumner to drop his campaign to break the Camden and Amboy railroad monopoly in New Jersey. Lincoln cut Ashley short, telling him that he could "do nothing with Mr. Sumner in these matters."[36] He was right—Sumner was far too stubborn and principled to go for such a deal—but even if the target had not been Sumner, Lincoln would have balked: he knew the importance of preserving a kingly distance from the marketplace of political haggling.

---

[34] George S. Boutwell gave a sense of the process in *Reminiscences of Sixty Years in Public Affairs* (New York: McClure, Phillips and Co., 1902) 36.

[35] Anson Herrick to William H. Seward, 3 July 1865, 8 August 1865, 29 August 1865, 5 February 1867, and Homer Nelson to Seward, 29 July 1865, 20 November 1866, all in William Henry Seward papers, Rush Rhees Library, University of Rochester, Rochester, New York; Montgomery Blair to Andrew Johnson, 16 June 1865, Andrew Johnson papers, Manuscripts Division, Library of Congress, Washington, DC.

[36] John G. Nicolay and John Hay, *Abraham Lincoln: A History* (New York: Century Company, 1890) 10:84–85; and Helen Nicolay, *Lincoln's Secretary: A Biography of John Nicolay* (New York: Longmans, Green and Co., 1949) 220–21.

For all of the backroom bargaining that took place in the days before the final vote on the amendment, it turns out that very few actual deals were struck—either by Lincoln or by anyone else. Most of those who were rewarded for their vote already had planned to support the amendment even before the lobbyists entered the fray. Perhaps their decision came from principle, perhaps it came from the *possibility* of future patronage. But in only a few cases does a clear, promised incentive seem to have been involved, and in those cases, the opposition member usually abstained instead of voting for the amendment. Certainly there was no outright bribery. One Washington insider told the story that the New York lobbyists for the amendment controlled a $50,000 fund, but that after the amendment had been adopted, only $27.50 had been spent, all for incidental expenses only, not for bribes. "Good lord," one of them exclaimed, "that isn't the way they do things at Albany!"[37]

Why, then, did so many people—especially Republicans—later tell a sordid story of Lincoln's corrupt actions in getting the amendment adopted?[38] As late as 1898, one New Jersey Republican reported that, years before, the famous radical congressman Thaddeus Stevens had told him that the amendment "was passed by corruption, aided and abetted by the purest man in America"—meaning Lincoln.[39] The reason for such tales was simple. Republicans in the highly partisan decades of the late nineteenth century refused to concede to the Democrats any credit for the amendment, even though a Democrat had proposed the initial version of the amendment, Democrats converted to the cause of antislavery had been the most persuasive speakers for the measure, and Democrats in state legislatures had been decisive in getting the amendment ratified.[40]

---

[37] *Cincinnati Gazette*, 14 February 1865, 1. A more detailed analysis of the bargaining surrounding the amendment appears in Vorenberg, *Final Freedom*, chapter 7.

[38] See, for example, George S. Boutwell, *Reminiscences of Sixty Years in Public Affairs* (New York: McClure, Phillips and Co., 1902) 36; Albert Gallatin Riddle, *Recollections of War Times: Reminiscences of Men and Events in Washington, 1860–1865* (New York: G. P. Putnam's Sons, 1895) 324–25; George W. Julian, *Political Recollections, 1840–1872* (Chicago: Jansen, McClurg and Company, 1884) 249.

[39] James M. Scovel, "Thaddeus Stevens," *Lippincott's Monthly Magazine* 61 (1898): 550.

[40] Not all Republicans dismissed the Democrats' support for the amendment as illegitimate. In the late nineteenth century, James M. Ashley, James G. Blaine, and

Republicans elevated rumors of corruption into an explanation of Democratic support for the amendment, and, to absolve Lincoln, they played up his noble purposes as they told of his scandalous methods. The place of the amendment in public memory was thus transformed from a symbol of well-intentioned bipartisanship—precisely the symbol Lincoln had hoped it would be become—to a symbol of political graft. Lincoln's delicacy in using his power on behalf of the amendment while preserving the White House's dignity was largely forgotten.

The fourth part of the story of Lincoln's involvement with the amendment, his efforts on behalf of its ratification by the states, has been the least studied. Lincoln's major contribution to ratification was his plea that the ex-Confederate states be included in the ratification process. Those like Charles Sumner who believed that these states should have no say in ratification had a solid argument—after all, if the states had seceded, had they not forfeited the right of amending the Constitution of the country they had left behind? But Lincoln recognized the importance of having these states participate. As he said in his last public address, to exclude the ex-Confederate states from ratification "would be questionable, while a ratification by three fourths of all the States would be unquestioned and unquestionable."[41] He therefore allowed Secretary of State Seward to accept as legitimate the ratifications of the amendment by newly formed Union legislatures in these states, even though Congress had not yet agreed to accept back into its ranks the representatives from these states.[42] At the Hampton Roads conference, he

---

Lyman Trumbull, all of whom were trying to attract Democrats into their constituency (Trumbull had actually become a Democrat), praised the Democrats for their role in securing the amendment's passage. For Ashley, see Ashley, "Address before the Ohio Society of New York, February 20, 1890," *Duplicate Copy of the Souvenir from the Afro-American League of Tennessee to Hon. James M. Ashley of Ohio,* ed. Benjamin W. Arnett (Philadelphia: A.M.E. Church, 1894) 713; and Robert F. Horowitz, *The Great Impeacher: A Political Biography of James M. Ashley* (New York: Brooklyn College Press, 1979) 168; for Blaine, see *Twenty Years of Congress,* 539; for Trumbull, see Ralph Roske, *His Own Counsel: The Life and Times of Lyman Trumbull* (Reno: University of Nevada Press, 1979) 169–70; Horace White, *The Life of Lyman Trumbull* (Boston: Houghton Mifflin Company, 1913) 412; and John A. Logan, *The Democratic Party. Did it Abolish Slavery and Put Down the Rebellion?* (Chicago: NP, 1881).

[41] Basler, *Collected Works,* 8:404.

[42] See Vorenberg, *Final Freedom,* chap. 8.

advised Alexander Stephens to return to Georgia and urge the legislature there to ratify the amendment. Years later, Stephens wistfully remembered that Lincoln had even said that the legislature might ratify the measure "*prospectively*, so as to take effect—say in five years."[43] If Lincoln was indeed worried about making ratification seem legitimate, he could hardly have counseled such an unorthodox action as "prospective" ratification. More likely, Stephens was inventing this statement to lend authority to the efforts of Southern state governments to check the progress of black freedom.

Lincoln wanted to see the amendment ratified quickly, not only to put black freedom on solid constitutional ground but also to hasten the process of reunion. Thus, in his last public address, he used ratification as a carrot to get Congress to accept the legitimacy of the new Southern state governments. Louisiana's legislature had ratified the amendment, Lincoln explained, "If we reject Louisiana [from the Union], we also reject one vote in favor of the proposed amendment."[44] Lincoln gave over to Congress the power of readmitting ex-Confederate states to the Union. Yet, while he avoided breaching the separation between the executive and legislature, as we might expect a good Whig president to do, he deftly used what power he did have—in this case, the power under the secretary of state's office to process state ratifications of a constitutional amendment—to apply gentle pressure. It was a king's style—just right for a king's cure.

The king's cure that Lincoln spoke of after Congress adopted the amendment turned out to be less a cure for the evils of actual slavery than a cure for the evils that had befallen American politics because of slavery. As Lincoln must have known, the amendment by itself did nothing to relieve the suffering of the African-Americans who had lived under slavery and now faced the threat of further indignities at the hands of those determined to keep them subjugated. Perhaps that was one of the reasons that Lincoln had moved so slowly to endorse the amendment. Only more elaborate equal rights legislation and a massive shift in white racial thought would heal the wounds and move the nation forward.

---

[43] Stephens, *A Constitutional View of the Late War Between the States*, 2:613–14.
[44] Basler, *Collected Works*, 8:404.

Lincoln had come to realize that the amendment was nonetheless momentous, not only as a measure that might authorize further legislation but also as a symbol of Americans' wish to make a break with the constitutional order that had sanctioned slavery and oriented politics around the institution. In part, the "king's cure" metaphor was mocking—Lincoln had used the same term in 1839 to ridicule a Democratic alternative to a national bank[45]—but mainly it represented the president's genuine wish that a nation that had condoned slavery for so long could someday find some forgiveness for its past sins. In France in 1825 a witness to the last public ritual of the royal touch observed that "if the King in the accomplishment of the [royal touch]...approached those unfortunate people in order to heal them, he must, as a right-thinking person, have been sensible that even if he could not remedy the sores of the body, he could at least lessen the sorrows of the soul."[46] Lincoln knew that no one could remedy all the wounds of slavery, but he had come to understand the amendment's potential power as a symbol that might lessen the sorrows of the souls, North and South, who had sustained slavery.

Lincoln did not live to see the amendment ratified in December 1865, but even in death he coaxed the measure toward life. While he was still alive, opponents of the amendment in the New York state assembly had successfully blocked ratification. Then Lincoln was assassinated, and as his casket headed by train to Albany, the opposition realized how unseemly it would be for the legislature to stand against emancipation in the presence of the murdered Great Emancipator. "Let us refuse to...ever *seem* in a disloyal position or as the defenders of Slavery," one New York editor advised.[47] Four days before Lincoln's casket arrived, an opposition faction changed its position, and the assembly finally carried

---

[45] Basler, *Collected Works*, 1:169 (Lincoln mocked the idea of a national penitentiary as a deterrent to fraud under the proposed subtreasury system, calling it a "king-cure-call").

[46] Bloch, *The Royal Touch*, 227.

[47] Calvert Comstock to Manton Marble, 21 April 1865, Manton M. Marble papers, Manuscripts Division, Library of Congress, Washington, DC.

ratification.[48] In death, as in life, Lincoln cajoled reluctant emancipators to embrace constitutional freedom. It was an appropriate final act, one that might have befit a martyred king.

---

[48] *Journal of the Assembly of the State of New York*, 88th sess., 1865, 1387–89; *New York Evening Express*, 24 April 1865, 1; *New York Herald*, 24 April 1865, 4

LINCOLN'S ROLE IN THE
PRESIDENTIAL ELECTION OF 1864

William C. Harris

The presidential contest of 1864 was arguably the most important election in American history. The defeat of Lincoln and the election of George B. McClellan on the Democratic party's war-failure platform, calling for a cease-fire and the restoration of the Constitution as it was, would have endangered the Union purposes in the war and indefinitely delayed emancipation. Lincoln's role in this election was of paramount importance to the success of the Union party, thereby guaranteeing the early end of the war on the basis of reunion and making possible the adoption in 1865 of the Thirteenth Amendment abolishing slavery everywhere in the United States.

Historians, however, have not always seen the 1864 contest in such a critical light. Scholars writing during the Cold War and influenced by the need for national democratic unity in the face of the Soviet threat contended that no fundamental differences existed between the Republican and Democratic parties in the election or between Lincoln and McClellan. Both parties and candidates, these historians argued, supported the war and only disagreed on particulars regarding the conduct of the conflict and reconstruction policy. According to these scholars, a Democratic victory could not have short-circuited or changed the outcome of the war, which, they maintained, had been settled by the fall of Atlanta in early September and other federal military successes. Furthermore, McClellan, who announced his support for the war, would have rejected pressure from the Vallandigham Democrats or

Copperheads for a peace short of reunion.[1] Even slavery would have ended under a McClellan presidency. "The peculiar institution," as Allan Nevins in his magisterial study of the Civil War period wrote, had been "too far mutilated and undermined to recover," and no Democratic administration, however sympathetic to the restoration of the Union "as it was," could save it. For Nevins and other scholars of his generation the real importance of the election lay in the fact that during a great civil war the election occurred at all.[2]

The 1990s saw a resurgence of interest in the 1864 election, as well as in the Civil War generally. Historians writing during this decade found significant differences between the two parties and their candidates, Lincoln and McClellan. They concluded that Lincoln's election emphatically reaffirmed the central purposes in the war—reunion and emancipation—to be achieved by armed might and not by compromise. A McClellan victory, David E. Long wrote in the best account of the election, would have resulted in political gridlock in Washington, failed to suppress the rebellion, and aborted emancipation.[3]

Contemporaries who supported the Union or Republican parties held a similar view of the critical importance of the election, not only for the immediate war purposes but also for the future of popular government and human progress everywhere (meaning Europe and the Americas). George William Curtis, editor of the influential *Harper's Weekly*, wrote that "the grandest lesson of the [election] result is its vindication of the American system of free popular government....

---

[1] J. G. Randall and Richard N. Current, *Lincoln the President: Last Full Measure* (Urbana: University of Illinois Press, 1991; originally published in 1955) 263; William Frank Zornow, *Lincoln & the Party Divided* (Norman: University of Oklahoma Press, 1954) 139–40; Zornow's book, which, as the title suggests, emphasizes the conflict within the Republican party in 1864, is the first book-length account of the election.

[2] Allan Nevins, *The War for the Union: Volume IV, The Organized War to Victory, 1864–1865* (New York: Charles Scribner's Sons, 1971) 119–20. See also Harold M. Hyman, "Election of 1864," *History of American Presidential Elections, 1789–1968*, ed. Arthur M. Schlesinger, Jr. (New York: Chelsea House, 1985) 1155.

[3] David E. Long, *The Jewel of Liberty: Abraham Lincoln's Re-election and the End of Slavery* (Mechanicsburg PA: Stackpole Books, 1994) 265–69. See also John C. Waugh, *Reelecting Lincoln: The Battle for the 1864 Presidency* (New York: Crown Publishers, Inc., 1997) x.

Thank God and the people, we are a nation which comprehends its priceless importance to human progress and civilization."[4] Literary giant James Russell Lowell exclaimed, "The reelection of Mr. Lincoln was a greater triumph than any military victory could be" for the principles of democracy and liberty in the world.[5] General U. S. Grant echoed the same sentiment, declaring that the election "proves the worthiness of free institutions, and our capability of preserving them without running into anarchy or despotism."[6] Ralph Waldo Emerson simply remarked: "Seldom in history was so much staked on a popular vote."[7] Protestant ministers proclaimed the triumph, as Henry Ward Beecher expressed it, of "pure moral forces over the Devil" as represented by the Democratic party and its rebel allies.[8]

Amazingly, most contemporaries gave Lincoln little immediate credit for the resounding Union victory at the polls. Of course, crestfallen Democrats, whose dislike for Lincoln had become obsessive, ignored any positive role that he had played in the election. The *Boston Courier*, for example, characterized the Republican triumph as a "sham election" carried by "the unscrupulous and profligate agents" of Lincoln and his "besotted followers."[9] Radical Republicans contended that northerners, in Henry Winter Davis's words, voted for Lincoln only "to keep out worse people—keeping their hands on the pit of their stomach the while!"[10] Another Radical wrote that opposition to the Democrats' platform, "and not the confidence of the people in Mr. Lincoln, re-elected him.... All our speakers bear the same testimony. Through large portions of the country, particularly in the West, men voted for Mr.

---

[4] *Harper's Weekly*, 19 November 1864.

[5] James Russell Lowell to Aubrey de Vere, 27 December 1864, *The Letters of Charles Eliot Norton*, 2 vols., ed. Sara Norton and M. A. DeWolfe Howe (New York: 1913) 1:283.

[6] Entry for16 November 1864, *Inside Lincoln's White House: The Complete Civil War Diary of John Hay,* ed. Michael Burlingame and John R. Turner Ettlinger (Carbondale and Edwardsville: Southern Illinois University Press, 1997) 251.

[7] Waugh, *Reelecting Lincoln*, 357.

[8] As reported in the *St. Louis Missouri Democrat*, 1 December 1864.

[9] As reported in the *Boston Daily Advertiser*, 10 November 1864.

[10] As quoted in Nevins, *Organized War to Victory*, 142.

Lincoln as they take calomel; it was a bitter pill."[11] Journalist Whitelaw Reid observed that "men voted for the cause and not for Mr. Lincoln.... Three-fourths of the leading speakers at the meetings could not be induced to give the Administration their indorsement. But there was a determination...that the Republic should stand, and its enemies should perish."[12]

However, some contemporaries, particularly in Lincoln's faction of the Union party, gave the president a share of the credit for the victory. The distinguished Edward Everett, a conservative Unionist who late in the campaign had agreed to serve as a Lincoln elector in Massachusetts, spoke to a dinner audience in Boston and praised Lincoln for his personal qualities and the "strategical skill" that he exercised in unifying the two opposing wings of the Union party in the election. Everett attempted to lay to rest the prevalent opinion in the Northeast that Lincoln was a person of "uncouth appearance and manners." He informed his elite audience that "on the only occasion on which I had the honor to be in the President's company, viz., the commemoration at Gettysburg, [Lincoln] sat at the table of my friend David Wills, by the side of several distinguished persons, ladies and gentlemen, foreigners and Americans,...and that in gentlemanly appearance, manners and conversation, he was the peer of any man at the table." Everett admitted that "the most important objection urged against Mr. Lincoln is that personally he lacks fixedness of purpose, and that his cabinet and administration have wanted unity of counsel." Without defending Lincoln on these points, Everett reminded his dinner audience "that precisely the same charges on the same grounds [were] brought against General Washington and his administration." Several times during Everett's address, whenever Lincoln's name was mentioned, the audience rose and cheered.[13] Among the New England elite, the apotheosis of the prairie lawyer-politician had begun.

---

[11] *Boston Commonwealth*, 12 November 1864.

[12] James G. Smart, ed., *A Radical View: the 'Agate' Dispatches of Whitelaw Reid, 1861–1865*, 2 vols. (Memphis: Memphis State University Press, 1976) 2:187.

[13] Unidentified newspaper clipping, sent by Edward Everett, 22 November 1864, in Papers of Abraham Lincoln, Manuscript Division, Library of Congress, Washington, DC., no. 38591 (microfilm).

Like many of his contemporaries, historians have viewed Lincoln as playing a relatively minor role in the 1864 election. Such a role was in keeping with the tradition that presidential candidates should not campaign and also that Lincoln had more important things on his mind in 1864—that is, winning the war. In support of this view, they cite Lincoln's comment during the campaign: "I cannot run the political machine; I have enough on my hands without that. It is the people's business—the election is in their hands."[14]

Lincoln, however, was far from inactive in the 1864 campaign, though he made no campaign speeches or wrote speeches to be delivered at Republican rallies. With the possible exception of Stephen A. Douglas in 1860, he probably took a greater part in the contest than did any previous presidential candidate. For Lincoln the issue in the election was not so much his own desire to continue as president, but it was his strong conviction that the fate of the Union, its government, republican institutions, and emancipation lay in the balance. A victory for McClellan and the Democrats, Lincoln believed, especially after that party's adoption of the war-failure platform at Chicago in late August, would mean the repudiation of all that the Union stood for and would inevitably tarnish America's reputation as "the last, best hope of Earth."[15]

In the heat of the campaign, Lincoln adopted the view of many Union zealots that the Democrats were disloyal Copperheads who would arrange an inglorious peace with the rebels if in control of the government. He wrote in late July: "The present presidential contest will almost certainly be no other than a contest between a Union and a Disunion candidate, disunion certainly following the success of the latter. The issue is a mighty one for all people and all time; and whoever aids

---

[14] Emanuel Hertz, *Abraham Lincoln: A New Portrait*, 2 vols. (New York: Horace Liveright, Inc., 1931) 2:941; David Donald, *Lincoln* (New York: Simon & Schuster, 1995) 537.

[15] This quote is taken from Lincoln's Annual Message to Congress, 1 December 1862, Roy P. Basler, ed., *The Collected Works of Abraham Lincoln*, 9 vols. (New Brunswick, New Jersey: Rutgers University Press, 1953–1955) 5:537.

the right, will be appreciated and remembered."[16] In this time of great crisis for the republic, with thousands of men fighting, suffering, and dying for the Union in the South, Lincoln found little legitimacy in an opposition political party, especially one like the Democratic party that reputedly gave aid and comfort to the enemy. The president only barely tolerated the Copperhead party, and this was because of his commitment to preserve the Constitution, uphold the laws, and avoid civil strife in the Union states. Only after the election did he take a more charitable view of the Democrats, publicly acknowledging their loyalty to the Union.

Historians have concluded that federal military successes at Atlanta and elsewhere in the South in September and October and the Democrats' defeatist platform made inevitable Lincoln's victory at the polls. Certainly these victories made probable, but not inevitable, the Republican triumph in November. The Union party's success in critical states like New York, Pennsylvania, Indiana, Illinois, and Missouri, still depended upon a skillful handling of political affairs by Republican leaders, the achievement of party unity, and the aid that the president could provide local supporters. Lincoln played an important role in each case. He did not, however, become involved in campaign details. The traditional practice of state and local activists and newspaper editors carrying their party's banner was still followed—and this by both sides in 1864—with an intensity and passion never before or since seen in the Northern states, especially in the critical lower North. Lincoln kept abreast of the political situation in these states and on occasion assisted local Republicans, particularly through his use of federal patronage. At times Lincoln wisely refrained from involvement lest it create unnecessary divisions in the Union coalition. The president's shrewd management of men and political affairs with the election in mind and his firmness in adhering to the Republican war platform made possible party unity and reduced conservative Unionists' support for the Democrats in the election. Furthermore, Lincoln's determination to resist pressure to abandon emancipation at a critical time in the campaign made possible important Radical Republican support for his candidacy.

---

[16] Abraham Lincoln to Abraham Wakeman, 25 July 1865, *Collected Works*, ed. Basler, 7:461.

Without the president's political efforts and steadfastness during the late summer and autumn, the fall of Atlanta and other military successes could have failed to produce the Republican victory in November.

Lincoln's adroit leadership in the 1864 campaign began with the Republican or National Union convention that met in Baltimore in June and nominated him for a second term as president. Though he did not attend, Lincoln spoke to Republican delegates when they visited Washington prior to the convention. He specifically asked Senator Edwin Morgan of New York, chairman of the National Republican Committee, to call in his keynote speech for a resolution supporting a constitutional amendment abolishing slavery in the United States. Morgan complied and made a stirring address in favor of such a plank in the Republican platform. Other speakers immediately followed with appeals for the adoption of the antislavery plank.[17] In taking a strong stand for the amendment, Republican leaders were influenced by the failure of Congress to initiate such an amendment and the action of dissident Radicals who had met two weeks earlier at Cleveland and nominated John C. Fremont for president on an antislavery platform. On his part, Lincoln wanted to have his emancipation policy validated and end the blot on American republicanism as well as the fundamental cause of sectional discord—slavery. The change of the party's name from Republican to National Union was probably suggested by Lincoln to delegates who visited him in Washington. The new title supposedly would make the party less sectional and more attractive to War Democrats and conservatives in areas like the lower North and the border states where the name Republican was associated with radicalism. Finally, the convention endorsed Lincoln's administration but called for unity in its councils, a thinly veiled demand for the dismissal of Postmaster General Montgomery Blair and Secretary of State William H. Seward, both of whom had made many enemies in the party, particularly among Radicals.

---

[17] James A. Rawley, *Edwin D. Morgan, 1811–1893: Merchant in Politics* (New York: Columbia University Press, 1955) 198–99; Richard N. Current, *The Lincoln Nobody Knows* (New York: Hill and Wang, 1958) 229; John G. Nicolay and John Hay, *Abraham Lincoln: A History*, 10 vols. (New York: The Century Co., 1890) 10:79–80.

Much has been written about the replacement of Vice President Hannibal Hamlin by Andrew Johnson on the National Union ticket. It has long been an article of faith among historians that Lincoln had a hand in the selection of Johnson as the vice-presidential nominee. Professor Don E. Fehrenbacher has convincingly demonstrated in a 1995 article that this was not the case. Lincoln permitted the delegates to make their own selection, which allowed the anti-Hamlin forces to sweep the vice president from office and thereby broaden the party ticket.[18] The choice of Johnson, a Southern Unionist hero in the North, had popular support and was quickly endorsed by Lincoln who believed that the Tennessean's selection would be seen as an affirmation of his lenient reconstruction policy. Radical Republican congressman Albert G. Riddle later wrote: "The President favored Johnson, though certain I am that he made no open declaration of his wishes, nor could there have been anyone authorized to speak for him. Lincoln would never permit himself to attempt to influence the convention."[19]

The Lincoln (and Republican) campaign soon ran into trouble. The federal military offensives of 1864, begun with great hope during the spring, had faltered and by mid-summer had become a stalemate. Distressing reports reached the North of horrendous Union casualties in Virginia and Georgia. The desire for peace increased dramatically, and the Northern people predictably blamed the Lincoln administration for the failure to win the war. The spectacle of General Jubal Early's raid across Maryland and to the gates of Washington before being repulsed shocked the North and added to the people's distress. Even members of Lincoln's cabinet admitted the "national humiliation" caused by the Confederate raid.[20] Peace Democrats or Copperheads like Clement

---

[18] Don E. Fehrenbacher, "The Making of a Myth: Lincoln and the Vice-Presidential Nomination in 1864," *Civil War History* 41 (December 1995): 289–90. For other strong evidence that Lincoln did not interfere in the vice-presidential nomination, see John Hay to John G. Nicolay, 6 June 1864, Michael Burlingame, ed., *At Lincoln's Side: John Hay's Civil War Correspondence and Selected Writings* (Carbondale and Edwardsville: Southern Illinois University Press, 2000) 84.

[19] Albert Gallatin Riddle, *Recollections of War Times: Reminiscences of Men and Events in Washington, 1860–1865* (New York: G. P. Putnam's Sons, 1895) 282.

[20] Entry for 15 July 1864, *Welles Diary*, 2:77.

Vallandigham at last saw their opportunity to gain control of the Democratic party, defeat the Republicans in the fall election, and end the war on the basis of restoring "the Union as it was."

At the other extreme, Radical Republicans, frustrated by military setbacks, by Lincoln's soft reconstruction policy, and by divisions within the administration, became bolder in both their private and public snipping at the president. Conservative Republicans like Senator Orville Browning of Illinois, a longtime friend of Lincoln, and Thurlow Weed, the New York wire-puller and Seward associate, began to doubt Lincoln's leadership abilities. In late June Salmon P. Chase's forced resignation as secretary of treasury caused concern among Republicans, especially Radicals, reinforcing their view that the administration lacked unity and a sense of direction. The president's appointment of William Pitt Fessenden to replace Chase did little to placate the Radicals, though it partly soothed the ruffled feathers of middle-of-the-road Republicans. Lincoln's promise to Senator Charles Sumner and others that he would appoint Chase as chief justice of the Supreme Court if the aging Roger B. Taney died or resigned also could have been influenced by his desire to deflect Radical concern regarding Chase's resignation.[21]

Emboldened by Lincoln's political vulnerability, Radicals in Congress, joined by other Republicans, in early July secured the passage of the Wade-Davis bill, directly challenging the president's mild reconstruction plan. Lincoln believed that the approval of the stringent bill would snuff out the work of civil reorganization in Louisiana and elsewhere in the South. It would also cost him and his party important conservative support in the North and the border states, losses that could throw the election to the Democrats in November. Lincoln pocket-vetoed the bill, but to soften the blow, he indicated that he would not object to any Southern state voluntarily reorganizing loyal governments under the provisions of the bill, an option that no state was likely to take. The president also reaffirmed his support for a constitutional amendment abolishing slavery in all the states. Though the veto brought down on

---

[21] For Lincoln's promise to appoint Chase as Chief Justice, see Charles Sumner to Francis Lieber, 12 October 1864, Edward L. Pierce, ed., *Memoir and Letters of Charles Sumner*, 4 vols. (Boston: Robert Brothers, 1878–1894) 4:207–209.

Lincoln's head the wrath of Wade and Davis, most Radicals, desirous of maintaining party harmony in view of the rising Copperhead threat, only privately condemned the president's "usurpation" of authority and awaited their opportunity to strike back at him.[22]

At the same time Lincoln sought to placate those who had charged that he was avoiding peace talks with the rebels. Horace Greeley, the powerful and eccentric editor of the New York *Tribune*, wrote the president on 7 July entreating him to meet with Confederate envoys in Canada who, Greeley claimed, had full authority to negotiate peace. On 9 July, the day after pocket vetoing the Wade-Davis bill, Lincoln replied that he or his representatives would meet with "any person anywhere professing to have any proposition of Jefferson Davis in writing, for peace, embracing the restoration of the Union and abandonment of slavery, whatever else it embraces." After some complicated correspondence, the president followed his reply with his famous "To Whom It May Concern" letter, reaffirming what he had told Greeley, but this one was published and used by the Democrats against him in the campaign.[23] The Democrats had considerable success in arguing that Lincoln was willing to sacrifice peace and reunion for emancipation, a position that was becoming increasingly untenable in the border states and the lower North as the military casualties mounted during the summer. Though conservatives in the Union coalition were unhappy with Lincoln's inflexibility on emancipation, other Republicans saw a steadfastness in the president that they thought had not existed before. Then, on 18 July Lincoln boldly issued a proclamation calling for 500,000 additional troops to replace the severe losses in the armies. This action, which created anxiety among Republican and condemnation by Peace Democrats, endeared Lincoln to the officers and soldiers in the trenches, many of whom would be voting in the fall.[24]

---

[22] William C. Harris, *With Charity for All: Lincoln and the Restoration of the Union* (Lexington: University Press of Kentucky, 1997) 186–87.

[23] Abraham Lincoln to Horace Greeley, 9 July 1864; "To Whom It May Concern," 18 July 1864, both in Basler, *Collected Works*, 7:435, 435–36 n. 451.

[24] Proclamation Calling for 500,000 Volunteers, 18 July 1864, *Collected Works*, ed. Basler, 7:448–49. This call for troops would be followed by a draft on 5 September on communities and counties who failed to meet their quotas of volunteers.

Late July and the whole month of August brought great anguish for Lincoln and the Republicans, accompanied by fear that the election—and perhaps the Union—would be lost. The military situation had continued to deteriorate with little hope that the stalemate near Petersburg and Atlanta would soon be broken. The disastrous Crater fiasco in Virginia and another Jubal Early raid north of the Potomac—this one as far as Chambersburg, Pennsylvania, on 30 July—compounded Lincoln's problems.

Prominent conservative Unionists, many of whom were old Whigs like Lincoln who had never voted Democratic, pronounced Lincoln a failure. They revived the Constitutional Union movement of 1860 and made plans to fuse with the Democrats when they met in Chicago on 29 August. Governor Thomas E. Bramlette of Kentucky, Maryland senator Reverdy Johnson, and the Boston brahmin and former Whig Speaker of the US House of Representatives Robert C. Winthrop announced their intention to support General George B. McClellan, the presumed Democratic candidate for president.[25] These conservatives believed that Lincoln had failed the test of leadership, and his policies, especially his unswerving commitment to emancipation, would make impossible the suppression of the rebellion.

Within Lincoln's own party, revolt flared. Richard Smith, editor of the *Cincinnati Gazette*, wrote: "The people regard Mr. Lincoln's candidacy as a misfortune. His apparent strength when nominated [in June] was fictitious, and now the fiction has disappeared, and instead of confidence there is distress. I do not know a Lincoln man."[26] Senator Charles Sumner of Massachusetts told a friend that Lincoln "has no instinct or inspiration," and he wanted him to step aside as the party's presidential candidate in favor of "any one of 100 names."[27] In mid August, a group of New York Republicans—not all of them

---

[25] William C. Harris, "Conservative Unionists and the Presidential Election of 1864," *Civil War History* 38 (December 1992): 300–305.

[26] Richard Smith to John Austin Stevens(?), 27 August 1864, printed in the *New York Sun*, 30 June 1889.

[27] Charles Sumner to John Bright, 27 September 1864, in Beverly Wilson Palmer, ed., *The Selected Letters of Charles Sumner*, 2 vols. (Boston: Northeastern University Press, 1990) 2:253.

Radicals—met and plotted to replace Lincoln as the party's standard-bearer. They issued a call for another Republican convention to meet in Cincinnati on 28 September for this purpose and also to breathe new life into the Union cause. Their appeal did not mention emancipation as an aim of the party.[28]

Several candidates were brought forth as possible replacements for Lincoln, including Chase, General John A. Dix, and General Benjamin F. Butler. Butler attracted the most attention, a fact that was not lost on Lincoln. The controversial general had become embroiled in a dispute over jurisdiction in the Norfolk area with Governor Francis H. Pierpont of the Restored (Union) Government of Virginia. Pierpont demanded that Lincoln remove Butler from command, an action that General Grant, for military reasons, also wanted. On 20 July the president discussed the Pierpont-Butler conflict with his cabinet. Several members, including Secretary of War Edwin M. Stanton, urged him to sustain Governor Pierpont and reprimand the controversial Butler, if not remove him from command. Lincoln hesitated; finally, on 9 August he drafted a letter to the general chastising him for instituting military rule for reasons other than military necessity. Lincoln did not send the letter; he feared that with the approaching election a reprimand would antagonize Butler's Radical friends, cause the irascible general's political stock to rise, and contribute to further divisions within the Union coalition.[29] Lincoln wisely waited until after the election before reining in the general. After Butler's embarrassing failure to take Fort Fisher in December, the president removed him from command.

Many Republicans refused to endorse a second Republican convention, correctly concluding that it would further divide the party. Lincoln also was not about to recognize the convention movement or step aside for Butler or any other candidate. The president realized that if the convention met it would be an admission that his administration and

---

[28] The *New York Sun* in its 30 June 1889, issue published the call for the Cincinnati convention and also a large collection of letters relating to it.

[29] Entries for 20 July, 4 August 1864, "The Diary of Edward Bates, 1859–1866," *Annual Report of the American Historical Association for 1930*, ed. Howard K. Beale, ed (Washington, DC: NP, 1930) 4:386–87, 397.

its policies had failed, and such an admission, he believed, would lead to the election of the Copperheads in November.

Still, during the bleak days of late August, Lincoln despaired of success at the polls. On 23 August Lincoln wrote a remarkable memorandum and secured, sight unseen, the endorsement of each cabinet member to it. The so-called "blind memorandum" read: "This morning, as for some days past, it seems exceedingly probable that this Administration will not be re-elected. Then it will be my duty to so co-operate with the President elect, as to save the Union between the election and the inauguration, as he will have secured his election on such ground that he can not possibly save it afterwards."[30] The next day, Lincoln drafted a letter authorizing Henry J. Raymond, editor of the New York *Times* and the new chairman of the national Republican committee, to go south and propose to Jefferson Davis that "upon the restoration of the Union and the National authority, the war shall cease at once, all remaining questions to be left for adjustment by peaceful means." But after sleeping on the matter and apparently consulting with several members of his cabinet, the president determined not to authorize the peace commission. He informed Raymond, who had suggested it, that to send a peace commission to Richmond at this juncture of the war and to break his promise to blacks who had been freed by the Emancipation Proclamation would be worse than losing the presidential contest. It would be an ignominious surrender of the Union purposes in the war.[31] On that morning, John Nicolay wrote his wife: today could be "the turning-point in our crisis. If the President can infect" Raymond and other "weak-kneed" Republicans "with some of his own patience and pluck, we are saved."[32]

One week later, Lincoln's steadfastness began to pay off. The Democrats, meeting in Chicago, did what Lincoln had presumed they would do. They adopted the Copperhead platform declaring the war a

---

[30] Memorandum Concerning His Probable Failure of Re-election, 23 August 1864, *Collected Works*, ed. Basler, 7:514.

[31] Abraham Lincoln to Henry J. Raymond, 24 August 1864, *Collected Works*, ed. Basler, 7:517, 518n.

[32] As reported in Helen Nicolay, *Lincoln's Secretary: A Biography of John G. Nicolay* (New York: Longman's Green, 1949) 212.

failure, calling for a cease-fire ostensibly to be followed by a national reunion convention, and demanding the restoration of the rights of states as they existed before the war, which implicitly included the invalidation of the Emancipation Proclamation. The Democrats then nominated General McClellan, who supported the war, for president and George H. Pendleton, a Copperhead, for vice president. However, it was the Democratic platform that attracted the most attention and produced an outraged reaction that worked to the advantage of Lincoln and the Republicans in the campaign.

Soon after the Chicago convention, Lincoln put on paper his view of the issues in the election. A supporter had asked him to attend a Union mass meeting in Buffalo and address local Republicans. In drafting a letter declining the invitation, the president wrote that the Democratic platform calling for "an armistice—a cessation of hostilities—is the end of the struggle, and the insurgents would be in a peaceable possession of all that has been struggled for. Any different policy in regard to the colored man, deprives us of his help, and this is more than we can bear. We can not spare the hundred and forty or fifty thousand now serving us as soldiers, seamen, and laborers."[33] He never finished the draft of the letter; instead, Lincoln sent a telegram to his Buffalo friend that it would not be proper "for one holding the office, and being a candidate for re-election" to participate publicly in the campaign.[34]

When Lincoln wrote this reply, the news was sweeping the nation that Admiral David Farragut had won a spectacular naval battle at the mouth of Mobile Bay and, even more thrilling for northerners, General William Tecumseh Sherman had taken Atlanta. After the successes at Mobile Bay and Atlanta, northerners believed that the stalemate had been broken and significant progress toward the suppression of the rebellion had been made. Union morale earlier had been bolstered by triumphs (for example, Gettysburg) only to be deflated by later military setbacks. If military reverses accompanied by heavy casualties occurred before the November election, public opinion could again swing against Lincoln

---

[33] Abraham Lincoln to Isaac M. Schermerhorn, 12 September 1864, *Collected Works*, ed. Basler, 8:1–2.

[34] Ibid., 8:2.

and his party. An inkling of this volatility occurred when Confederate General Sterling Price's army of 12,000 entered Missouri in September and moved rapidly toward St. Louis. Though stopped and turned westward in October before reaching the city, the raid caused consternation, especially in the West, and apprehension that rebel forces were still formidable.[35] Under the circumstances, the unity of the Union coalition in the election remained crucial, and Lincoln was the key to maintaining it.

Sobered by the Democratic platform and the threat posed by the Vallandigham Copperheads, Radicals and other dissident Republicans abandoned their plan to meet in Cincinnati in late September, reorganize the party, and remove Lincoln from the ticket. Then, on 23 September John C. Fremont, under pressure from fearful Union supporters, withdrew from the race. At the same time Lincoln sought to consolidate discontented Republican support for his candidacy by securing the resignation of Postmaster General Montgomery Blair, the bête noir of the Radicals. He refused, however, to remove Secretary of State William H. Seward, another important target of discontented Republicans. Instead, Lincoln made clear his support for Seward by replacing Chase men with members of the Seward faction in the important federal Treasury offices in New York.[36] This action also regained the support of Seward's sidekick, Thurlow Weed, and invigorated the conservative Republican forces in the state. An effort by Henry J. Raymond, Republican chairman and editor of the New York *Times*, to sweep the large Brooklyn Navy Yard of McClellan supporters, however, met with Lincoln's disapproval. Secretary of Navy Welles applauded the president's resistance to Raymond's pressure. He wrote in his diary that Lincoln's "good sense and sagacity are against such exercise or abuse of power and patronage."[37]

The forced resignation of Blair, whom Lincoln admired, was a bitter pill for the president to swallow, but he knew that he must sacrifice him

---

[35] Boston *Daily Advertiser*, 17 October 1864.

[36] Charles S. Bartles to Lyman Trumbull, 1 September 1864, Lyman Trumbull Papers, Manuscript Division, Library of Congress, Washington, DC; Randall and Current, *Lincoln the President*, 249–50.

[37] Entry for 5 September 1864, *Welles Diary*, 2:136–37.

for the good of party unity. However, there was a risk involved in the resignation: Blair had a devoted conservative and War Democratic following that could be lost to the National Union party, especially if he were replaced by a Radical. Lincoln relieved conservative fears with the appointment of William Dennison, a friend of Blair's and chair of the party's Baltimore convention. Blair immediately published a letter reaffirming his wholehearted support for the administration and the party's principles adopted at Baltimore.[38]

Whether the removal of Blair, as historians have believed, was a quid pro quo for Fremont's withdrawal from the race is debatable.[39] The timing might have been coincidental. From the beginning, Lincoln did not seem concerned about Fremont's candidacy. Furthermore, the Pathfinder's support had faded during the summer, and few disaffected Republicans endorsed his third party movement. Lincoln probably knew that many of Fremont's followers were German-Americans or Democrats who disliked the Republicans and would not vote for him anyway.[40] Earlier Lincoln had dismissed the Fremont threat by comparing him with Jim Jett's brother in Illinois. "Jim used to say," Lincoln recalled, "that his brother was the biggest scoundrel that ever lived, but in the infinite mercy of Providence he was also the biggest fool."[41]

In September, Radicals, fearful of a McClellan victory, reluctantly fell in line behind the Lincoln ticket and took to the stump in their states. Benjamin F. Wade wrote his Radical friend Senator Zachariah Chandler of Michigan: "Were it not for the country there would be poetic justice in [Lincoln] being beaten by that stupid ass McClellan.... I can but wish the

---

[38] Entry for 23 September 1864, *Welles Diary*, 2:156–58; William Earnest Smith, *The Francis Preston Blair Family in Politics* (New York: The Macmillan Company, 1933) 290–91.

[39] For the view that Fremont's withdrawal was tied to Blair's removal, see James M. McPherson, *Battle Cry of Freedom: The Civil War Era* (New York and Oxford: Oxford University Press, 1988) 776. For a contrary view, see Nevins, *War for the Union*, 105–06.

[40] Entry for 8 June 1864, *Diary of George Templeton Strong*, 4 vols. (New York: The Macmillan Company, 1952) 3:455; John Tapley to James R. Doolittle, 3 July 1864, James R. Doolittle Papers, Wisconsin State Historical Society, Madison; *National Anti-Slavery Standard*, 2 July 1864.

[41] Entry for 22 May 1864, Burlingame and Ettlinger, *Hay Diary*, 197–98.

d—l had Old Abe. But the issue is now made up and we have got to take him, or Jeff Davis, for McClellan and all who will support him, are meaner traitors than are to be found in the Confederacy."[42] Francis Lieber, a German-American friend of Charles Sumner and a prominent Columbia University professor who in early September had called for Lincoln to withdraw in order to avoid a Union disaster at the polls, now wrote a pamphlet, *Lincoln or McClellan*, promoting the president's candidacy. The pamphlet, which was issued in English, German, and Dutch and designed mainly for German-Americans, had an important effect among foreign-born voters, a contribution to the campaign that Lincoln acknowledged.[43] Other Republicans, inspired by Union military successes and Lincoln's determination to stand by the party's platform—though many of them had wavered in August on the antislavery plank—entered the crusade to save the republic.

Lincoln also sought to resolve intraparty disputes in such faction-ridden states as Missouri and thereby unite Union forces behind his candidacy. In October he dispatched his private secretary, John G. Nicolay, to Missouri where the Radicals and the Claybanks, or conservative Unionists, battled for control. The division had threatened to give the election to McClellan. Lincoln instructed Nicolay to bring the two sides together and report to him regarding his prospects in that state. In a long written report to the president, Nicolay indicated that personal animosities and ambitions, not ideology, had poisoned the political environment among Missouri Unionists. However, he wrote Lincoln that in view of the critical nature of the election, personal obstacles to party unity "were fast giving way," though many Claybanks planned to vote for McClellan and some Radicals were still alienated by their dislike for Lincoln.[44]

Northeastern intellectuals contributed their pens to the National Union campaign. Having recovered from the shock of a crude, joke-

---

[42] As quoted in Waugh, *Reelecting Lincoln*, 308.

[43] John Hay to Francis Lieber, 29 September 1864, Michael Burlingame, *At Lincoln's Side: John Hay's Civil War Correspondence and Selected Writings* (Carbondale: Southern Illinois University Press, 2000) 95–96, n. 124.

[44] John G. Nicolay to the President, 18 October 1864, Lincoln Papers, Robert Todd Lincoln Collection, Library of Congress, Washington, DC.

telling Western prairie lawyer occupying the White House, writers, poets, and editors of prominent literary journals found that Lincoln possessed a great deal of traditional American common sense and honesty. More importantly, as James Russell Lowell wrote, Lincoln "is the exponent of principles vital to our peace, dignity, and renown,—of all that can save America from becoming Mexico, and insure popular freedom for centuries to come."[45] In early 1864 Lincoln had flattered Lowell, the influential poet, essayist, and editor of the *North American Review*, when he wrote the magazine's publishers expressing his delight with a favorable article that the New Englander had written on the president's war and antislavery policies. Rarely did Lincoln respond to commentaries in magazines or newspapers, but in this case, because of the strength of Lowell's essay in support of his administration, he made an exception and told its publishers that the article "will be of value to the country."[46] Inspired by the president's letter, Lowell, before the fall election, wrote three additional political essays in aid of Lincoln and the National Union party.

The support that Northern Protestant churches gave to the Republican party in the 1864 campaign is fairly well-known among students of the war's political history. though a recent book on religion and the Civil War ignores the election.[47] However, neither the mutual relationship that developed between Lincoln and the Protestant establishment or the crucial importance of church bishops, ministers, and editors in the campaign have been adequately described. The Methodist Episcopal Church, the leading denomination in the North, provided the greatest aid to the Republican or National Union campaign. While not as prominent, other Protestant churches joined in the Union crusade with a religious and moral fervor probably not known before or since in an American election. Having fought the slavocracy and its Southern church

---

[45] James Russell Lowell, "The Next General Election," *North American Review* 99 (October 1864): 569–71.

[46] Abraham Lincoln to William Crosby and Henry P. Nichols, 16 January 1864, *Collected Works*, ed. Basler, 7:132, 132–33n.

[47] A recent book on religion and the Civil War ignores the election. See Randall M. Miller, Harry S. Stout, and Charles Reagan Wilson, eds., *Religion and the American Civil War* (New York and Oxford: Oxford University Press, 1998).

apologists before the war, Northern Protestant leaders had become more intensely Union and antislavery as the war progressed, a position that Lincoln certainly appreciated. Though the president had not moved as quickly against slavery as they wanted, Protestant leaders in 1864 applauded his support of the proposed abolition amendment, his recognition of God's moral purposes in the war, his strong commitment to Republican institutions, and his uncompromising determination to suppress the rebellion. These clergymen also admired his honesty and personal probity. They viewed his reelection as a necessity to defeat the evil forces at work in the Southern rebellion and in the Copperhead movement of the North.

A skeptic in early life, on several occasions during the war Lincoln met with Protestant delegations and expressed his conviction that God was working his way through the terrible ordeal and "will give us the rightful result." He reportedly told a group of ministers in late 1862 that he considered himself "an instrument of Providence" in the war.[48] In June 1863 Lincoln informed a committee of the Presbyterian General Assembly, who presented him with resolutions supporting his administration, that "from the beginning I saw that the issues of our great struggle depended on Divine interposition and favor." He promised the delegation: "Relying, as I do, upon the Almighty Power, and encouraged as I am by...the support which I receive from Christian men, I shall not hesitate to use all the means at my control to secure the termination of this rebellion."[49] Church leaders concluded that Democrats showed no such determination to suppress the Southern insurrection.

As the war became long and tragic, Lincoln proclaimed days of humiliation, fasting, and prayer to get the nation right with God. During the 1864 political campaign, he issued two such proclamations. In the first proclamation on 7 July, he requested that all loyal citizens, including those in the military, "assemble in their preferred places of public worship" on 4 August for the observance of "a day of national

---

[48] Richard N. Current, *The Lincoln Nobody Knows* (New York: Hill and Wang, 1958) 72–73.

[49] Reply to Members of the Presbyterian General Assembly, 2 June 1863, *Collected Works*, ed. Basler, 6:244–45.

humiliation and prayer," and ask for the speedy suppression of the rebellion and the end of the war.[50] Then, on 20 October Lincoln issued a proclamation setting aside the last Thursday in November "as a day of Thanksgiving and Praise to Almighty God" and requesting Americans to "reverently humble themselves in the dust and from thence offer up penitent and fervent prayers and supplications to the Great Disposer of events for a return of the inestimable blessings of Peace, Union and Harmony throughout the land."[51] Protestant leaders and at least one Catholic bishop praised Lincoln's action in proclaiming days of prayer, repentance, and thanksgiving for the successful end of the war.[52]

One should not conclude, as some historians have, that Lincoln had mainly, if not exclusively political purposes in mind in his religious pronouncements.[53] His frequent reference to the role of Providence in the war, especially during the conflict's later stages, is evidence of his growing spirituality, prompted by a psychological need to explain the tragic conflict in the context of the religious culture that he understood. On one occasion in September 1864, when presented with a Bible by a group of Baltimore blacks who had no political constituency, Lincoln expressed to them that "all the good the Savior gave to the world was communicated through this book.... It is the best gift that God has given to man."[54] On another occasion in September the president wrote Eliza P. Gurney that:

> The purposes of the Almighty are perfect, and must prevail, though we erring mortals may fail to accurately perceive them in advance.... We [should] acknowledge His wisdom and our own error therein. Meanwhile we must work earnestly in the best

---

[50] Proclamation of a Day of Prayer, 7 July 1864, *Collected Works*, ed. Basler, 7:431–32.

[51] Proclamation of Thanksgiving, 20 October 1864, *Collected Works*, ed. Basler, 8:55–56.

[52] *Christian Advocate and Journal*, 24 November 1864; Nicolay and Hay, *Lincoln*, 6:325.

[53] Allen Guelzo, *Abraham Lincoln: Redeemer President* (Grand Rapids MI: William B. Eerdmans Publishing Co., 1999) 313–14.

[54] Reply to Loyal Colored People of Baltimore upon Presentation of a Bible, 7 September 1864, *Collected Works*, ed. Basler, 7:542.

light He gives us, trusting that so working still conduces to the great ends He ordains. Surely He intends some great good to follow this mighty convulsion, which no mortal could make, and no mortal could stay."

Lincoln assured Ms. Gurney that "I am much indebted to the good christian people of the country for their constant prayers and consolations."[55] Lincoln could not reasonably be charged with having a political motive or with hypocrisy in expressing his religious sentiments to the Baltimore blacks and Ms. Gurney who could not vote. Like Protestant leaders and others in 1864, he blended the presumed purposes of Providence with those of the Union in the war. Due partly to Lincoln, civil religion had become a powerful force for the Union, Republicans, and emancipation in the 1864 campaign.

The Methodist Church was in the forefront of the Protestant effort to sustain Lincoln and the Union cause in the election. Meeting in a general (national) conference in Philadelphia in May 1864, three weeks before the Republican convention that renominated Lincoln, Methodist leaders passed a resolution supporting Lincoln and his efforts to end slavery, suppress the "wicked rebellion," and restore an undivided Union "founded on the Word of God, and securing in righteousness liberty and equal rights to all." On 18 May a delegation from the general conference officially presented the address to the president, a copy of which he had obtained before the meeting. Lincoln, in a carefully written response, praised all of the churches for their support of the government, singling out the Methodists "as the most important of all." "The Methodist Church," he declared, "sends more soldiers to the field, more nurses to the hospital, and more prayers to Heaven than any. God bless the Methodist Church—bless all the churches—and blessed be God, Who, in this our great trial, giveth us the churches."[56]

---

[55] Abraham Lincoln to Eliza P. Gurney, 4 September 1864, *Collected Works*, ed. Basler, 535.

[56] Response to Methodists, 18 May 1864, *Collected Works*, ed. Basler, 7:350–51. Lincoln wrote this response on the day before the meeting. William Warren Sweet, *The Methodist Episcopal Church and the Civil War* (Cincinnati: Methodist Book Concern Press, 1912) 89–90.

Methodist leaders proved true to their promise of support for Lincoln in the presidential campaign. Bishop Matthew Simpson, whose good will Lincoln cultivated, delivered "lectures on patriotic themes" in several northeastern cities, ending his tour on 3 November with a stirring Union speech to a standing-room only audience at New York's Academy of Music.[57] Bishop Gilbert Haven of New England in a sermon preached in Boston on 11 September admonished all Methodists to "march to the ballot-box, an army of Christ...and deposit a million of votes for [the church's] true representative, and...the final blow" will be given "to the reeling [rebel] fiend." Haven insisted that "the Church must do her duty in this hour, and that duty is, by every righteous means in her power to secure the reelection of Abraham Lincoln."[58] Except for Kentucky pastors, few Methodist ministers or army chaplains during the campaign failed to preach the pure Union gospel from their pulpits. On 6 September Lincoln reportedly remarked to Joseph H. Thompson, a New York Congregation minister, that "I rely upon the religious sentiment of the country" in this election, "which I am told is very largely for me."[59]

Beginning in August and until after the election, Lincoln remained in Washington, where he gave close attention to the canvass as well as to the war effort. Though declining to make explicit political addresses, he still contributed to the National Union campaign. The president spoke to Union regiments returning from the front, visited soldiers and sailors in the many hospitals in Washington, and attended charitable events to raise money for the troops. On these occasions Lincoln talked about the virtues of the Union and free government while carefully avoiding specific appeals for support at the polls.[60] His presence among the troops and his obvious sympathy for those who were suffering carried great political weight, extending well beyond the bounds of the District of Columbia. Lincoln pointedly remarked to a group of Maryland

---

[57] New York *Tribune*, 7 November 1864; *Harper's Weekly* (15 October 1864) 659.

[58] Gilbert Haven, *National Sermons: Sermons, Speeches and Letters on Slavery and its War, From the Passage of the Fugitive Slave Bill to the Election of President Grant* (Boston: Lee and Shepard, 1869) 86.

[59] Fehrenbacher, ed., *Recollected Words of Lincoln* (Stanford CA: Stanford University Press, 1996) 446.

[60] Nicolay and Hay, *Lincoln*, 10:354–55.

serenaders on 19 October that in support of his "purpose to save the country and it's [sic] liberties, no classes of people seem so nearly unanamous [sic] as the soldiers in the field and the seamen afloat. Do they not have the hardest of it? Who shall quail while they do not? God bless the soldiers and seamen with all their brave commanders."[61] Lincoln probably understood that these remarks would receive wide circulation in the press and contribute to his identification with the sacrifices of the men fighting for the Union. Such patriotic comments were political and designed mainly to aid him and the National Union party in the election.

In response to a frantic appeal from Governor Oliver Morton for aid, Lincoln's faith in the support of the troops prompted him to write General Sherman and request that he release his Indiana soldiers to return home and vote in the crucial October state election. The president told Sherman that the loss of Indiana "to the friends of the Government would go far toward losing the whole Union cause" in November. He reminded Sherman that "Indiana is the only important State, voting in October, whose soldiers cannot vote in the field. Any thing you can safely do to let her soldiers, or any part of them, go home and vote at the State election, will be greatly in point. They need not remain for the Presidential election." Lincoln made it clear to the general that "this is, in no sense, an order, but is merely intended to impress you with the importance, to the army itself, of your doing all you safely can" to aid the Union cause in Indiana.[62]

Sherman, who thought of himself above politics, was sufficiently impressed by the president's appeal, and whether ordered or not, he permitted several thousand Indiana soldiers to return home and vote. The furloughed soldiers, with their votes and political influence in the

---

[61] Response to a Serenade, 19 October 1864, *Collected Works*, ed. Basler, 8:52–53.

[62] Abraham Lincoln to General William Tecumseh Sherman, 19 September 1864, *Collected Works*, ed. Basler, 11 and note. Lincoln, however, rejected Morton's plea for him to suspend the draft in the state until after the elections. William D. Foulke, *Life of Oliver P. Morton, Including his Important Speeches*, 2 vols. (Indianapolis: Bowen-Merrill, 1899) 1:366–68.

communities, contributed to the overwhelming victory of the National Union party in Indiana.[63]

Lincoln also encouraged troops to vote in the field. Republican Congressman Elihu B. Washburne remarked, perhaps with exaggeration regarding Lincoln's anxiety: The president was so anxious to have the soldiers vote that "if it could be done in no other way, [he] would take a carpet bag and go around and collect those votes himself."[64] Lincoln's confidence in the troops was rewarded on election day; nine out of ten of them voted for "Father Abraham," as they affectionately called him.[65]

The 11 October elections in Indiana, Ohio, and Pennsylvania foretold a Lincoln victory in November. In Indiana and Ohio, the Union party won almost all of the congressional seats, easily returned Governor Morton to office, and won a narrow victory in Pennsylvania. On the same day, the adoption by Maryland voters of a new constitution abolishing slavery especially pleased Lincoln, who had lobbied for its approval.[66] Though historians have assumed that his election was inevitable after the Republican successes in October, Lincoln remained anxious about the outcome. Two days after the victories in the lower Union states, the president, while waiting in the War Department's telegraph office for military dispatches, jotted down his "estimated electoral vote" for each state in the November election. Lincoln calculated that he would win by a close margin of 120 votes to McClellan's 114.[67]

A few days later the president received a frantic appeal from Congressman Washburne to send the Illinois troops home to vote in order to "save the State from the most appalling calamity"—a loss to the Democrats. Despite the fact that Lincoln believed the vote would be

---

[63] Kenneth Stampp, *Indiana Politics during the Civil War* (Indianapolis: Indiana Historical Bureau, 1949) 252.

[64] As cited in Donald, *Lincoln*, 544.

[65] William C. Davis, *Lincoln's Men: How President Lincoln Became Father to An Army and A Nation* (New York: The Free Press, 1999) 222–23.

[66] Response to a Serenade, 19 October 1864, *Collected Works*, ed. Basler, 8:52.

[67] Estimated Electoral Vote, 13 October 1864, *Collected Works*, ed. Basler, 8:46; David Homer Bates, *Lincoln in the Telegraph Office* (New York: The Century Co., 1907) 278.

close in his home state and the "Copperheads," as he labeled the McClellan forces, might win it, he refused to act. He filed Washburne's letter with the notation on the envelope: "Stampeded."[68]

As it turned out, Lincoln won handily in the electoral vote. McClellan carried only 3 states, despite winning 45 percent of the national popular vote. A swing of 31,500 total votes in 8 states would have given him the election. The Democrats, Lincoln reportedly remarked, would have won the election "if, instead of resolving that the war was a failure, [they] had resolved that I was a failure and denounced me for not more vigorously prosecuting it."[69] Though partly correct, Lincoln must have realized that military successes at Atlanta and elsewhere at least made his reelection possible if not probable. Furthermore, the vigorous campaign work of hundreds of aroused Republican activists at home and in the military forces and Protestant leaders in the North also contributed mightily to his success. In addition, the president's own shrewd and quiet management of political affairs in Washington proved important in achieving the victory and the success of his party, which not only won the presidential election but also increased its strength in Congress and in state offices throughout the North. Without Lincoln's skillful leadership, occurring during the Union's greatest crisis, it is reasonable to conclude that the Republican victory in the election would not have happened. Lincoln's defeat would have inevitably changed the timing of the war's end, the pace of emancipation, and the course of reconstruction. Furthermore, this president's reputation in history would have been severely diminished by a defeat in 1864. Instead, Lincoln's 1864 victory made possible the fulfillment of the

---

[68] Elihu B. Washburne to Abraham Lincoln, 17 October 1864, Lincoln Papers; Nicolay and Hay, *Lincoln*, 9:372.

[69] Hugh McCulloch, *Men and Measures of Half a Century* (New York: Charles Scribner's Sons, 1882) 162. For state election returns, see Hyman, "Election of 1864," Appendix, 1244

war's purposes and Lincoln's apotheosis as America's greatest statesman and folk hero.

RESHAPING THE MARRIAGE:
MARY LINCOLN AND POST-ASSASSINATION MEMORY

Jennifer Fleischner

By the time Mary Lincoln began to emerge from the shock of her husband's assassination and started sharing her memories of her dead husband in letters to her personal correspondents, William H. Herndon had already conceived the idea of collecting other people's memories of Abraham Lincoln in order to write and publish something of his own on Lincoln's "inner life." Both were participants in the creation of Lincoln memory, yet from the start their visions of what that memory should be diverged. In a note to Charles Sumner that she wrote 9 May to accompany her gift to him of one of Lincoln's many canes, Mary made her first known references to her "idolized Husband" and to his cane as a "relic," a word resonant of the sacred.[1] One month later, on 10 June, while engaged in a battle with Illinois dignitaries over the burial and placement of a monument to commemorate Lincoln, she would invoke sacred rhetoric again and call her dead husband the "immortal Savior& Martyr for Freedom."[2] Meanwhile, Herndon, bent on creating a different Lincoln memory, had begun gathering reminiscences about Lincoln in May, and on 8 June, wrote fellow prospective Lincoln biographer, Josiah G. Holland, of his own intention to search for *"the facts & truths of*

---

[1] Mary Lincoln to Charles Sumner, 9 May 1865, *Mary Todd Lincoln: Her Life and Letters,* ed. Justin G. Turner & Linda Levitt Turner (New York: Alfred A. Knopf, 1972) 227–28.

[2] Mary Lincoln to Richard J. Oglesby, 10 June 1865, *Mary Todd Lincoln,* 243–44.

Lincoln's life—not fictions—not fables—not floating rumors, but *facts—solid facts & well attested truths.*"[3]

Mourning and biography are closely related. Both require calling up memories of the life of the person. In both, memory serves not merely to *give* shape to the past life, but to *reshape* it—in part, to make the life commensurate to the aims and needs of those doing the remembering. In the years following the assassination, Mary Lincoln needed the memory of Lincoln to take a certain shape for many understandable reasons: for private, emotional reasons as she mourned her husband of twenty-three years and for more public, social, and economic reasons, as she sought to secure a home for herself that matched not only her idea of what she was due as the president's widow, but also the kind of home that she said Lincoln had promised her once his second term was over. This is a memory she shared with her friend Sally Orne in August 1865 when the matter of finding a suitable home that she could afford was pressing upon her, and she was beginning to enlist her friends' aid in fundraising for herself.[4]

The conflict between Mary Lincoln and the first generation of Lincoln biographers was inevitable, emerging out of a clash of memory goals and needs. Mary wanted to preserve Lincoln's memory for her private use, and she was more than willing to enlist the rhetoric of Lincoln's martyrdom for her own ends. But the Civil War and the assassination made Lincoln's memory crucial to the unfolding of the national narrative, and Lincoln's memory was a lucrative business. As wife and widow, Mary Lincoln could not escape her fate as a subordinate figure in the evolving narrative of her husband's life. How Lincoln was to be remembered, in what terms, was anything but clear. Meanwhile, the letters Mary Lincoln wrote in the several years following the assassination show her increasing awareness of the high stakes for her in Lincoln memory. Above all, they demonstrate her growing alarm at the

---

[3] William H. Herndon to Josiah G. Holland, 8 June 1865, *Herndon's Informants: Letters, Interviews, and Statements about Abraham Lincoln,* ed. Douglas L. Wilson and Rodney O. Davis (Urbana: University of Illinois Press, 1998) xiv.

[4] Mary Lincoln to Mrs. Sally Orne, 31 August 1865, *Mary Todd Lincoln,* 269–71.

rising tide of public revelations about Lincoln's private life and the marriage.

To explore the question of post-assassination Lincoln memory and Mary Lincoln's relation to it, I focus on several critical moments that form a trajectory in Mary's confrontation with Lincoln memory during the first three years of widowhood. The first is a period in December 1865 during which she wrote letters in reaction to Holland's Lincoln biography; the next, in March 1867, concerns her reaction to Herndon's lectures on Lincoln, particularly the widely disseminated fourth lecture of November 1866, about Lincoln's tragic romance with Ann Rutledge; and her subsequent summons of her dressmaker and confidante, the ex-slave Elizabeth Keckley, in order to propose what would later become known as the "old clothes scandal." After this, I turn to May 1868, and the aftermath of the publication of Keckley's memoir, in which Keckley revealed the "secret history" (Keckley's words) of the old clothes scandal and published letters she received from Mary. I end in December 1868, after Mary fled to Europe with her son Tad and could look back across the ocean and judge those "boastful Americans" who—as she now saw it—had exploited their proximity to her for their own gain.

During this three-year period, from December 1865 through December 1868, Mary Lincoln engaged in an intensifying effort to preempt, rebut, and reshape Lincoln's memory as she watched it evolve in ways beyond her control. Her only access to the shaping of public memory was through personal letters, through which she hoped to influence the circulation of information, particularly about her marriage and her finances. It would have been unthinkable for her—even for *Mary Lincoln,* some Lincoln scholars might feel moved to add—to write a memoir herself. As Nathaniel Hawthorne once remarked upon his wife's fleeting ambitions to write, it would be like going to bed in public. Not that women were not publishing memoirs, but they were already fallen outsiders—for instance, lady spies, former slaves, journalists. If Mary felt that her life's history was not her own, she was right. Yet certainly, she was not about to give it up without comment or a fight.

On 6 December 1865, Mary Lincoln wrote her friend Mary Jane Welles about the new biographies that were coming out about her husband:

I have been trying to interest myself of late, in the different Biographies, of my Husband that have been sent me, from time to time. The last one, from the pen of Dr Holland, I have been looking over, this week. Some of his accounts are very minute & *one*, especially that he publishes, would have *pained* my husband, very much, if at *this* distant day, he had ever supposed, it would have appeared in print.[5]

  Two days earlier she had written Holland, thanking him for sending her a copy of his biography, but she also registered her concern about the same issue she would raise with her friend: the *minuteness* of Holland's information on a subject that at this "distant day" would have pained her husband. She wrote, "After a careful perusal of the work, I find the statements, in *most* instances, so very correct, that I feel quite surprised of the extent of your *minute* information."[6] Evidently, Mary was struck by Holland's knowledge of the details of Lincoln's abortive duel with James Shields back in Springfield in August/September 1842. She wrote, "After the reconciliation between the *contending* parties, Mr. L & myself mutually agreed, never to refer to it & except in an occasional light manner, between us, it was never mentioned. I am surprised, at *so* distant a day, you should have heard of the circumstance."

  The duel was an affair that occurred six weeks before their marriage and involved Mary; and given the circumstances it may have become a comical memory for the long-married couple. However, it is not likely the memory would have "pained" Lincoln as Mary contends (neither man was dishonored, and no one was injured); instead, Mary's anxiety about Holland's extensive information may have sprung from her realization that the period about which Holland knew such minutia coincided with the Lincolns' broken engagement, a detail Mary herself might have wished to forget. This period lasted from late December

---

[5] Mary Lincoln to Mary Jane Welles, 6 December 1865, *Mary Todd Lincoln*, 294–96.

[6] Mary Lincoln to Josiah G. Holland, 4 December 1865, *Mary Todd Lincoln*, 292–94.

1840, after Lincoln broke off from Mary, to their reconciliation in October 1842, after the Shields episode as recounted in Holland's book. During this time, Mary was deeply unhappy, as indicated by the letter she wrote her friend Mercy Ann Levering in June 1841: "The last two or three months have been of *interminable* length, after my gay companions of last winter have departed, I was left much to the solitude of my own thoughts, and some *lingering regrets* over the past," among these her flirtations that she worried may have driven a more important suitor (thought to be Lincoln) away.[7]

Holland said nothing about the couple's engagement in his book, but Mary may have wondered what he had heard about it, so in her letter to Holland she may have been eager to give him her own version of events for the time period surrounding the Shields duel. This she did, as she continued, "It is exceedingly painful to me, *now*, suffering under such an overwhelming bereavement to recall *that* happy time. My beloved husband, had so entirely devoted himself to me, for two years before my marriage, that I doubtless trespassed, many times & oft, upon his great tenderness & amiability of character." Perhaps as reinforcement, she repeated her memory of their happy two-year engagement in her letters to Mary Jane Welles on 6 December and to the Lincoln memoirist, the painter Francis Bicknell Carpenter, on 8 December. Moreover, the Shields affair, occurring when it did, seems to have worried another old wound—the memory of Lincoln's constancy, or inconstancy, of affection. In a passage written to Mary Jane Welles alone, not to Holland or Carpenter, Mary wrote, "It was always, music in my ears, both before & after our marriage, when my husband, told me, that I was the only one, he had ever thought of, or cared for. It will solace me to my grave."[8]

That this kind of recollection is more intimate than anything she might have readily told Holland or Carpenter—it is the sort of thing told to a girlfriend—could explain Mary's silence on this point to the men. Yet coming when it does, with no apparent prompting by what anyone

---

[7] Mary Todd to Mercy Ann Levering, June 1841, *Mary Todd Lincoln,* 25–28.

[8] Mary Todd Lincoln to Josiah G. Holland, 4 December 1865 and Mary Todd Lincoln to Mary Jane Welles 6 December 1865, *Mary Todd Lincoln,* 292–94.

has actually said about Lincoln having had other attachments, it seems that this particular memory was generated at this particular point out of Mary's concerns not about anything Holland said, but rather about what he might have left out.

In the months following her husband's assassination, Mary often spoke of her husband's devotion to her, but these letters to Holland, Welles, and Carpenter are the first recorded times that she specifically recalled their two-year engagement. If Mary could not with assurance know what Holland had heard, she likely knew whom he heard it from: her husband's old law partner, William H. Herndon, who had met Holland in Springfield in May earlier that year and become Holland's greatest source of information on Lincoln. If Mary connected Holland to Herndon, then her desire to tell her three correspondents about her two-year engagement—and her additional confidence to her friend that Lincoln had loved only her—was a preemptive strike against future Herndon revelations. At that point, she may not have been thinking as far back as Ann Rutledge (whose engagement to Lincoln prior to Mary Herndon had yet to report to the world). She need only have been remembering back to the time of their engagement and her brother-in-law's cousin, Mathilda Edwards. For as Mary had known and probably remembered, Mathilda had been her rival in the winter of 1840: the woman Lincoln may have believed he loved when he broke his engagement with her.[9]

By December 1865 Mary had reason to think about both the potential power and dangers of putting her memories of her marriage in her letters. Carpenter, for instance, had already published a portion of what she wrote to him on 15 November about her last intimate carriage ride with her husband. It is a now famous dialogue, quoted often to illustrate the Lincolns' sadness and the distance that developed between them after the death of their twelve-year son, Willie. Confiding to Carpenter, Mary had recalled her husband telling her: "We must *both*, be more cheerful in the future—between the war & the loss of our darling

---

[9] For the chronology of the courtship and the Mathilda Edwards episode, I rely on Douglas L. Wilson's, *Honor's Voice: The Transformation of Abraham Lincoln* (New York: Alfred A. Knopf, 1998).

Willie—we have both, been very miserable."[10] By the time of her next letter to the painter, the one of 8 December, she had seen her own words in print, and it bothered her. So after commenting on Holland's account of the Shields affair, she turned her attention to Carpenter's public use of her private letter: "I must say, I was greatly surprised, to see a simple letter of mine, written, when my heart was bursting, with its great sorrow, in print. I will forgive you—in the hope, it may never occur again."[11]

Ironically, after she was out of the White House the lack of privacy troubled Mary in ways it had not when she was there. No doubt Lincoln's presence had been a protection. As 1865 drew to a close, Mary split her focus between managing the past, by intervening in Lincoln memory and commemoration, and in managing her future, by trying to secure an income and a home. By the end of December, she had grown despondent about her financial situation and her homelessness. Embittered by the decision of Congress to grant her only one year of Lincoln's salary with no hope of receiving the remaining three years or any form of assistance, she felt that an ungrateful American public and their representatives were denying her the home that—according to her memory—her husband had promised. By this time, she had begun to speak of her desire for a home in connection to a wish for privacy, as if exposure in hotels were now associated in her mind with the exposure she was feeling as memoirs and biographies of her husband began to emerge. On 30 December she wrote Sally Orne: "We, as an afflicted family, *well knew*, we had lost our *all*—the *nation*, has sealed the decree, by their vote, that there, is to be, no privacy, for us, in the future, our grief & we, ourselves—can have, no retirement."[12]

The retirement she sought came no time soon; indeed, the following year gave Mary Lincoln more reason to feel exposed. Herndon had been enormously successful in collecting letters, interviews, and statements about Lincoln and by January 1866 had delivered three lectures on

---

[10] Mary Lincoln to Francis B. Carpenter, 15 November 1865, *Mary Todd Lincoln,* 283–85.

[11] Mary Lincoln to Francis B. Carpenter, 8 December 1865, *Mary Todd Lincoln,* 297–300.

[12] Mary Lincoln to Sally Orne, 30 December 1865, *Mary Todd Lincoln,* 318–20.

Lincoln. Hoping to interview Mary Lincoln, he had written Robert with a request, and Mary responded in a friendly, flattering letter. One imagines that her positive response was a strategy, since in Herndon's note to Robert there had been something that worried her, and she wanted Herndon to explain: "You will excuse me, enclosing you, this sentence, of yours & asking its meaning." The sentence Mary had clipped from Herndon's letter and enclosed contained his express interest in writing about her: "I want to give a sketch—a short life of your mother in my biography up to her marriage to your father—or say up to 1846—or 1858—. I wish to do her justice fully—so that the world will understand things better. You understand me."[13] Several years later, Herndon would say that when they met for the interview Mary tried to convince him to leave her out of his biography, that she said, "It was not unusual to mention the facts, the history of the wife, in the biography of her husband, further than to say that the two were married at such and such a place."[14] If Mary made this request—and it seems plausible given the circumstances and Herndon's hinting sentence—it had little effect. In November Herndon delivered his fourth lecture, a bomb dropped on the Lincoln marriage: the tragic "true history" of Lincoln's early love for Ann Rutledge, with Herndon's speculation how after Ann's death in 1835, Lincoln "never addressed another woman" with love and affection. Although it was not the sketch of her life that Herndon delivered into the hands of the public, as Mary had feared, it was something far worse for her—a total undermining of the marriage.

Herndon's argument that the Ann Rutledge story dissolved Mary's culpability in the difficulties of the marriage was no consolation for Mary, who had just seen the world informed that Lincoln never loved her. Nor could she have cared about Herndon's theory of the biographer's responsibility to tell the "*necessary* truth"—as he put it in a letter to Charles Hart.[15] As a shaper of Lincoln memory, Herndon was

---

[13] Mary Lincoln to William H. Herndon, 28 August 1866, enclosure cited in Wilson and Davis, *Herndon's Informants*, 326.

[14] "Mrs. Lincoln's Denial, and What She Says," printed broadside, Illinois State Historical Library.

[15] William H. Herndon to Charles H. Hart, 26 November 1866, *The Hidden Lincoln: From the Letters and Papers of William H. Herndon*, ed. Emanuel Hertz

shifting the terms of remembrance from a notion of sacred memory to sacred history, an important theoretical move. In the lecture, published first as a broadside then widely disseminated in the newspapers, Herndon defended himself with an argument that *history* was sacred—that is, not the biographical life, not even Lincoln's life:

> I am willing that my character among you may stand or fall by the substantial truthfulness of this lecture, *in every particular.* Truth in history is my sole and only motive for making this sad story now public for the first time. History is sacred, and should be so held eternally by all men. What would you give for a manly, honest, candid and noble biography of Washington.... I dare not keep these facts longer. Men need to read history by a blazing light. This is my apology for the publication of these facts *now*, and I appeal to time for my defense.[16]

Not surprisingly, appeals to sacred *history* held no interest for Mary Lincoln, who needed the idea of sacred memory. The anxiety raised by Holland's familiarity with the minutia of her husband's life was nothing compared to the humiliation and rage Herndon's revelations made her feel. It is not known when she first learned of the lecture, but 4 March 1867 found her writing what must have been one in a series of rebuttals of Herndon's narratives in the only venue available to her: personal letters. To her husband's executor, David Davis, who had evidently tried to soothe her, she wrote:

> As you justly remark, each & every one has had, a little romance in their early days—but as my husband was *truth itself,*

(Garden City NY: Blue Ribbon Books, 1940) 40. For more on Herndon's relationship with Mary Lincoln, see Douglas L. Wilson, "William H. Herndon and Mary Lincoln," *Journal of the Abraham Lincoln Association* 22:1 (Summer 2001): 1–27. I am indebted to Dr. Wilson for making his article available to me before publication.

   [16] William H. Herndon, "Lincoln, Ann Rutledge and The Pioneers of New Salem," delivered November 16, 1866, in Springfield, Illinois; printed broadside, Illinois State Historical Society; reprinted in limited edition, Harry Rosecrans Burke, ed. (Herrin, Illinois: Trovillion Private Press, 1945) 5–6.

and as he always assured me, he had cared for no one but myself, the false W. H. (au contraire) I shall assuredly remain firm in my conviction—that *Ann Rutledge*, is a myth—for in all his confidential communications, such a romantic name, was never breathed, and concealment could have been no object, as Mr. H's vivid imagination, supposed this pathetic tragedy to occur when Mr L was eighteen & I did not know him, until he was thirty years old! Nor did his life or his joyous laugh, lead one to suppose his heart, was in any unfortunate woman's grave—but in the proper place with his loved wife & children—I assure you, it will not be *well with him*—if he makes the *least* disagreeable or false allusion in the future. *He* will be closely watched.[17]

Two days later, encouraged by the negative criticism Herndon's lecture was reaping, including Robert's reaction, and having just read an open letter that her former pastor, Dr. James Smith, had sent to the Chicago *Tribune,* denouncing Herndon's betrayal of his friend and the family, she escalated her threats against Herndon, and wrote Davis:

W[illiam] H[erndon] may consider himself a ruined man, in attempting to disgrace others, the vials of wrath, will be poured upon his own head...if W.H-utters another word—and is not silent with his infamous falsehoods in the future, *his* life is not worth, living for—I *have* friends, if his *low* soul thought that my great affliction—had left me without them. In the future, he may well say, his *prayers*—"Revenge is sweet, especially to womankind but there are some of mankind left, who will wreak it upon him—He is a dirty dog.[18]

It was about this time that Mary wrote a letter to Elizabeth Keckley with a bold and, in the end, disastrous request: "Now, Lizzie, I want to ask a favor of you. It is imperative that I should do something for my relief, and I want you to meet me in New York, between the 30th of

---

[17] Mary Lincoln to David Davis, 4 March 1867, *Mary Todd Lincoln,* 414–15.
[18] Mary Lincoln to David Davis, 6 March 1867, *Mary Todd Lincoln,* 415–16.

August and the 5th of September next, to assist me in disposing of a portion of my wardrobe."[19] On all fronts, her efforts to manage her private affairs were faltering. In June the year before, she had bought a house on the expectation of financial support from Simon Cameron, among others. This support never materialized, leaving her financially overwhelmed and emotionally desperate. It may be that in March 1867, after the blow of reading Herndon's lecture, she decided to take matters into her own hands. Lizzie had been an emotional mainstay in the White House, particularly after Willie's death and the assassination; she may have turned to her now out of the memory of those former offices. She may have also felt that Lizzie, her former servant, would be one person she could count on to actually do what she wanted.

The two women met at the St. Denis Hotel in New York in September; it was a year after Mary had met Herndon at the St. Nicholas in Springfield. In some respects, these interviews were comparable: as she had with Herndon, Mary went to meet Keckley expecting to engineer a certain outcome for herself; yet as with Herndon, her interview with Keckley yielded results practically the opposite of what she desired. Keckley remained in New York through the fall and winter to handle the business of auctioning of Mary's clothes and jewelry through a brokerage house, while Mary retreated to Chicago, where she posted letters of direction to Keckley. But sometime between October and April, while she was living in New York, Keckley wrote a memoir, without Mary's knowledge, focusing on her relationship with Mary Lincoln and devoting the entire last section to an account of Mary's machinations "behind the scenes" in New York during the fall. It was published in April 1868, under the inviting title, *Behind the Scenes; or, Thirty Years a Slave and Four Years in the White House: Concerning various things, including her service for Senator Jefferson Davis and in the Lincoln White House.*

For Mary, Keckley's public betrayal of her confidence—she even published Mary's letters to her—must have felt like *déjà vu*. It was not just Herndon, for by then the once-forgiven Carpenter had joined the ranks of betraying biographers in her eyes, "the *indefatigable* F. B.

---

[19] Mary Lincoln to Elizabeth Keckley, March [undated] 1867, *Mary Todd Lincoln,* 417–18.

Carpenter" she now called him, "a second edition of Mr. L's crazy drinking law partner Herndon endeavoring to *write* himself into notice leaving truth, far, far, in the distance."[20] In her book, Keckley even defended her telling "the secret history" of the old clothes scandal with a theory of sympathetic truth-telling that mirrored Herndon's:

> The veil of mystery must be drawn aside; the origin of a fact must be brought to light with the naked fact itself. If I have betrayed confidence in anything I have published, it has been to place Mrs. Lincoln in a better light before the world. A breach of trust—if breach it can be called—of this kind is always excusable.... The world have [sic] judged Mrs. Lincoln by the facts that float upon the surface, and through her have partially judged me, and the only way to convince them that wrong was not meditated is to explain motives that actuated us. I have written nothing that can place Mrs. Lincoln in a worse light before the world than the light in which she now stands, therefore the secret history that I publish can do her no harm.[21]

The newspapers that had been attacking Mary Lincoln for her vulgarity and greed in the fall now leapt to her defense in the spring. The issue for them was not simply one of privacy, but that Keckley had

---

[20] Mary Lincoln to Henry C. Deming, 16 December 1867, "Unpublished Mary Todd Lincoln," ed. Thomas F. Schwartz and Kim M. Bauer, *Journal of the American Lincoln Association,* 17:2 (1996) 14. What had set Mary off against Carpenter was an article in which he described Lincoln and Seward, whom Mary disliked, sharing a speaking engagement together in Boston after the end of the session of Congress in late summer 1848 and also, perhaps more pertinently, Carpenter's suggestion that Lincoln knew a lady by the name of "Fanny." According to Mary, "Neither Mr. L. or myself knew any *young or old* lady by the name of Fanny Mc____." As she continued, "C. intruded frequently into Mr. L's office when *time* was too precious to be idled. *Of this fact,* I am well aware. To think of this *stranger,* silly adventurer, daring to write a work, entitle "The inner life of Abraham Lincoln." Each scribbling writer, almost strangers to Mr. L. subscribe themselves, *his most* intimate friend!!"

[21] Elizabeth Keckley, Formerly a Slave, but More Recently Modiste, and Friend to Mrs. Abraham Lincoln, *Behind the Scenes: or, Thirty Years a Slave, and Four Years in the White House* (New York: G. W. Carleton & Co., Publishers, 1868) xiv–xv.

violated the social hierarchies of class and race relations. One alarmed reviewer at the influential Washington *National Intelligencer* demanded:

> If the negro servant in one conspicuous home may be tolerated in spreading to the world her representations of all the most secret and unguarded words that are uttered in the bosom of such a family, what family of eminence that employs a negro is safe from such desecration? Where will it end? What family that has a servant may not, in fact, have its peace and happiness destroyed by such treacherous creatures as the Keckley woman?[22]

A reviewer at the Springfield *Republican* (where Holland worked) warned against the dangerous consequences of universal education:

> The theories about the diffusion of knowledge and the education of the masses, are all very fine, and within certain limits work well. It is not pleasant, to be sure, to have a cook so literally inclined as to be continually removing all your pet books from the library to the kitchen, and who insists on the first reading of the morning paper while she is getting breakfast; or a housemaid who prefers reading your letters to attending to her own proper duties. But all these can be patiently endured in consideration of the many benefits that are supposed to accrue to Bridget and Dinah on account of a smattering of knowledge. But when Bridget and Dinah takes to writing books instead, and selects for themes the conversations and events that occur in the privacy of the family circle, we respectfully submit that it is carrying the thing a little too far. The line must be drawn somewhere, and we protest that it had better be traced before all the servant girls are educated up to the point of writing up the private history of the families in which they are engaged.[23]

---

[22] *National Intelligencer*, 25 April 1868.
[23] *Springfield Republican*, 22 April 1868.

Keckley made one public response to her critics, in a letter to the editor of the *New York Citizen*:

> I maintain that all I have written of Mrs. Lincoln has had a tendency to place her in a better light before the world.... The impartial reader of the book, if I mistake not, will...agree that it is not written in the spirit of "an angry Negro servant." All through the book I have spoken kindly of Mrs. L [sic]. I have simply written the truth, because I felt confident that, where slander has been so free and vile, there was no occasion to shrink from the truth.[24]

Herndon had not responded publicly to his critics, but in a private letter to a friend rationalized that was not unlike Keckley's: "Mrs. Lincoln must be put properly before the world. She hates me, yet I *can* and *will* do her justice; she hates me on the same grounds a thief hates a policeman who knows a dangerous secret about him.... Poor woman! The world has no charity for her and yet justice must be done her, being careful not to *injure* her husband. All that I know ennobles them both."[25]

Mary Lincoln's letters reveal no extended reaction to Keckley's memoir; perhaps because this time the newspapers had taken up her defense, because Keckley, as a black dressmaker, was basically dismissible, and because Keckley's revelations exposed Mary's botched finances, not a botched marriage. In fact, in her book, Keckley took Mary's side, if not her tone, against Herndon: "Mr. Herndon's story...is a pleasant piece of fiction. When it appeared Mrs. Lincoln felt shocked that one who pretended to be the friend of her dead husband should deliberately seek to blacken his memory."[26] Yet in May, just weeks after *Behind the Scenes* was published, Mary did challenge Keckley's charge of debt in a letter, discussing a prospective European tour, written to her friend Rhoda White (wife of James W. White, former justice in New

---

[24] Elizabeth Keckley, Letter to the editor of the *New York Citizen*, 21 April 1868.

[25] Herndon to Charles H. Hart, 26 November 1866, in Hertz, *The Hidden Lincoln*, 40.

[26] Keckley, *Behind the Scenes*, 235.

York Superior Court): "This proposition [of a tour] from me, does not argue *a debt of $70,000!! As the colored* historian asserts."[27]

It is not understood why Keckley wrote and published *Behind the Scenes* nor what role her collaborator, the former war correspondent and anti-slavery journalist James Redpath, played. Keckley maintained that she never intended to betray her former employer or that Mary's letters be published. She also apparently suggested that Mary knew that she was writing a book. In any event, the publication of Keckley's memoir was a culminating blow against Mary's efforts to shape her own public image. For, indeed, since she was still very much alive, it was her *image*, not her *memory*, that concerned her.

Mary Lincoln and Tad sailed for Europe in September that year. Living abroad among people who never heard of Herndon or Keckley took the sting out of Mary Lincoln's recent battles with memoirists and biographers. Distance and novelty temporarily gave her a sense of escape, even of triumph, over those who had used *her* to promote themselves—as she now more philosophically viewed the Lincoln chroniclers. Things were done differently in Europe; the privacy of royalty was respected. As she wrote Eliza Slataper from Frankfort in December:

> [T]he most charming of *all* dressmakers, [a man named Popp], who receives orders from America, and makes for the royal family of Prussia & all the nobility, has just made me up some heavy mourning silks, richly trimmed with crape.... He [Popp] has made dresses for Queen Victoria's daughters so long, that a few years since, shen [she passed] through [F. and] stopped at this house—she sent for him & of course he obeyed the summons. He is a very modest man & never speaks of it himself. How different *some* of our boastful Americans, would be.[28]

---

[27] Mary Lincoln to Rhoda White, 2 May 1868, *Mary Todd Lincoln,* 475–77.

[28] Mary Lincoln to Eliza Slataper, 13 December 1868, *Mary Todd Lincoln,* 493–96.

LINCOLN'S LEGACY FOR OUR TIME

James M. McPherson

When Abraham Lincoln breathed his last at 7:22 A.M. on 15 April 1865, Secretary of War Edwin M. Stanton intoned: "Now he belongs to the ages."

Stanton's remark was more prescient than he knew, for Lincoln's image and his legacy became the possession not only of future ages of Americans but also of people of other nations. On the centenary of Lincoln's birth in 1909, Leo Tolstoy described him as "a Christ in miniature, a saint of humanity." An Islamic leader projected a more militant image of Lincoln, declaring that America's sixteenth president "spoke with a voice of thunder...and his deeds were as strong as the rock." When Jacqueline Kennedy lived in the White House, she sought comfort in the Lincoln Room in times of trouble. "The kind of peace I felt in that room," she recalled, "was what you feel when going into a church. I used to feel his strength, I'd sort of be talking to him."[1]

Martin Luther King, Jr., tried to persuade Jacqueline Kennedy's husband to issue a second Emancipation Proclamation on the hundredth anniversary of the first. John Kennedy demurred, so King went ahead on his own. When he stood on the steps of the Lincoln Memorial in August 1963 to deliver his "I have a Dream" speech, King declared: "Fivescore years ago, a great American, in whose shadow we stand today, signed the Emancipation Proclamation. This momentous decree came as a great

---

1 Tolstoy and Kennedy quoted in Merrill D. Peterson, *Lincoln and American Memory* (New York: Oxford University Press, 1994) 185, 324n.

beacon of hope to millions of Negro slaves who had been scarred in the flames of withering injustice."[2]

Lincoln could not anticipate the reverence that millions would feel for him in future ages, but he *was* intensely aware, as he told Congress in December 1861 when America was engulfed in a tragic Civil War, that this struggle to preserve the Union "is not altogether for today—it is for a vast future also." More than any other president of the United States except perhaps Thomas Jefferson, Abraham Lincoln had a profound sense of history. He did not acquire it by formal education. Unlike Woodrow Wilson, Lincoln did not have a Ph.D. He did not study history in college or high school; indeed, he did not study it in school at all, for he had less than a year of formal schooling, which included no history courses. The only work of history Lincoln seems to have read as a boy was "Parson," Weems's famous filiopietistic biography of George Washington, with its apocryphal story of the hatchet and cherry tree.

That book made a lasting impression on Lincoln. Forty years after he first read it, President-elect Lincoln addressed the New Jersey legislature in Trenton, near the spot where George Washington's ragged troops had won a victory the day after Christmas 1776 that saved the American Revolution from collapse. Lincoln told the legislators:

> I remember all the accounts [in Weems's book] of the battle-fields and struggles for the liberty of the country, and none fixed themselves upon my imagination so deeply as the struggle here at Trenton.... The crossing of the river; the contest with the Hessians; the great hardships endured at that time, all fixed themselves on my memory more than any single revolutionary event.... I recollect thinking then, boy even though I was, that there must have been something more than common that those men struggled for.[3]

---

2 Ibid., 355–56.
[3] Roy P. Basler, ed., *The Collected Works of Abraham Lincoln*, 9 vols. (Rutgers University Press, New Brunswick, 1953–1955) 4:235–36.

These words were not merely an exercise in nostalgia. As always, Lincoln invoked the past for a purpose. On this occasion he shifted from the Revolution to the present and future. Prospects for the United States in that present and future were dark. The country of which Lincoln would become president eleven days later was no longer the United States, but the *dis*-United States. Seven slave states, fearing for the future of their peculiar institution in a nation governed by the new antislavery Republican party, had seceded from the Union in response to Lincoln's election. Several more slave states were threatening to do the same. Even as Lincoln spoke in Trenton, delegates from those first seven states were meeting in Montgomery, Alabama, to form the independent nation of the Confederate States of America. Civil War or a permanent division of the country with its dire precedent for further divisions—or both—loomed on the horizon. Thus it is not surprising that when Lincoln shifted from his discussion of the Revolution to the present, he began: "I am exceedingly anxious" that what those men fought for, "that something even more than National Independence; that something that held out a great promise to all the people of the world [for] all time to come; I am exceedingly anxious that this Union, the Constitution, and the liberties of the people shall be perpetuated in accordance with the original idea for which that struggle was made."[4]

The next day, Washington's birthday, Lincoln spoke at Independence Hall in Philadelphia where he spelled out more clearly what he believed was at stake both in the Revolution and in the crisis of 1861. "I have often inquired of myself," said Lincoln, "what great principle or idea it was that kept this [Union] so long together. It was not the mere matter of the separation of the colonies from the mother land, but that sentiment in the Declaration [of Independence] which gave liberty, not alone to the people of this country, but hope to the world for all future time." At this point in Lincoln's remarks, the newspaper text indicated "Great applause" from the audience, which included the city council and leading citizens of Philadelphia. Lincoln told them: "I have never had a feeling politically that did not spring from the sentiments embodied in the Declaration of Independence" ("Great cheering,"

---

[4] Ibid., 4:236.

according to the press). The ringing phrases that "all men are created equal, that they are endowed by their Creator with certain unalienable Rights, that among these are Life, Liberty and the pursuit of Happiness," said Lincoln in 1861, "gave promise" not just to Americans, but "hope to the world" that "in due time the weights should be lifted from the shoulders of all men, and that *all* should have an equal chance. (Cheers)"[5]

The sincerity of some in the audience who cheered Lincoln's egalitarian sentiments might be questioned, but Lincoln was quite sincere in his endorsement of them. He was painfully aware that many Americans enjoyed neither liberty nor equality. Four million were slaves, making the United States—the self-professed beacon of liberty to oppressed masses everywhere—the largest slaveholding country in the world. Lincoln grasped this nettle. "I hate...the monstrous injustice of slavery," he said in his famous Peoria speech of 1854. "I hate it because it deprives our republican example of its just influence in the world—enables the enemies of free institutions, with plausibility, to taunt us as hypocrites."[6]

As for equality, said Lincoln on another occasion, the author of the Declaration of Independence and the founding fathers who signed it clearly "did not intend to declare all men equal *in all respects.*" They did not even "mean to assert the obvious untruth" that all men in 1776 were equal in rights and opportunities. Rather, "they meant to set up a standard maxim for free society, which should be...constantly looked to, constantly labored for, and even though never perfectly attained, constantly approximated, and thereby constantly spreading and deepening its influence, and augmenting the happiness and value of life to all people of all colors everywhere."[7]

Like Thomas Jefferson, Lincoln asserted a universality and timelessness for the principles of liberty, equal rights, and equal opportunity on which the nation was founded. Lincoln acknowledged his intellectual debt to Jefferson—not Jefferson the slaveholder, not

---

[5] Ibid., 4:240.
[6] Ibid., 2:255.
[7] Ibid., 2:405–406.

Jefferson the author of the Kentucky resolutions of 1799 asserting the superiority of state over federal sovereignty, not even Jefferson the president—but Jefferson the philosopher of liberty, author of the Northwest Ordinance that kept slavery out of future states comprising 160,000 square miles at a time when most existing states of the Union still had slavery, and the Jefferson who, though he owned slaves, said of the institution that "he trembled for his country when he remembered that God was just." This was the Jefferson, said Lincoln in 1859, who "in the concrete pressure of a struggle for national independence by a single people had the coolness, forecast, and capacity to introduce into a merely revolutionary document"—the Declaration of Independence—"an abstract truth, applicable to all men and all times."[8]

Universal and timeless this truth may be, but in Jefferson's time it remained mostly as Lincoln described it—abstract. Fate decreed that it fell to Lincoln, not Jefferson, to give substance and meaning to what Jefferson had called a self-evident truth. Ironically, it was the slaveholders who provided Lincoln the opportunity to do so, for by taking their states out of the Union they set in train a progression of events that destroyed the very social and political order founded on slavery that they had seceded to preserve.

Secession transformed the main issue before the country from slavery to disunion. When Lincoln became president, he confronted the question—not what to do about slavery—of what to do about secession. On this question, Lincoln did not hesitate. Branding secession as "the essence of anarchy," he insisted in 1861 that "the central idea pervading this struggle is the necessity that is upon us, of proving that popular government is not an absurdity. We must settle this question now, whether in a free government the minority have the right to break up the government whenever they choose. If we fail it will go far to prove the incapability of the people to govern themselves."[9]

---

[8] Ibid., 3:376.

[9] Ibid., 4:268; Michael Burlingame and John R. Turner Ettlinger, eds., *Inside Lincoln's White House: The Complete Civil War Diary of John Hay* (Carbondale: Southern Illinois University Press, 1997) 20.

I Lincoln had come a long way in his understanding of history since his boyhood reading of Weems's biography of Washington. Like other thoughtful Americans, he was acutely conscious of the unhappy fate of most republics in the past. The United States stood almost alone in the mid-nineteenth century as a democratic republic in a world bestrode by kings, queens, emperors, czars, petty dictators, and theories of aristocracy. Some Americans alive at mid-century had seen two French republics rise and fall. The hopes of 1848 for the triumph of popular government in Europe had been shattered by the counterrevolutions that brought a conservative reaction in the Old World. Would the American experiment in government of, by, and for the people also be swept into the dustbin of history?

Not if Lincoln could help it. "Our popular government has often been called an experiment," he told a special session of Congress that met on 4 July 1861. "Two points in it, our people have already settled—the successful *establishing*, and the successful *administering* of it. One still remains—its successful *maintenance* against a formidable internal attempt to overthrow it." If that attempt succeeded, said Lincoln, the forces of reaction in Europe would smile in smug satisfaction at this proof of their contention that the upstart republic launched in 1776 could not last.[10]

Many in the North shared Lincoln's conviction that democracy was on trial in this war. "We must fight," proclaimed an Indianapolis newspaper two weeks after Confederate guns opened fire on Fort Sumter:

> We must fight because we *must*. The National Government has been assailed. The Nation has been defied. If either can be done with impunity neither Nation nor Government is worth a cent.... War is self preservation, if our form of Government is worth preserving. If monarchy would be better, it might be wise to quit fighting, admit that a Republic is too weak to take care of

---

[10] Basler, *Collected Works*, 4:439.

itself, and invite some deposed Duke or Prince of Europe to come over here and rule us. But otherwise, *we must fight.*[11]

The outbreak of war brought hundreds of thousands of Northern men to recruiting offices. A good many of them expressed a similar sense of democratic mission as a motive for fighting. "I do feel that the liberty of the world is placed in our hands to defend," wrote a Massachusetts soldier to his wife in 1862, "and if we are overcome then farewell to freedom." In 1863, on the second anniversary of his enlistment, an Ohio private wrote in his diary that he had not expected the war to last so long, but no matter how much longer it took it must be carried on "for the great principles of liberty and self government at stake, for should we fail, the onward march of Liberty in the Old World will be retarded at least a century, and Monarch, Kings, and Aristocrats will be more powerful against their subjects than ever."[12]

Some foreign-born soldiers appreciated the international impact of the war more intensely than native-born men who took their political rights for granted. A young British immigrant in Philadelphia wrote to his father back in England explaining why he had enlisted in the Union army. "If the Unionists let the South secede," he wrote, "the West might want to separate next Presidential Election...others might want to follow and this country would be as bad as the German states." Another English-born soldier, a forty-year-old corporal in an Ohio regiment, wrote to his wife in 1864 explaining why he had decided to reenlist for a second three-year hitch: "If I do get hurt I want you to remember that it will be not only for my Country and my Children but for Liberty all over the World that I risked my life, for if Liberty should be crushed here, what hope would there be fore the cause of Human Progress anywhere else?" An Irish-born carpenter, a private in the 28th Massachusetts Infantry of the famous Irish Brigade, rebuked both his wife in Boston and his father-in-law back in Ireland for questioning his judgment in

---

[11] Indianapolis *Daily Journal*, 27 April 1861.
[12] Josiah Perry to Phebe Perry, 3 October 1862, Josiah Perry Papers, Illinois State Historical Library, Springfield; Robert T. McMahan diary, entry of 3 September 1863, State Historical Society of Missouri, Columbia.

risking his life for the Union. "This is the first test of a modern free government in the act of sustaining itself against internal enemys," he wrote almost in echo of Lincoln. "If it fail then the hopes of millions fall and the designs and wishes of all tyrants will succeed the old cry will be sent forth from the aristocrats of europe that such is the common lot of all republics."[13] It is worth noting that both this Irish-born private and the English-born Ohio corporal were killed in action in 1864.

The American sense of mission invoked by Lincoln and by these soldiers—the idea that the American experiment in democracy was a beacon of liberty for oppressed people everywhere—is as old as the Mayflower Compact and as new as apparent American victory in the Cold War. In our own time this sentiment sometimes comes across as self-righteous posturing that inspires more resentment than admiration abroad. The same was true in Lincoln's time, when the resentment was expressed mainly by upper-class conservatives, especially in Britain. But many spokesmen for the middle and working classes in Europe echoed the most chauvinistic Yankees. During the debate that produced the British Reform Act of 1832, the London Working Men's Association pronounced "the Republic of America" to be a "beacon of freedom for all mankind," while a British newspaper named the *Poor Man's Guardian* pointed to American institutions as "the best precedent and guide to the oppressed and enslaved people of England in their struggle for the RIGHT OF REPRESENTATION FOR EVERY MAN."[14]

In the preface to the twelfth edition of his *Democracy in America*, written during the heady days of the 1848 democratic uprisings in Europe, Alexis de Tocqueville urged the leaders of France's newly

[13] Titus Crenshaw to father, 10 November 1861, *Invisible Immigrants: The Adaptation of English and Scottish Immigrants in Nineteenth Century America,* ed. Charlotte Erickson (Coral Gables: University of Miami Press, 1972) 348; George H. Cadman to Esther Cadman, 6 March 1864, Cadman Papers, Southern Historical Collection, University of North Carolina, Chapel Hill; Peter Welsh to Mary Welsh, 3 February 1863 and Peter Welsh to Patrick Prendergast, 1 June 1863, *Irish Green and Union Blue: The Civil War Letters of Peter Welsh*, ed. Laurence Frederick Kohl and Margaret Cosee Richard (New York: Fordham University Press, 1986) 65–66, 102.
[14] Quoted in G. D. Lillibridge, *Beacon of Freedom: The Impact of American Democracy upon Great Britain 1830–1870* (Philadelphia: University of Pennsylvania Press, 1955) 5, 28.

created Second Republic to study American institutions as a guide to "the approaching irrestible and universal spread of democracy throughout the world." When instead of democracy France got the Second Empire under Napoleon III, the republican opposition to his regime looked to the United States for inspiration. "Many of the suggested reforms," wrote the historian of the French opposition, "would have remained utopic had it not been for the demonstrable existence of the United States and its republican institutions." The existence of the United States remained a thorn in the side of European reactionaries, according to a British radical newspaper, which stated in 1856 that "to the oppressors of Europe, especially those of England, the [United States] is a constant terror, and an everlasting menace" because it stood as "a practical and triumphant refutation of the lying and servile sophists who maintain that without kings and aristocrats, civilized communities cannot exist."[15]

Once the war broke out, French republicans, some of them in exile, supported the North as "defenders of right and humanity." In England, John Stuart Mill expressed the conviction that the American Civil War "is destined to be a turning point, for good and evil, of the course of human affairs." Confederate success, said Mills, "would be a victory for the powers of evil which would give courage to the enemies of progress and damp the spirits of its friends all over the civilized world."[16]

Some European monarchists and conservatives did indeed make no secret of their hope that the Union would fall into the dustbin of history. The powerful *Times* of London considered the likely downfall of "the American colossus" a good "riddance of a nightmare.... Excepting a few gentlemen of republican tendencies, we all expect, we nearly all wish, success to the Confederate cause." The Earl of Shrewsbury expressed his cheerful belief "that the dissolution of the Union is inevitable, and that

---

[15] Alexis de Tocqueville, *Democracy in America*, 12th ed., trans. George Lawrence, ed. J. P. Mayer (New York: Harper & Row, 1966) xiii; Serge Gavronsky, *The French Liberal Opposition and the American Civil War* (New York: Humanities Press, 1968); Lillibridge, *Beacon of Freedom*, 80.

[16] *Revue des Deux Mondes* 15 August 1861, and John Stuart Mill, *Autobiography*, both quoted in Belle Becker Sideman and Lillian Friedman, eds., *Europe Looks at the Civil War* (New York: Orion Press, 1960) 81, 117–18.

men before me will live to see an aristocracy established in America."[17] In Spain the royalist journal *Pensamiento Español* found it scarcely surprising that Americans were butchering each other, for the United States, it declared editorially, "was populated by the dregs of all the nations of the world.... Such is the real history of the one and only state in the world which has succeeded in constituting itself according to the flaming theories of democracy. The example is too horrible to stir any desire for emulation." The minister to the United States from the Czar of all Russians echoed this opinion in 1863. "The republican form of government, so much talked about by the Europeans and so much praised by the Americans, is breaking down," he wrote. "What can be expected from a country where men of humble origin are elevated to the highest positions?" He meant Lincoln, of course. "This is democracy in practice, the democracy that European theorists rave about. If they could only see it at work they would cease their agitation and thank God for the government which they are enjoying."[18]

Clearly, opinion in Europe supported Lincoln's conviction that the very survival of democracy was at stake in the Civil War, but in the first year and one-half of the war, the problem of slavery muddied the clarity of this issue. The Confederacy was a slave society, which should have strengthened the Union's image abroad as the champion of liberty and equal rights. As Lincoln put it in a private conversation in January 1862: "I cannot imagine that any European power would dare to recognize and aid the Southern Confederacy if it became clear that the Confederacy stands for slavery and the Union for freedom." The problem was that the Union did not yet stand for the freedom of slaves. Constitutional constraints plus Lincoln's need to keep Northern Democrats and the border slave states in his war coalition inhibited efforts to make it a war against slavery. This restraint puzzled and alienated many potential

---

[17] *Times* quoted in Frank L. Owsley, *King Cotton Diplomacy: Foreign Relations of the confederate States of America*, 2d ed., rev. Harriet C. Owlsey (Chicago: University of Chicago Press, 1959) 186; Earl of Shrewsbury quoted in Ephraim D. Adams, *Great Britain and the American Civil War*, 2 vols. (New York: Russell & Russell, 1925) 2:282.

[18] *Pensamiento Espanol*, September 1862, quoted in Sideman and Friedman, *Europe Looks at the Civil War*, 173–74; Stoeckl quoted in Albert A. Woldman, *Lincoln and the Russians* (Cleveland: World Publishing Co., 1952) 216–17.

European friends of the Union cause. An English observer asked in September 1861: Since "the North does not proclaim abolition and never pretended to fight for anti-slavery," how "can we be fairly called upon to sympathize so warmly with the Federal cause?"[19]

Lincoln recognized the validity of this question. In September 1862 he agreed with a delegation of antislavery clergymen that "emancipation would help us in Europe, and convince them that we are incited by something more than ambition." When he said this, Lincoln had made up his mind to issue an emancipation proclamation. The balance of political forces in the North and military forces on the battlefield had shifted just enough to give this decision the impetus of public support. Basing his action on the power of the commander in chief to seize enemy property being used to wage war against the United States—slaves were property and their labor was essential to the Confederate war economy—Lincoln issued a preliminary Emancipation Proclamation in September 1862 and the final Proclamation on 1 January 1863, justifying it as both a "military necessity" and an "act of justice."[20]

The Emancipation Proclamation laid the groundwork for the total abolition of slavery in the United States, which was accomplished by the Thirteenth Amendment to the Constitution in 1865. It also emancipated Lincoln from the contradiction of fighting a war for democratic liberty without fighting a war against slavery. Emancipation deepened Lincoln's sense of history. As he signed the Proclamation on that New Year's Day 1863, he said to colleagues who gathered to witness this historic occasion: "I never, in my life, felt more certain that I was doing right than I do in signing this paper. If my name ever goes into history it will be for this act, and my whole soul is in it."[21]

---

[19] Lincoln quoted in *The Reminiscences of Carl Schurz*, 3 vols. (New York: The McClure Company, 1907–08) 2:309; *Saturday Review*, 14 September 1861, quoted in Adams, *Great Britain and the American Civil War*, 1:181; *Economist*, September 1861, quoted in Karl Marx and Friedrich Engels, *The Civil War in the United States*, ed. Richard Enmale (New York: International Publishers, 1937) 12.

[20] Basler, *Collected Works*, 5:53, 537.

[21] Frederick W. Seward, *Seward at Washington as Senator and Secretary of State* (New York: Derby & Miller, 1891) 2:151.

Lincoln connected the act of emancipation with the future, as he had earlier connected the war for the Union with a past that had given Lincoln's generation the legacy of a united country. Just as the sacrifices of those who had fought for independence and nationhood in 1776 inspired Lincoln and the people he led, their sacrifices in the Civil War would leave a legacy of democracy and freedom to future generations. In his first annual message to Congress—we call it today the State of the Union Address—Lincoln declared that "the struggle of today is not altogether for today—it is for a vast future also." Lincoln sent his second annual message to Congress in December 1862, just before he issued the final Emancipation Proclamation. On this occasion he defined the war's meaning by linking past, present, and future in a passage of unsurpassed eloquence and power:

> Fellow-citizens, we cannot escape history. We of this Congress and this administration, will be remembered in spite of ourselves.... The fiery trial through which we pass, will light us down, in honor or dishonor, to the latest generation.... We shall nobly save, or meanly lose, the last, best hope of earth.... The dogmas of the quiet past, are inadequate to the stormy present.... In *giving* freedom to the *slave*, we *assure* freedom to the *free*.... We must disenthrall ourselves, and then we shall save our country.[22]

I said above that Lincoln's eloquence in this passage was unsurpassed, but he did surpass himself nearly a year later, in the prose poem of 272 words that we know as the Gettysburg Address. In this elegy for Union soldiers killed at the battle of Gettysburg, Lincoln wove together past, present, and future with two other sets of three images: continent, nation, battlefield and birth, death, rebirth. The Gettysburg Address is so familiar that, like other things we can recite from memory, its meaning sometimes loses its import. At the risk of destroying the speech's poetic qualities, let us disaggregate these parallel images of past, present, future; continent, nation, battlefield; and birth, death,

---

[22] Ibid., 5:53, 2:537.

rebirth. To do this will underscore the meaning of the Civil War not only for Lincoln's time but also for generations into the future, indeed for the new millennium we have just entered:

Four score and seven years in the *past*, said Lincoln, our fathers *brought forth* on this *continent* a *nation* conceived in liberty. *Today*, our generation faces a great test whether a nation so conceived can survive. In dedicating the cemetery on this *battlefield*, the living must take inspiration to finish the task that those who lie buried here so nobly advanced by giving their last full measure of devotion. Life and *death* in this passage have a paradoxical but metaphorical relationship: men died that the nation might live, yet metaphorically the old Union also died, and with it would die the institution of slavery. After these deaths, the nation must have a *"new birth* of freedom" so that government of, by, and for the people that our fathers conceived and brought forth in the past "shall not perish from the earth" but live into the vast *future*, even unto the next millennium.

Although Lincoln gave this address at the dedication of a cemetery, its rhetoric was secular. As the war went on, however, Lincoln's efforts to come to grips with the mounting toll of death, destruction, and suffering became more infused with religious inquiry. Perhaps God was punishing Americans with "this terrible war" for some great sin. By the time of his inauguration for the second term, Lincoln believed he had identified that sin. "Fondly do we hope—fervently do we pray—that this mighty scourge of war may speedily pass away," said Lincoln in his second inaugural address. "Yet, if God wills that it continue, until all the wealth piled by the bond-man's two hundred and fifty years of unrequited toil shall be sunk, and until every drop of blood drawn with the lash, shall be paid by another drawn with the sword, as was said three thousand years ago, so still it must be said 'the judgments of the Lord, are true and righteous altogether.'"[23]

Fortunately, the war lasted only another few weeks after Lincoln's second inauguration. In this new millennium, we may well wonder if we are still paying for the blood drawn with the lash of slavery. The impact abroad of Union victory was almost immediate. In Britain a disgruntled

---

[23]Ibid., 2:333.

Tory member of Parliament expressed disappointment that the Union had not broken in "two or perhaps more fragments," for he considered the United States "a menace to the whole civilized world." A Tory colleague described this menace as "the beginning of the Americanizing process in England. The new Democratic ideas are gradually to find embodiment." Indeed they were. In 1865 a liberal political economist at University College London, Edward Beesly, who wanted the expansion of voting rights in Britain, pointed to the moral of Union victory across the Atlantic. "Our opponents told us that Republicanism was on trial" in the American Civil War, said Beesly:

> They insisted on our watching what they called its breakdown. They told us that it was forever discredited in England. Well, we accepted the challenge. We staked our hopes boldly on the result.... Under a strain such as no aristocracy, no monarchy, no empire could have supported, Republican institutions have stood firm. It is we, now, who call upon the privileged classes to mark the result.... A vast impetus has been given to Republican sentiments in England.[24]

Queen Victoria's throne was safe, but a two-year debate in Parliament, in which the American example figured prominently, led to enactment of the Reform Bill of 1867, which nearly doubled the eligible electorate and enfranchised a large part of the British working class for the first time. With this act the world's most powerful nation took a long stride toward democracy. What might have happened to the Reform Bill if the North had lost the Civil War, thereby confounding liberals and confirming Tory opinions of democracy, is impossible to say.

The end of slavery in the re-United States sounded the death knell of the institution in Brazil and Cuba, the only other places in the western hemisphere where it still existed. Commending the Brazilian

---

[24] Sir Edward Bulwer-Lytton to John Bigelow, April ?, 1865, quoted in Sideman and Friedman, eds., *Europe Looks at the Civil War*, 282; Harold M. Hyman, ed., *Heard Round the World: The Impact Abroad of the Civil War* (New York: Alfred A. Knopf, 1969) xi, 73.

government's first steps toward abolition of slavery in 1871, an abolitionist in that country was glad, as he put it, "to see Brazil receive so quickly the moral of the Civil War in the United States."[25] Even without Northern victory in the war, slavery in the United States, Brazil, and Cuba would have been unlikely to survive into the next millennium, but it might well have survived into the next century. And without the Fourteenth and Fifteenth Amendments to the US Constitution, which like the Thirteenth were a direct consequence of the war and which granted equal civil and political rights to African-Americans, the United States might have developed into even more of an apartheid society in the twentieth century than it did.

These amendments consummated a new interpretation of liberty in the American polity, an interpretation that may be the most important legacy of the Civil War for the new millennium. Lincoln played a crucial role in the evolution of this new concept of liberty. In April 1864 he chose the occasion of a public speech in Baltimore to define the difference between two meanings of this word that is so central to America's understanding of itself. "The world has never had a *good* definition of the word liberty," Lincoln declared in that state of Maryland which still had slavery but was about to abolish it:

> We all declare for liberty, but in using the same *word* we do
> not mean the same *thing*. With some the word liberty may mean
> for each man to do as he pleases with himself, and the product of
> his labor; while with others the same may mean for some men to
> do as they please with other men, and the product of other men's
> labor. Here are two, not only different, but incompatible things,
> called by the same *name*—liberty.

As he often did, Lincoln went on to illustrate his point with a parable. One of the first books he had read as a child was *Aesop's Fables*, and throughout his life Lincoln told apparently simple stories about animals to make subtle and profound points about important matters. He said:

---

[25] Hyman, *Heard Round the World*, 323.

The shepherd drives the wolf from the sheep's throat, for which the sheep thanks the shepherd as a *liberator*, while the wolf denounces him for the same act as a destroyer of liberty, especially as the sheep is a black one. Plainly the sheep and the wolf are not agreed upon a definition of the word liberty; and precisely the same difference prevails to-day among us human creatures, even in the North, and all professing to love liberty. Hence we behold the processes by which thousands are daily passing from under the yoke of bondage, hailed by some as the advance of liberty, and bewailed by others as the destruction of all liberty.[26]

The shepherd in this fable was Lincoln himself; the black sheep was the slave, and the wolf was the slave's owner. The point of this fable was similar to a barbed comment Lincoln had made a decade earlier about Southern rhetoric professing a love of liberty. "The perfect liberty they sigh for," said Lincoln on that occasion, "is the liberty of making slaves of other people."[27] More subtly, Lincoln in this parable was drawing a distinction between what the late philosopher Isaiah Berlin described as "negative liberty" and "positive liberty."[28] The concept of negative liberty is perhaps more familiar. It can be defined as the absence of restraint, a freedom from interference by outside authority with individual thought or behavior. Negative liberty is best described as freedom *from*. Positive liberty can be defined as freedom *to*.

The example of freedom of the press perhaps provides an illustration. This freedom is usually understood as a negative liberty—freedom from interference with what a writer writes or a reader reads. But an illiterate person suffers from a denial of positive liberty. He is unable to enjoy the freedom to read or write whatever he pleases not because some authority prevents him from doing so, but because he

---

[26] Basler, *Collected Works*, 7:301–302.

[27] Ibid., 2:250.

[28] Isaiah Berlin, *Four Essays on Liberty* (New York: Oxford University Press, 1974) 118–72.

cannot read or write anything. The remedy lies not in removal of restraint but in achievement of the capacity to read and write—positive liberty.

Another way of defining the difference between these two concepts of liberty is to describe their relation to power. Negative liberty and power are at opposite poles; power is the enemy of liberty, especially power in the hands of a central government. Negative liberty was the preeminent concern of Americans in the eighteenth and first half of the nineteenth centuries. Many feared the federal government as the main threat to individual liberty; some still do today. Americans fought their Revolution against the overweening power of King and Parliament. In the Constitution, they fragmented power among the three branches of the federal government, between the two houses of Congress, and between the national and state governments. Even this was not enough, in James Madison's words, to prevent the "tendency in all Governments to an augmentation of power at the expense of liberty."[29] So the founders wrote a Bill of Rights, which, in the first ten amendments to the Constitution, imposed limits on the power of the federal government.

Throughout early American history, political leaders remained vigilant against concentration of power. Andrew Jackson vetoed the charter renewal of the Second Bank of the United States in 1832 because, he said, such a combination of private wealth and government power would cause "our liberties to be crushed." In 1854 the famous reformer of mental hospitals, Dorothea Dix, persuaded Congress to pass a bill granting public lands to the states to subsidize improved facilities for the mentally ill. President Franklin Pierce vetoed the bill because if Congress could enact such a law, "it has the power to provide for the indigent who are not insane, and thus...the whole field of public beneficence is thrown open to the care and culture of the Federal Government." This would mean "all sovereignty vested in an absolute consolidated central power, against which the spirit of liberty has so often and in so many countries struggled in vain." Therefore, a law to improve mental hospitals, concluded Pierce, would be "the beginning of the end...of our blessed

---

[29] Gordon S. Wood, *The Creation of the American Republic*, 1776–1787 (Chapel Hill: University of North Carolina Press, 1969) 413.

inheritance of representative liberty."[30] Owners of slaves also relied on
this bulwark of negative liberty to defend their right of property in
human beings. John C. Calhoun and other Southern political leaders
constructed an elaborate structure of state sovereignty and limitations on
national power. No exercise of federal power escaped the censure of
these proslavery libertarians. As Senator Nathaniel Macon of North
Carolina explained: "If Congress can make banks, roads, and canals
under the Constitution, they can free any slave in the United States."[31]
The ultimate manifestation of negative liberty was secession. Southern
states left the Union in 1861 because they feared that sometime in the
future the growing Northern antislavery majority embodied in the
Republican party would exercise its power to free the slaves—a form of
positive liberty that might even go so far as to empower them to read and
write, to vote, and to aspire to equality with whites—a truly frightening
scenario of positive liberty. Ironically, by seceding and provoking a war,
Southern whites hastened the very achievement of positive liberty they
had gone to war to prevent. By 1864, when Lincoln told his parable
about the shepherd protecting the black sheep from the wolf, that
shepherd wielded a very big staff as commander in chief of the largest
army yet known in the United States. It took every ounce of this power to
accomplish the "new birth of freedom" that Lincoln invoked at
Gettysburg.

   Tragically, Lincoln did not live to oversee advancement toward that
goal. His earlier definition of equality as a "maxim for free
society...even though never perfectly attained...constantly labored
for...and thereby constantly spreading the deepening its influence, and
augmenting the happiness and value of life to all people of all colors"
suggests the policies of positive liberty he would have pursued had he
lived. But at Ford's Theatre, John Wilkes Booth ended that possibility as
he shouted Virginia's state motto, "sic semper tyrannis" (thus always to
tyrants)—the slogan of negative liberty.

---

[30] Robert Remini, *Andrew Jackson and the Bank War* (New York: Norton, 1967)
45; James D. Richardson, comp., *Messages and Papers of the Presidents*, 20 vols.
(Washington, DC: Government Printing Office, 1897) 4:2780–84.
   [31] Norman K. Risjord, *The Old Republicans: Southern Conservatism in the Age of
Jefferson* (New York: Columbia University Press, 1965) 242.

But Lincoln's party carried on the tradition of positive liberty with its efforts to legislate and enforce equal civil rights, voting rights, and education during Reconstruction. As Republican Congressman George Julian noted in 1867, the only way to achieve "justice and equality...for the freedmen of the South" was by "the strong arm of *power*, outstretched from the central authority here in Washington." As Congressman James Garfield, a future Republican president, put it also in 1867, "we must plant the heavy hand of...authority upon these rebel communities, and...plant liberty on the ruins of slavery."[32]

That is what the Thirteenth, Fourteenth, and Fifteenth Amendments to the Constitution tried to do. These amendments radically transformed the thrust of the Constitution from negative to positive liberty. Instead of the straitjacket of "thou shalt nots" imposed on the federal government by the Bill of Rights, the Civil War amendments established a precedent whereby nine of the next fourteen constitutional amendments contained the phrase "Congress shall have the *power*" to enforce the provisions. Lincoln himself set this precedent by helping to draft the Thirteenth Amendment, which was the centerpiece of the platform on which he was reelected in 1864.

Lincoln's party continued its commitment to positive liberty at least through the presidency of Theodore Roosevelt. In the twentieth century, however, the two major parties gradually reversed positions. The Democratic Party, once the bastion of negative liberty, states' rights, and limited government, donned the mantle of positive liberty while most Republicans invoked the mantra of negative liberty. How these matters will play out in the new millennium remains to be seen. But whatever happens, Lincoln's legacy of one nation, indivisible, with freedom for four million slaves and their descendants, seems likely to persist far into the millennium.

A few years ago the Huntington Library sponsored an essay contest on Lincoln for high school students in connection with its major Lincoln exhibit. One of the finalists was a seventeen-year-old girl from Texas,

---

[32] *Congressional Globe,* 39 Cong., 2d Sess. (28 January 1867) Appendix, 78; Burke A. Hinsdale, ed., *The Works of James Abram Garfield,* 2 vols. (Boston: J. R. Osgood & Company, 1882) 1:249.

whose forebears had immigrated to the United States from India. She wrote, "If the United States was not in existence today, I would not have the opportunity to excel in life and education. The Union was preserved, not only for the people yesterday, but also for the lives of today."[33]

Lincoln would surely have applauded this statement. In 1861 he said that the struggle for the Union involved not only "the fate of these United States" but also "the whole family of man." It was a struggle "not altogether for today" but "for a vast future also." We are living in that vast future. Lincoln's words resonate in the twenty-first century with as much relevance as they did seven score years ago.

---

[33] Reena Mathew, "One Set of Footprints," essay in author's possession

CONTRIBUTORS BY ORDER
OF APPEARANCE

CHARLES M. HUBBARD is Director of the Abraham Lincoln Library and Museum and Associate Professor of History at Lincoln Memorial University in Harrogate, Tennessee. Included in his publications are: *The Burden of Confederate Diplomacy* (1997) and his most recent publication, *Historic Reflections on U.S. Governance and Civil Society* (2001). He resides in Signal Mountain, Tennessee.

FRANK J. WILLIAMS is Chief Justice of the Rhode Island Supreme Court and a leader in the Lincoln community for over thirty years. His books include: *Abraham Lincoln: Sources and Styles of Leadership* (1994*)* and *Abraham Lincoln Contemporary* (1995). He is a regular contributor and the literary editor of the *Lincoln Herald*. A native of Providence, he now resides in Hope Valley, Rhode Island.

GERALD J. PROKOPOWICZ received his Ph.D. in History from Harvard University where he studied with David Herbert Donald. He is Director of Public Programs at the Lincoln Museum in Fort Wayne, Indiana. His most recent publication is *All for the Regiment: The Army of Ohio, 1861-1862* (2001). He is the editor of *Lincoln Lore* and has published numerous articles and reviews.

JOHN R. SELLERS is the historical specialist on the American Civil War at the Library of Congress. His best known book is *Civil War Manuscripts: A Guide to Collections in the Manuscript Division of the Library of Congress* (1986). For over thirty years Dr. Sellers has assisted researchers and scholars at the Library of Congress and his frequent appearances on the History Channel and C-Span have demonstrated his familiarity with original Lincoln sources.

MICHAEL BURLINGAME is the May Buckley Sadowski Professor of History at Connecticut College in New London, Connecticut. He has written and edited over twenty books about Abraham Lincoln and his contemporaries. His book, *The Inner World of Lincoln* (1994) was one of the first inquiries into the psychological world of the sixteenth president. He is presently completing the revisions for a three-volume biography of Abraham Lincoln.

PHILIP SHAW PALUDAN is one of the nation's foremost authorities on Abraham Lincoln and the Civil War and occupies the Naomi B. Lynn distinguished Chair of Lincoln Studies at the University of Illinois at Springfield. His book, *The Presidency of Abraham Lincoln,* received the 1995 Lincoln Book Prize. Another of his books, *Victims, A True Story of the Civil War* (1981), is a bestselling History Book Club Selection.

WILLIAM LEE MILLER is the scholar in Ethics and Institutions at the Miller Center for Public Affairs at the University of Virginia. He is the author of: *Lincoln's Virtues: An Ethical Biography* (2002), as well as *Arguing About Slavery: John Quincy Adams and the Great Battle in the American Congress* (1996), which won the D.B. Haldeman Award for the best book on Congress in 1996.

LUCAS E. MOREL received his Ph.D. from Claremont Graduate School in 1994 and teaches American Government and Political Philosophy at Washington and Lee University. His most recent book, *Lincoln's Sacred Effort: Redefining Religion's Role in American Self-Government* (2002), has received critical acclaim.

MICHAEL VORENBERG is Assistant Professor of History at Brown University and was a post-Doctoral Fellow at the W.E.B. Du Bois Center at Harvard University. He is the author of *Final Freedom: The Civil War, the Abolition of Slavery, and the 13th Amendment* published by Cambridge University Press (2001). He is presently doing research for a book entitled: *Written Constitutions and Radical Constitutions in Nineteenth Century America.*

WILLIAM C. HARRIS is Professor of History, North Carolina State University. His biography of William Woods Holden received the Jefferson Davis Book Award in 1988 as the best book on Confederate History. The Lincoln Book Prize was awarded for Harris's book, *With Charity for All: Lincoln and the Restoration of the Union* (1998). He is currently working on a study of the final months of Abraham Lincoln's presidency.

JENNIFER FLEISCHNER is the Associate Professor of English at State University of New York in Albany and is the author of *Mastering Slavery: Memory, Family, and Identity in Women's Slave Narratives* (1996). She is completing another book titled *Mrs. Lincoln and Mrs. Keckly.*

JAMES M. McPHERSON is Professor of History at Princeton University and has written extensively on Abraham Lincoln and the Civil War. Among his many books is a history of America in the mid-nineteenth century, *The Battle Cry of Freedom* (1988), which won a Pulitzer Prize in History.